Essential Articles 11

Editors: Christine Shepherd & Chas White

D0248719

CAREL PRESS
www.carelpress.com

Introduction

Welcome to Essential Articles 11, the latest volume of this highly praised series.

We are very pleased with the feedback about the new format. Customers have told us that they find the bound volume useful, attractive and accessible. As we had hoped, changing to a yearly publication has meant that Essential Articles can be both currently relevant and of lasting value.

We are continuing to strengthen the connection between Essential Articles and its sister publication, Fact File. Statistics in Fact File support and develop relevant articles in Essential Articles, while those same stories bring the figures to life.

This means you will find Essential Articles indispensable for both browsing and researching. Students researching with Essential Articles can quickly find relevant and appropriate material, rather than wasting hours on fruitless internet searches. Because it can be copied, it's also invaluable in the library and the classroom for exploring today's issues and controversies; considering opposing views; looking at models of the best writing and gaining an insight into the press.

We have selected pieces of writing that offer opinions on current affairs rather than news stories. Even where the details have changed, the opinions contained in the articles remain both valid and valuable. Once again, distressingly,

a number of features deal with violence and killing amongst young people. Writers reflect on the factors which contribute to the situation and what can be done about it, which is why Carmen Batmanghelidjh's piece appears in *Britain & its citizens* rather than in the *Law & order* section. *Britain & its citizens* looks at a variety of aspects of our society, both serious and humorous. In every section you will find contrasting views and opinions. In *Family & relationships*, for example, you can read personal accounts from a mother who gave away her baby and from a woman who sought out the mother who had deserted her. In the *Education* section you can contrast the highly disciplined Chinese education system with a relaxed Scandinavian regime which is soon to be used in the UK.

As always, we have sought to provide material from sources which are not easily accessible as well as presenting pieces from well known and respected national media.

While each volume in the series can be considered as a separate item, all the volumes taken together make up a unique resource on important issues and controversies, offering balanced argument, personal accounts, strong viewpoints and humour.

A free digital, searchable guide to the whole series is available on our website. This guide also links articles with the statistics in Fact File.

Published by Carel Press Ltd
4 Hewson St, Carlisle CA2 5AU
Tel +44 (0)1228 538928, Fax 591816
info@carelpress.com
www.carelpress.com (for a free digital guide to the series)
This collection © 2009 Christine A Shepherd & Chas White

Acknowledgements
Additional illustrations: Adrian Burrows
Designers: Adrian Burrows, Anne Louise Kershaw, Debbie Maxwell, Dean Ryan
Editorial team: Anne Louise Kershaw, Debbie Maxwell, Christine A Shepherd, Chas White, Jack Gregory
Subscriptions: Ann Batey (Manager), Brenda Hughes, Anne Maclagan

We wish to thank all those writers, editors, photographers, cartoonists, artists, press agencies and wire services who have given permission to reproduce copyright material. Every effort has been made to trace copyright holders of material but in a few cases this has not been possible. The publishers would be glad to hear from anyone who has not been consulted.

Once again, we are particularly grateful to Laura Hitchcock of PA for her helpfulness and efficiency.

Cover design: Anne Louise Kershaw

Front cover photo: Mohammed Abed/AFP/Getty Images

British Library
Cataloguing in Publication Data
Essential Articles 11: The articles you need on the issues that matter
1. Social problems – Study and teaching (Secondary) – Great Britain
2. Social sciences – Study and teaching (Secondary) – Great Britain
    I. Shepherd, Christine A   II. White, C
    361.00712 41
    ISBN   978-1-905600-16-8

Printed by Finemark, Poland

Contents

'If you are not being eulogised by white liberals... you are being verbally abused by a white racist'
page 36

Contents

'Had I been selfish having a baby knowing I had a 50:50 chance of passing on my disability?'
page 54

For up-to-date statistics on consumers, disability and drugs, as well as many other topics in Essential Articles see:

Fact File

Contents

> ‘But at some point death comes into the equation and who better to pull the trigger than the consumer’
> page 100

Contents

For up-to-date statistics on family, food and health, as well as many other topics in Essential Articles see:

Fact File

'I was briefly unable to handle the social cues that most people take for granted; that's why I talked to total strangers on buses. But society seems to be terrified of mental illness'
page 118

Look into my eyes!
Madeleine McCann was abducted from Praia Da Luz, Portugal on 03/05/2007

Should you have any information please contact Crimestoppers UK
0800 555111

Contents

> 'Youth and social services only became involved when they no longer had a choice, by which time my daughter was well and truly an "habitual offender" with a serious drug and alcohol problem'
>
> *page 143*

Contents

'The accident was the easy bit, it was waiting for treatment back home that was a nightmare... No one likes to watch their life ebb away.'
page 164

WORK

'At 13 years old, I hit my lowest point. I was drinking up to three litres of wine a day and a litre of vodka"
page 200

YOUNG PEOPLE

Stuff the tiger – long live extinction

By Jeremy Clarkson

As the population of China becomes more wealthy, demand for illegal tiger parts is booming. Up to 600m Chinese people believe that tiger bones, claws and even penises will cure any number of ailments, including arthritis and impotency. And as a result we've just been told, for about the hundredth time, that if nothing is done extinction looms.

Well, not complete extinction. Obviously tigers will continue to exist in Las Vegas for many years to come. And in Asia there are so many backstreet big cat farms that they outnumber cows. But they will cease to exist in the wild.

Right. And what are we supposed to do, exactly? Send an international force tooled up with the latest night-vision gear and helicopter gunships to hunt down and kill the poachers?

Really? And what are these mercenaries supposed to say to the locals? "Yes, I realise that you have no fresh water, no healthcare, little food and that your ox is broken, but we are not here to do anything about that. In fact we're going to put an end to the only industry you have."

Yes, say the conservationists, who argue that unless this is done now our children will grow up never being able to see a tiger in the wild. And that this is very sad.

Is it? I have never seen a duckbilled platypus in the wild or a rattlesnake. I've never seen any number of creatures that I know to exist. So why should I care if my children never see a tiger? In fact, come to think of it, if they're on a gap year trekking through the jungles of Burma I fervently hope they don't.

There's an awful lot of sentimentality around the concept of extinction. We have a sense that when a species dies out we should all fall to our knees and spend some time wailing. But why? Apart from for a few impotent middle-class Chinamen, or if you want a nice rug, it makes not the slightest bit of difference if Johnny tiger dies out. It won't upset our power supplies or heal the rift with Russia. It is as irrelevant as the death of a faraway star.

So far this century we've waved goodbye to the Pyrenean ibex – did you notice? – and the mouthful that is Miss Waldron's red colobus monkey. Undoubtedly both extinctions were blamed on Shell, McDonald's, the trade in illegal diamonds, Deutsche Bank or some other spurious shareholder-led attempt to turn all of the world into money and carbon dioxide.

Unless you want a nice rug, it makes not the slightest bit of difference if Johnny tiger dies out

But if we look back to a time before oil, steam and German bankers, we find that species were managing to die off all on their own. The brontosaurus, for example. And who honestly thinks it's sad that their children will never get to see a tyrannosaurus rex in the wild?

In the 19th century 27 species went west, including the great auk, the thicktail chub, the quagga, the Cape lion and the Polish primitive horse. Apparently the Poles tried their hardest but it was no good. It was just too primitive.

Between 1900 and 1919 eco-mentalists ignore the fact that we lost most of the young men in Europe and prattle on about the passing of the passenger pigeon, the Carolina parakeet, and the Tasmanian wolf.

Eco-mentalists ignore the fact that between 1900 and 1919 we lost most of our young men in Europe

Honestly, who cares because there are quite literally millions more fish in the sea. Only last week we heard that scientists in the South American rainforest have found 24 previously unknown species including 12 dung beetles, a whole new ant, some fish and a rather fetching frog.

It may not be as cuddly as a baby tiger or as primitive as a Polish horse, but it is groovier since its purple fluorescent hoop markings appear to have been drawn by Steve Hillage himself.

So is the world rejoicing at the sensational news that we've been joined on earth by a hippie frog? Is it hell as like. What the world is doing instead is crying into its eco-handkerchief because of what's going on in the Arctic.

We're told that because of the Range Rover, HSBC and Prince Bandar all the ice at the North Pole is melting and that as a result the polar bear has nowhere to live. Apart that is for the 3m square miles of northern Canada that are completely untouched by any form of human encroachment.

Anyway, ignoring that, we are told that the polar bear is now at risk and as a result we're all supposed to kill ourselves.

Why? Contrary to what you may have been led to believe by Steiff's cute and squishy cuddly toys, the polar bear is a big savage brute; the colour of nicotine, with a mean ugly pointy face and claws that, if they were to be found in

Nottingham on a Saturday night, would be confiscated as offensive weapons.

If the polar bear dies out it will make not a jot of difference to you or anyone you've ever met. The only people who'll even notice are the Innuits, and its passing will actually improve their lives because they'll be able to go out fishing and clubbing without running the risk of being eaten to death.

We are told that the polar bear is now at risk and as a result we're all supposed to kill ourselves

I do not believe that we should deliberately kill stuff because we find it ugly or offensive. Unless it's a virus or a mosquito. But I do wish the world's conservationists would learn a lesson from some of the more enlightened species in the animal kingdom: that when push comes to shove, the only creatures that really matter are those in our social group. And our children.

The Sunday Times 10 June 2007

Photo: Soeren Stache/DPA/PA Photos

Berlin's famous young polar bear 'Knut', weighing 125 kg, plays with a toy bone in his enclosure in the zoo in Berlin, Germany

'PSYCHO' POLAR BEAR IS 'ADDICTED TO HUMANS'

Tony Paterson

Berlin Zoo does little to prepare visitors for the shock of a first encounter with Knut, the world's most famous polar bear. Placards advertising the ursine celebrity at its entrance gate show a cuddly, snowy-white creature not much bigger than a domestic cat.

A kiosk next door is stuffed full of miniature Knuts. The souvenir toy bears are still cat sized, fluffy and white but this time, at about £11.00 apiece, they are synthetic, machine washable and have grins on their faces.

A good hundred yards inside, past the pelican pond and the African warthogs, an almost permanent 200-strong crowd of children and camera-waving adults braving a January afternoon, belie the near divine

presence of the real Knut — the bear turned future Hollywood film star who has a following of millions.

Knut close up is disconcerting to say the least: he is not white but mired a filthy brownish grey by the mud and dirty pools of water in his enclosure. At a year old, and weighing more than 17 stone he is bigger than a man when standing on his hind legs.

On a wet day last week Knut stood alone in his enclosure playing to his gallery of adoring visitors like an accomplished RADA graduate.

Somebody had thrown him a six-inch-long plastic toy. Knut rolled it around in his mouth, threw it into a pool and dived after it, snatched it up with his paw and then rose up on to his hind legs before quickly flipping the object back into his mouth again.

His audience roared with approval. It was more circus than zoo.

The Knut phenomenon is currently causing a major debate about the rights of caged animals in Germany. The debate will come into even sharper focus in a few weeks' time when another polar bear cub, this time a female called Flocke will go on show in Nuremberg zoo in what promises to be a repetition of the Knut treatment.

While some insist that bears born in zoos have a right to human intervention to save and secure their lives, others, such as German animal rights activist Frank Albrecht, argue that they become so dependent on man that they end up divorced from nature and turn into hyperactive, disturbed freaks.

"Knut is a problem bear who has

Flocke plays with a dish cloth at Nuremberg Zoo, Germany

Photo: Ralf Schedlbauer/DPA/PA Photos

become addicted to human beings," he said. The German zoologist Peter Arras has described Knut as a "psychopath". The debate has grown following the birth of three polar bear cubs at Nuremberg Zoo to two different female bears. A team of highly experienced zoologists initially argued that nature must be allowed to take its course. They allowed one of the females to kill and eat her offspring because they were too weak to survive.

But the zoo's "bear infanticide" policy coincided with television pictures designed to melt the heart of anybody who cannot help assuming that polar bears are just like human beings. They showed the zoo's other female polar bear, Vera, carrying her female cub, called Flocke or Snowflake, by the scruff of its neck through her enclosure.

Within hours of the images being broadcast, Nuremberg Zoo had performed a complete policy U-turn: a keeper was sent into Vera's enclosure and Flocke was removed "for its own

safety". Amid growing fears that the last remaining cub might also be eaten the zoo promptly announced that the cub would be fed from a bottle.

"I don't think anyone could have stood it, if we had allowed our last bear cub to be eaten by its mum," said Nuremberg's deputy mayor.

Knut stood alone in his enclosure playing to his gallery of adoring visitors like an accomplished RADA graduate

Without Knut, it is unlikely that the events at Nuremberg would have taken the course that they did. He was also rejected by his mother, a disturbed circus bear called Tosca, and faced the prospect of being eaten.

Enter Thomas Dörflein. Within days Knut was placed in the 44-year-old Berlin zookeeper's care. Dörflein instantly fulfilled the role

of Knut's surrogate mother, hand-feeding his charge day and night.

When Knut first appeared in public in March last year, there were more than 500 journalists present.

The Knut marketing machine shifted into top gear. The first 2,400 Knut stuffed toys produced by the zoo sold out in four days. Within a matter of weeks Knut was sharing the front cover of Vanity Fair magazine with Leonardo DiCaprio. There are games, posters, T-shirts, pop songs, a children's book and silver coins bearing Knut images and an animated film featuring Knut is in the works.

Sigmar Gabriel, Germany's Environment Minister, has adopted the bear, claiming him as a symbol of the world's endangered species. Yet evidence suggests that polar bears are not facing extinction, even if the ice caps are melting. Alaska, home to a fifth of the world's 25,000 polar bears, currently has its largest bear population in 40 years.

Independent 2 February 2008

Chain reaction

Children who are violent to animals grow up to be violent to people. True or false? Does a man who ill-treats his dog do the same to his wife and children? And do the children who see this happening go on to do the same thing?

The connection between cruelty to animals and violence towards others has long been argued about. Finally an RSPCA study proves there is a link. Animal abuse should be treated as a matter of serious concern as it forms part of a pattern of violence within the family and society as a whole.

83% of those who had abused an animal also admitted to being violent towards another person

Child abuse, animal abuse and domestic violence are not isolated and unrelated patterns of behaviour. Where one occurs it is quite likely that all three may take place in almost a chain reaction.

Previously, low levels of reporting of all three have often lead to connections going unseen. However in 2001, the multi-agency Links Group was set up to encourage organisations to work together to help prevent and detect cases of interlinked abuse.

One of the main achievements of the Links Group has been the introduction of a joint RSPCA/NSPCC inspector training programme to encourage

greater cross-reporting. Last year social services referred over 600 cases to the RSPCA. Data collected by domestic violence charities, Refuge and Women's Aid, shows there were almost 400 cases of violence to animals last year with pets being used to coerce, control and intimidate partners.

Further alarming news has been revealed by a new scientific study conducted on behalf of the RSPCA. The research conducted over seven years among a group of 4,300 school children aged 13-17, revealed that 13% admitted they had deliberately harmed an animal. Furthermore 83% of those who had abused an animal also admitted to being violent towards another person – establishing the link between violence towards animals and that towards humans.

When animals are abused, people are at risk; when people are abused, animals are at risk. "Cruelty whether towards animals, children or vulnerable adults, is simply not acceptable in our society," says RSPCA acting chief executive Mark Watts.

For many women and children leaving a violent relationship is difficult because they cannot leave their pets behind in a violent situation and the refuges

When animals are abused, people are at risk; when people are abused, animals are at risk

they are going to won't allow pets. A number of pet fostering services have been set up around the country by various charities, including the Dogs Trust and the RSPCA. These offer foster places to pets when domestic violence has occurred and demand for these services is high.

The RSPCA is calling on the government and other agencies to do further research into the relationship between such abuses and to find effective ways to prevent such behaviour. In the meantime, for most involved, the chain reaction continues.

> For further information about pet fostering or if you need help with your pet go to:
> www.pawsforkids.org.uk
> www.rspca.org.uk
> www.dogstrust.org.uk

How do you tackle a dangerous dog?

Zoe Williams

The story of James Rehill's death, mauled by his own rottweiler, has a horrible familiarity to it. It is only a month since Archie-Lee Hirst was killed by a family pet of the same breed; in the intervening time, a dog kennel worker, Mandy Peynado, had to have her arm amputated after a savage attack by a stray with predominantly rottie traits. This emphasis on breed is misleading – all dogs can be dangerous, given the wrong training and the right conditions. But rottweilers, along with bull breeds, have extremely strong jaws, and it will give even the most hardboiled dog-lover pause to note that nearly 20 people went to help Rehill, and none were able to get the dog off him. So if a dog is attacking someone else, what technique should you use?

Behaviourist and trainer Stan Rawlinson (doglistener.co.uk) says, first of all, "Don't try to grab the dog's head, because you could get redirected aggression." Instead, follow the techniques you would use to break up a dog fight, namely: "Lift the dog's hindquarters off the ground and then drag it backwards by the tail. This will confuse the dog and may cause it to relax its grip. For dogs without tails, don't drag by the hind legs, as the dog can easily turn around and bite the person holding it."

You can also throw a blanket or a coat over the dog's head, or you can spray it with water, though this is not always effective and will probably not be fast enough unless you have a hose on you. Rawlinson says he personally would use the hindquarters method, with the option of going nuclear with a kick in the groin. Things are much harder if the dog is attacking you – bear in mind that movement stimulates their prey drive, so stay as still as possible, having first curled into a ball with your arms over your head.

The Guardian 30 January 2008
© Guardian News & Media Ltd. 2008

Number of hospital admissions as a result of dog bites and strikes

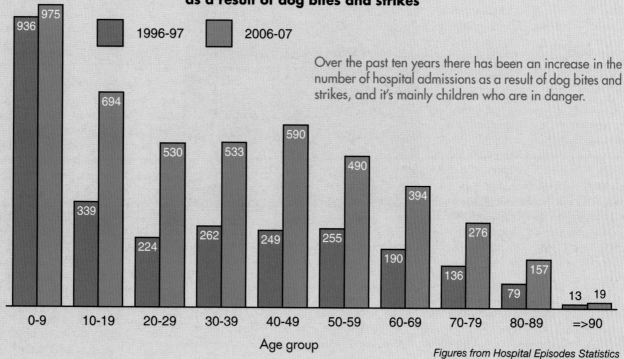

Legend: 1996-97, 2006-07

Over the past ten years there has been an increase in the number of hospital admissions as a result of dog bites and strikes, and it's mainly children who are in danger.

Age group	1996-97	2006-07
0-9	936	975
10-19	339	694
20-29	224	530
30-39	262	533
40-49	249	590
50-59	255	490
60-69	190	394
70-79	136	276
80-89	79	157
=>90	13	19

Figures from Hospital Episodes Statistics
http://hesonline.nhs.uk

Diamond Dogs

From canine cocktail gowns to poochy perfumes — pampering your pet is now at a whole new level, says Danny Buckland

The elegant coat is designer indulgence, the diamonds are sparkling and, with the scent of a fine perfume lingering, there is more than a hint of diva in the air. Hair care is with organic products, naturally, and nail polish and a boutique handbag add a little extra glitz.

But this little vignette of super style has a surprising twist. For once, it is the celebrities who are under-dressed as dogs take centre stage in a fashion trend that is confounding market forces – and, some might say, common sense.

Barely a decade ago, the canine accessory list was functional rather than fashionable with leather leads, a rubber bone, flea powder and a tartan waistcoat fastened with Velcro forming the basic wardrobe. Now the inventory stretches across frontline design houses such as Hermes, Chanel, Aquascutum and Ralph Lauren.

It is easy to view pet pampering as the preserve of slightly mad celebrities adopting miniature dogs as fashion statements and, as some psychologists would contend, comfort blankets against a hostile world. But, whatever the motives of pooch-toting stars such as Paris Hilton, Nicole Richie, Sandra Bullock and Charlotte Church, it seems that it is not only the famous who are going crazy for canine couture.

There is a profit-hungry machine capitalising on the UK's obsession with dogs and the canine grooming and accessory business is now a phenomenon with huge growth rates that have made it the darling of the struggling stock market.

The pets business has grown by more than 40% in five years and is now worth an astonishing £2.5 billion to the British economy. It is a sobering thought that, as the nation braces itself for financial doom next year, forecasters gleefully predict that more than £35 million will be spent on pets this Christmas.

In the US, the market is worth more than £20 billion which is more than many countries' gross domestic product. Put simply, Americans spend more on their pets than they do on music, computer

games and videos combined. And if you think Britain will escape, it's already too late.

Canine couture is big business already and the high spot of the calendar will be at Harrods with its Pet-à-Porter show featuring celebrated designers Vivienne Westwood and Ben de Lisi and trendy

jeweller Stephen Webster (whose clients include Johnny Depp, Madonna and Sharon Stone), who has crafted a diamond-encrusted dog collar worth more than £500,000 to showcase at the event.

> "In the US, the market is worth more than £20 billion which is more than many countries' gross domestic product"

"Interest has grown rapidly over the five years we've held the show and with the introduction of dog accessories from top fashion brands, there is now a trend that sees your dog as well dressed as yourself, or in some cases better," says a Harrods spokesperson.

"Our doggy customers love it and we have people reserving tickets for the next show. The pet shop is now a confirmed destination in Harrods." The show – guests will be served champagne and canapés – attracts more than 300 clients prepared to spend £35 on a ticket and fortunes on their dogs.

The range of designer goodies on sale is startling, but new heights of cosseting were reached last week with the launch of the Petite Armande dog fragrance. Slick advertising unveils it as "inspired by nature with notes of French blackcurrant, Tunisian neroli, mimosa and violet leaf on a base of sweet vanilla bourbon with a little almond" – which should make a change from that heady whiff of decaying leaves and muddy puddles. The perfume comes in 50ml bottles at £38 each with the instructions to "spray lightly on to coat."

The manufacturer Mungo and Maud, which also sells a dog balm made from "botanical infusions and essential oils" for precious paws, is believed to have Liz Hurley, Sienna Miller and Graham Norton interested in the line for their treasured dogs.

Traditional pet shops are now finding competition from boutiques that specialise in sparkle rather than sawdust, with tuxedos, evening dresses, hoodies and gleaming bowls that would probably self-destruct if owners had the temerity to serve leftovers in them.

The US dog fashion line Little Lily has produced a Red Carpet Collection for pooches that are taken to awards ceremonies, cocktail parties and weddings. They have made mini versions of the Marchesa gown J-Lo wore to the Golden Globe Awards and of the sweeping Versace dress Penelope Cruz sported at the Oscars.

For the chaps, there is a miniature copy of Leonardo DiCaprio's Armani tux. The firm's only problem is keeping pace with demand.

Paul Mitchell's dog-care range of shampoos and conditioners, launched at Crufts this March, has reported monthly double-digit growth, proving that the trade is not just about showy accessories.

Celebrities are also realising a doggy dividend with Paris Hilton designing jewellery, Pamela Anderson launching a pet range and the ubiquitous Playboy logo now branded onto rhinestone collars.

Away from the glamour, pets generate the sort of numbers that have accountants and investors purring. The company Pets At Home, which has grown from a single shop in Chester in 1991 into a nationwide chain of pet superstores, is considering going public and has been valued at £600m.

CLARISSA BALDWIN, chief executive of Dogs Trust, which homes thousands of stray and abandoned dogs, sounds a note of caution, however: "It is wonderful that people love and care for their dogs because they give us so much and there is nothing wrong with buying them something smart that is practical, but dressing them up in expensive, unnecessary clothes is ridiculous," she says.

> "Dogs are wearing goggles and bandanas. People are transferring human desires to their pets"

"We don't need to humanise them in this way. I think this sort of showy dressing up says more about the owner than the dog. Putting a dog in an Elvis Presley costume and having dog weddings makes a mockery of the animal – they don't deserve it.

"I only wish these people with this amount of disposable income would give it to us to care for the 150,000 unwanted dogs each year.

"It might be seen as fun but I hope and pray that this does not become something where dogs are seen as playthings to be dressed up and then cast away when the fashion for this has gone." She reveals that despite the boom in pampering, 8,000 unwanted dogs are put down each year in the UK.

> "I hope that this doesn't become something where dogs are seen as playthings to be dressed up and cast away when the fashion for this has gone"

But the dog business is predicted to have many good years to come. "The industry has taken advantage of current human trends for natural, organic, 'light', and convenience products. There are even detox supplements and, naturally, probiotics are everywhere, too," says Karen Pickwick, editor of Pet Business World News magazine.

"Luxury and lifestyle products even feature four-poster beds and dogs are wearing goggles and bandanas. People are transferring human desires to their pets; if they need detox, 'good' bacteria, low-calorie/low fat diets and fresh breath chews then their dogs must need them too. And if they enjoy summer pudding or apple crumble then the pet industry is happy to oblige by making desserts for dogs along with 'up-market' recipes.

"We might mock, but if it's good for the animals and for the British industry, with far more science behind feeding and pets apparently living longer and healthier lives, then long may it continue."

So, if you are considering taking your dog for a walk today you had better make sure that both of you are in your Sunday best before you go.

Sunday Express 25 November 2007

So You Think You're Vegan?!

Everyone reading this knows what veganism is. Even my dictionary knows: a vegan is 'a person who does not eat or use animal products' (*The Concise Oxford Dictionary*)

John Davis

And yet, put a group of vegans in the same room, and sooner or later a discussion will begin about what it means to be a vegan. Are you a vegan if you still wear your old leather belt? Are you a vegan if you eat eggs that your rescue hens have laid? What if you eat a meal a friend has carefully prepared thinking that it is vegan, but which you discover contains honey? Are you a vegan if you took medicine containing an animal product when you were ill?

A strict vegan will be quick to say no. Vegans do not eat or use animal products, so if you do so, you are not a vegan. End of story. But if this is the case then it raises the question, who is a vegan? Is there really anyone out there who has not, at one time or another, knowingly or accidentally, used or consumed an animal product? I doubt it. The sad truth is that it is simply not possible to live in a modern Western society as a perfect vegan. So does this mean that there are no vegans on this planet? Of course not.

Let us turn instead to the Vegan Society's definition of veganism: 'Veganism may be defined as a way of living which seeks to exclude, as far as possible and practical, all forms of exploitation of, and cruelty to, animals for food, clothing or any other purpose.'

There are, I believe, two things that are very important to note in this definition. Firstly, it accepts that it is not possible to avoid animal products entirely. Veganism 'seeks to exclude': it is an attempt to exclude animal products, it is not the act of flawlessly doing so. It wasn't possible to avoid animal products entirely when the vegan movement began, and it isn't now. So if, on occasion, we find that we have consumed something containing an animal product, or need to take a medicine containing an animal product, this is no reason to give in to feelings of guilt, or consider ourselves no longer a vegan as a result.

Secondly, the definition places emphasis not on dogmatic adherence to the avoidance of all animal products for its own sake, but in order to avoid exploitation of animals. And it is this aim of avoiding exploitation of animals that is of primary importance. Of course, most of the time, the way in which we can best avoid animals being exploited for our benefit is to avoid animal products. But consider again one of the examples I gave at the start of this article: A friend, knowing that you are vegan, spends time and effort preparing what they think is a vegan meal for a dinner party. Unfortunately, it contains honey, which they had not realised was not vegan.

So you have two options available to you. You can refuse to eat the meal, thereby maintaining your veganism. All right, so you offend your friend, leaving them with the impression that vegans are ungrateful and fanatical, and of the opinion that they won't bother making the effort in future.

Or you can thank them for their thoughtfulness, eat the meal in the knowledge that everyone else is enjoying a virtually vegan meal whereas, had you not have been present, they would have been eating meat, and perhaps, if the opportunity arises, point out that honey is not actually strictly vegan, opening up the opportunity to talk about veganism to people who might not otherwise have considered it. Personally, I know which option would seem to most 'reduce the exploitation of, and cruelty to, animals'.

Similar reasoning, with the emphasis on minimising cruelty to animals, can be applied to the other examples I mentioned. Personally I would probably not eat an egg laid by a rescue hen, since to do so would promote the idea that it is acceptable to eat eggs, which in general causes harm to animals. And similarly, I would not wear even a second-hand leather belt as it promotes the idea that it is acceptable to wear leather. But I am aware that there are reasonable counter-arguments which say that is better to eat the egg than let it go to waste, and it is better for people to use old leather products than throw them away. However, although there is not always an easy answer, what is clear is that if, in these instances, through your decision you are attempting to 'reduce the exploitation of, and cruelty to, animals', you are acting as a vegan.

Veganism is an attempt to minimise animal cruelty through avoiding animal products. It is not possible to always avoid all animal products, and there may even be circumstances where one could argue that it is better not to do so. But in my opinion that does not mean that if one does, knowingly or accidentally, occasionally use an animal product, then one is no longer a vegan. I think an appropriate analogy can be found through comparison to religion. A person may still call themselves a Christian even if, on occasion, they sin. And a person is still a vegan if, on occasion, circumstances force them to consume an animal product.

For in the final reckoning, the root of veganism lies not in avoiding of animal products: that is simply a result of veganism. The essence of veganism is the attempt to 'reduce the exploitation of, and cruelty to, animals'. That is what is important.

Note: *This article considers veganism to be synonymous with ethical veganism. I am aware that there are those who are vegan only for health reasons, and for those people, other definitions of veganism might be held as being of paramount importance.*

The Vegan Autumn 2007

Veganism is an attempt to exclude animal products, it is not the act of flawlessly doing so. It wasn't possible to avoid animal products entirely when the vegan movement began, and it isn't now

Why I use laboratory animals

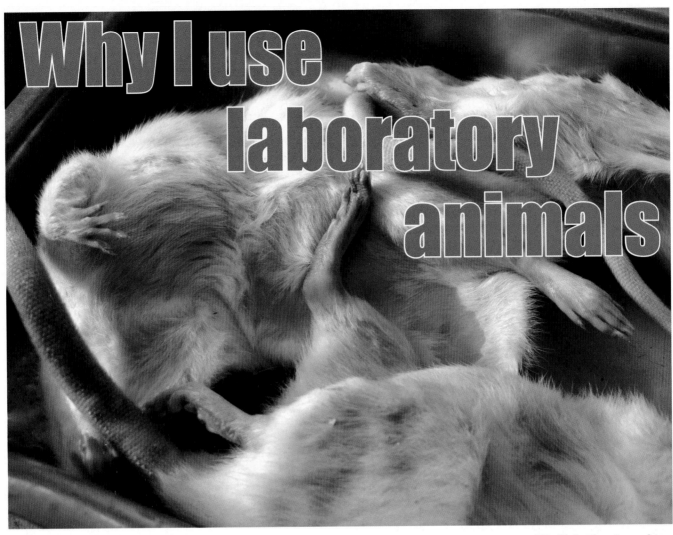

By Edythe London

A UCLA scientist targeted by animal rights militants defends her research on addiction and the brain

For years, I have watched with growing concern as my UCLA colleagues have been subjected to increasing harassment, violence and threats by animal rights extremists. In the last 15 months, these attempts at intimidation have included the placement of a Molotov cocktail-type device at a colleague's home and another under a colleague's car – thankfully, they didn't ignite – as well as rocks thrown through windows, phone and e-mail threats, banging on doors in the middle of the night and, on several occasions, direct confrontations with young children.

Then, several weeks ago, an article in the *San Francisco Chronicle* about the work I have been doing to understand and treat nicotine addition among adolescents informed readers that some of my research is done on primates. I was instantly on my guard. Would I be the next victim? Would the more extremist elements of the animal rights movement now turn their sights on me?

The answer came this week when the Animal Liberation Front claimed responsibility for vandalism that caused between $20,000 and $30,000 worth of damage to my home after extremists broke a window and inserted a garden hose, flooding the interior. Later, in a public statement addressed to me, the extremists said they had been torn between flooding my house or setting it afire. Maybe I should feel lucky.

Having come to the United States as the child of Holocaust survivors who had lost almost everything, I appreciate that perhaps "only in America" could I have fulfilled my dream of becoming a biomedical scientist, supported in doing research to reduce human suffering. But it is difficult for me to understand why the same country that was founded on the idea of freedom for all gives rise to an organisation like the Animal Liberation Front, a shadowy group identified by the FBI as a domestic terrorism threat, which threatens the safety of researchers engaged in animal studies that are crucial to moving medicine forward.

I have devoted my career to understanding how nicotine, methamphetamine and other drugs can hijack brain chemistry and leave the affected individual at the mercy of his or her addiction. My personal connection to addiction is rooted in the untimely death of my father, who died of complications of nicotine dependence. My work on the neurobiology of addiction has spanned three decades of my life – most of this time as a senior scientist at the National Institutes of Health. To me, nothing could be more important than solving the mysteries of addiction and learning how we can restore a person's control over his or her own life. Addiction robs young people of their futures, destroys families and places a tremendous burden on society.

Animal studies allow us to test potential treatments without confounding factors, such as prior drug use and other experiences that complicate human studies. Even more important, they allow us to test possibly life-saving treatments before they are considered safe to test in humans. Our animal studies address the effects of chronic drug use on brain functions, such as decision-making and self-control,

It would be immoral to decline an opportunity to increase our knowledge about addiction, especially when teens are involved

that are impaired in human addicts. We are also testing potential treatments, and all of our studies comply with federal laws designed to ensure humane care.

While monkeys receive drugs in the laboratory, they do not become "addicted" in the same sense that humans become addicted. Still, we are able to see how changes in brain chemistry alter the way the brain works – knowledge that is vital to the design of effective medications.

My colleagues and I place a huge value on the welfare of our research subjects. We constantly strive to minimize the risk to them; however, a certain amount of risk is necessary to provide us with the information we need in a rigorously scientific manner. Since the incident at my house, our research has gotten a lot of attention. Some anti-smoking groups have raised questions about the fact that our work was funded by Philip Morris USA. Is it moral to allow the tobacco industry to fund research on addiction? My view is that the problem of tobacco dependence is enormous, and the resources available for research on the problem are limited. It would, therefore, be immoral to decline an opportunity to increase

our knowledge about addiction and develop new treatments for quitting smoking, especially when teens are involved. Few people are untouched by the scourge of addiction in their friends or family. It is through work like ours that the understanding of addiction expands and gives rise to hope that we can help people like my father live longer, healthier lives.

Thousands of other scientists use laboratory animals in other research, giving hope to those afflicted with a wide variety of ailments. Already, one scientist at UCLA has announced that he will not pursue potentially important studies involving how the brain receives information from the retina, for fear of the violence that animal rights radicals might visit on his family. We must not allow these extremists to stop important research that advances the human condition.

Edythe London is a professor of psychiatry and bio-behavioral sciences and of molecular and medical pharmacology at the David Geffen School of Medicine at UCLA (University of California, Los Angeles)

LA Times 1 November 2007

The last word on diets

Kira Cochrane

I finally have to bow to the inevitable. For a few years now I've been avoiding the evidence – the clothes I can no longer wear, the sight of myself in photographs, the fact that, if I so wished (which would, admittedly, be really weird), I could fit my head quite happily into one of my bra cups. I have also been avoiding the fact that my father died of a massive heart attack at the age of 34, and that if I don't lose a stone or four I could be on a fast track to the same fate. Fun! Yes, it is time to lose weight.

This brings me to the dread word "diet". Dieting strikes fear into my soul – and not just because I know it'll involve imbibing vats full of bean sprout juice. No, diets scare me because they involve buying into something hateful, a system that makes women feel terrible about themselves.

Now, before you say it, I know that men are made to feel crap about their bodies, too; absolutely, no doubt. Yet there are some differences. One, a man's achievements are not judged through the prism of his size to the extent that women's tend to be. Two, the "ideal" male body shape is predicated on a healthier template – strength and a wee bit of brawn – rather than utter diminishment.

By comparison, we women are taught from an early age that our success is dependent on our looks. In this context, looking good has nothing to do with strength or agility or being healthy and everything to do with being "bird-like", "delicate", or that modern confection, "size zero". In other words, it's about negation.

And, having been taught that our bodies are our most important asset, and that the key is to remain slim, small and unthreatening, women very often (not always, but often) naturally proceed to police themselves and others.

A friend had to stop his mother commenting on his daughter's thighs – said daughter is three years old

Last month, for instance, a More magazine survey revealed that, in an effort to lose weight, a third of young women (34%) had taken slimming pills and 30% had made themselves sick. 11% had taken speed or cocaine specifically to quicken their metabolism. Only 5% felt that they could possibly be happy as a size 14 and only 1% could raise a smile as a size 16 – a shame at the very least, when you consider that size 16 is the UK average.

This unhappiness starts young – a poll for the BBC's Newsround this month found that more than a quarter of girls aged six to 12 wanted to be thinner or to change their body shape. This is hardly surprising. Mothers police their daughters from an incredibly early age, sometimes without even knowing it. My mother's pet name for me as a kid was "fairy elephant", which was no doubt meant affectionately, but...

A male friend of mine had to ask his mother to stop making comments about his daughter's thighs – specifically, "You'll never get a boyfriend or get married if you don't lose some weight, darling." Said daughter is three. Friends police their friends: "A moment on the lips, a lifetime on the hips."

Ugh, ugh, ugh. One of the most depressing lines I have ever read was in an extract from a book by Candida Crewe on the subject of her eating habits. Of being in social situations, she wrote: "I cannot settle until I have taken into account where I am in the pecking order of fatness, and therefore where I am in the pecking order generally."

It is possible to opt out of all this. I haven't weighed myself in years and I can honestly say I don't judge people by their weight. Nor have I (amazing, I know!) ever taken cocaine to keep my weight down.

But the problem is that while you can opt out of the diet side of the equation, there is still the flipside to deal with – an obesogenic environment in which food is constantly available, in which high-calorie, big-portion meals are advertised to us endlessly, and in which sitting on one's arse all day (especially if you have an office job) is a virtual inevitability.

Ignore the "deprive yourself!" part of the equation, and you still have the "gorge yourself!" one to wrestle with.

I have read arguments which say that a woman committing to losing weight must give up her right to be taken seriously, as she is clearly self-obsessed and shallow. I'm also aware that a man carrying at least a few stone too many, at the risk of serious health complications, would simply be seen as quite sensible for taking action. To say that women can be considered intelligent only if they completely ignore their body seems to take the idea that women's bodies define us to its apotheosis.

I guess the key to making the whole thing less hateful is, first, not to call losing a bit of weight a "diet"; second, not to buy into the hideous diet industry and its products; and third, not to talk about it constantly, both boring the hell out of your friends and making them feel self-conscious about their own eating habits.

That's it then. Let's never speak of this again.

New Statesman 13 December 2007

Model health inquiry

The fashion industry has long been blamed for the increase in eating disorders among young people. Madrid Fashion week has already banned girls with a BMI of less than 18.5. Now London fashion week has responded too.

Twiggy, now aged 57, who is fronting the current M&S advertising campaign, is the picture of good health. However, if she were starting her career today she wouldn't be allowed onto the catwalks. Not only was Twiggy the face of the swinging Sixties, she was Britain's first teenage supermodel. Under the recommended rules she would be considered too young, too thin and too unhealthy.

When Twiggy, who was signed up in 1966 by Justin de Villeneuve, began modelling she was 5ft 6ins tall and weighed six-and-a-half stone (41 kgs). She was exceedingly skinny, with a Body Mass Index (BMI) of 14.6, well below the 18.5 regarded as the healthy minimum. Yet despite this, she soon became an icon of the age and an influence to future modelling generations.

The final report of the Model Health inquiry, set up by the British Fashion Council to tackle health problems among London Fashion Week models, states that models should be required to provide "good health" certificates from doctors specialising in eating disorders. Agencies would have to check the certificates before taking the models on. The inquiry will also specifically look into whether or not BMI is a useful measure for identifying eating disorders.

The inquiry rejected the idea of a weigh-in system, fearing that it would actually contribute to eating disorders as well as being demeaning. It is hoped that the system of medical certificates combined with monitoring will be a better way to support the health of catwalk models.

The report contained 14 recommendations including chaperones for 16-18 year old models, random drug tests and a "rigorous scientific study" into the extent of eating disorders within the industry.

The inquiry was sparked by the deaths of Uruguayan model Luisel Ramos, 22, and her sister, Eliana, 18, within months of each other last year as a result of eating disorders.

Models will have to provide health certificates

Shaping up to look good

Having a different body shape doesn't mean you're a fashion victim

Michael Shamash

Double amputee model Aimee Mullins strides down the catwalk on intricately carved wooden legs designed by Alexander McQueen

LAURA WOOLNOUGH/IPA Archive/IPA Photos

Fashion is seen as something marginal in the lives of disabled people. We look at the images of the catwalks in Paris, Milan and New York with emaciated bodies wearing histrionic clothing costing ludicrous sums and question how we can relate to this.

Yet, for many disabled people our impairments mean that we have far more in common with the catwalk than we could possibly imagine. Body shapes and sensory perceptions that heighten our profile and accentuate difference define us. I am not able to retreat into

Yet the relationship between the disabled person and fashion has historically been a tortuous one. Look at a picture of a residential establishment and the disabled people would all be wearing similar clothes, dull colours, possibly striped.

a world of anonymous conformity.

When I was a teen I bought a pink sweater. My father told me not to wear it as it made me conspicuous to which I replied that even if I wore the least flamboyant clothes, as a person of restricted growth I would always be very noticeable so I might just as well wear what I wanted.

I grew up in a fashion-conscious family and from an early age was aware of the power of clothing. Clothes are both camouflage and statement. They are both profound and superficial. They show that we belong and yet we have our own

> **Even if I wore the least flamboyant clothes, as a person of restricted growth I would always be very noticeable**

independence of spirit. Clothes can provide us with any number of images to present to the world, drawing on a creative melting pot of influences. For example, you have a meeting. You could look neat and conventional or you could choose bright and assertive. Your clothes set the agenda.

Yet the relationship between the disabled

person and fashion has historically been a tortuous one. Look at a picture of a residential establishment and the disabled people would all be wearing similar clothes, dull colours, possibly striped. Garments were the symbol of subordination and control. Looking through archive photos of disabled people one sees elegant dignitaries patronising the dowdy disabled. Even in the post institutional era, clothes would be cast-offs frequently chosen by others.

Our appearance doesn't have to be something we're ashamed of, but could and should be a celebration of strength and dignity. The fashion

media has assiduously avoided suggesting that disabled people have any relationship with style. Disabled people were deemed too ugly. This orthodoxy was briefly challenged in the late '90s.

The style magazine Dazed and Confused in late 1998 had a fashion shoot of disabled people wearing outfits designed

by top fashion designers including Alexander McQueen, with the photography undertaken by Nick Knight, a doyen of fashion shoots. These were stylish clothes presented in stylish images suggesting alternative

> **Clothes are both camouflage and statement. They are both profound and superficial. They show that we belong and yet we have our own independence of spirit**

ways of defining beauty. For a short period, there was interest in the idea that disabled people could be stylish and fashionable.

I became involved in an inclusive fashion show entitled, "In our Fashion", in 2001. This was organised in London by the arts access organisation, Artsline. Top designers would create designs for disabled models. It was an exciting period, with newspaper articles and radio broadcasts. Disability fashion had become a serious issue with the clothing retail forum Awear being established in Nottingham, and local organisations ran inclusive fashion shows. There was even the possibility that major retailers would start to address the issue. This sadly amounted to nothing. There has never been a major inclusive fashion show since and

nor has a major style or fashion paper or magazine looked at disabled people as worthy of coverage. A lack of will and financial failure were the prime causes. "In our Fashion" was an honourable failure. Things need to be done

urgently to regain the lost momentum. Despite two Disability Discrimination Acts, little has been done to make the fashion retail environment any more inclusive or accessible. In many boutiques, style seems to equal stairs, poor lighting and an absence of signage. Designers are still loath, with a few honourable exceptions, to use the challenges of different bodies and sensory perspectives in a challenging way that could have genuine applications for all.

Disabled people need to revel in our thrilling differences. The world may need redesigning but in the meantime let's celebrate by acknowledging our style and poise. Disabled people must be an equal part of a style-conscious world. Let's put on our glad rags and join the party.

Disability Now
17 December 2007

Longevity: Isn't it time we acted our age?

Madonna's genes and gym-enhanced shape are the exception, says Karen Krizanovich

The trouble with longevity is how long it goes on for. Way back when we, as a societal group, died at 30, life was shorter and more compacted.

We married at 16, had children at 17 and were toothless by 25.

While there are parts of the country where this still happens, it is more common now for humans to live a protracted life, one that's as slow as a metaphorical sloth.

We move out of the family home to attend university, slink back to mum and dad at 30, and ponder marriage at about 40. After finding our perfect mate (online) at about the mid-40 mark, we are then heartbroken to learn that a scientist has to help us reproduce.

"Honey, we're too old to have kids!" We ask ourselves, "How did that happen? We're so young..."

Well, actually, you're not – you just feel that way. With the magic bullets of superior diet, expert dermatology, increased prosperity, medical miracles and that fountain of youth called daily exercise, we're finding ourselves with extra time on our hands.

Normal mortals now verge on immortal and, not being slouches, they want to make use of every minute they've got. So we end up with centenarians running marathons, 60-year-olds giving birth and 80-year-old men marrying women in their twenties.

Of course, Madonna, who keeps reminding us that her 50th birthday this year is a great excuse for a party, is our team leader. She's the icon of a new generation who refuses to grow old or grow up – as anyone who has seen her displaying her toned limbs on the latest cover of Vanity Fair can attest.

Closer to home, my 86-year-old father has just taken up the saxophone and Skypes me every day. My mum exercises daily for an hour and she's 84. They walk without canes and often have to produce ID to prove they qualify for senior citizen discounts. They are typical of a newfound longevity of mind, body and spirit.

While I love them desperately, I am not sure I would want to live that long. They've lost all their friends, have permanent visitors' parking spaces at the local hospital and cling to each other in a loving combat. They are each other's entire world.

We are all supposed to wither and die, otherwise our judgment of youth and age slides away from its traditional moorings.

Things are already starting to slip. Many of my generation are looking at new careers, new relationships, new families and new adventures when, 40 years ago, we would have been wearing support hose and bifocals.

We're in our late forties but some of us feel like teenagers, ready for a new life, despite looking like a saddlebag with eyes.

And that is the crux of the matter. Not everyone has good genes, an endless supply of sun block or a clever dermatologist. Although we feel surges of vigour, one look in the mirror says: "Whoa. Who are you kidding?"

Madonna is our team leader. She is the icon of a new generation who refuses to grow old or grow up.

Even with laser peels and non-surgical facelifts, from a certain age we can no longer look youthful; we can only appear well-rested.

There will be women and men at your gym whose bodies, despite their fitness, are not "youthening". With age, the bum goes flat, the shoulders stoop, the movements slow – and no amount of superior DNA, plastic surgery or nutrition can fix that.

As my mother once said when, as a teenager, I complained of spots, lank hair and being overweight: "Be happy. You're young. Young is good."

But even when you're 50, chances are you think deep down inside that you're not. In a recent survey of 1,200 adults between the ages of 40 and 70, nutritional analysts nutriprofile.org discovered that the average 50-year-old feels 12 years and four months younger than they really are – which means a perceived age of 37.

"We end up with centenarians running marathons, 60-year-olds giving birth and 80-year-old men marrying women in their twenties."

It's commendable that we're all so young at heart. But that does not change the fact that none of us gets out of this alive.

We can't all be Madonna who, with her wealth and fame, seems able to achieve the appearance of everlasting youth. By 50, most of us will be going the way of another of the world's most powerful and successful women, Oprah Winfrey, and filling out just as impressively. Ultimately, we are what we are.

Although we feel surges of vigour, one look in the mirror says: 'Whoa. Who are you kidding?'

While the nutriprofile.org findings are new, what the survey purports to tell us is not. Some of us have always considered ourselves a whole lot younger than we really are, knocking a couple of years off our age whenever it suits us.

This way, when our time finally comes, at least we won't feel old.

Daily Telegraph 2 April 2008
© Telegraph Group Ltd. 2008

Spectacles? Cool? Can't see it, myself

By Simon Round

One of the pivotal events of my school career occurred when I was seven.

My teacher, Mrs Soames, had noticed that I was struggling to read what she was writing on the blackboard. In fact, to get a decent view of what she was writing, I needed to get so near the blackboard I practically ended up with chalk on my nose. Soon she tired of my constant trips to the front of the class and my mother was informed that I needed a sight test.

The optician prescribed me glasses – to be precise, one pair of standard issue National Health specs of the type specifically designed to maximise the humiliation for any child. They worked a treat. From being a kid with poor eyesight and moderately high esteem I became a kid with good eyesight and low self esteem.

I was at the time the only myopic pupil in the class, though soon I was joined by some of the other smaller, weedier Jews. In an instant my football career was almost dead. If I wanted to head the ball, it meant leaping athletically while removing my glasses in the same instant, then putting them back on to see where the ball had gone – this stuff never happened to Johann Cruyff.

Then there was the shape of the glasses. They were round – so was my name. This lead to some hilarious jokes. The jokes got even better a couple of years later when I switched to square frames (you could probably make up your own here).

"I have been mentally scarred by specciness."

Then there was the attitude of my classmates who now saw me as a swot. My teachers, unimpressed with my progress, had me down for a dunce. Glasses were ruining my life.

Thankfully, it seems that the current generation of children are not going through this experience. According to a new survey, kids with glasses are now seen as cool. Indeed, 43% of speccy four-eyed (I'm sorry – I mean bespectacled) children now claim that having the right pair of glasses makes them more popular than their deprived un-myopic mates. They cite the influence of Johnny Depp and Harry Potter for making specs acceptable, which is ironic because Harry wears precisely the same kind of glasses which ruined my own image back in the 70s.

Still, on the plus side, at least I was in tune ethnically with my own people (there are very few employees at the Jewish Chronicle who don't wear glasses and we always gang up on them at playtime).

There is also scientific research undertaken (er, by me) which indicates that short-sighted people are cleverer than their counterparts with 20/20 vision. It stands to reason. If you are unable to see well enough to spear a wildebeest as it roams majestically across the plain, you need to come up with an alternative strategy to corner your prey (going to the supermarket works for me).

"Specs specifically designed to maximise the humiliation for any child"

To this day, I prefer not to wear glasses. I have been mentally scarred by specciness. Contemporaries who were not subjected to glasses in childhood, happily sport designer frames. Me? However cool the specs, they always bring back that mental image of me pinned to the floor in the playground as my "friends" all tried on my glasses while making the stupidest face they could manage (Richard Josephs didn't actually have to try that hard).

Thankfully, this kind of thing happens slightly less often when you are a grown-up. But then you can't be too careful – that's why I'm wearing lenses now.

Jewish Chronicle
9 November 2007

Britain – land of yobs and morons?

Other countries have them – so why not Britain? The concise phrase that sums up everything a nation stands for. France can do it in three words: *Liberté, égalité, fraternité* – the very rhythm of the country's revolutionary heartbeat. For America, the original motto: *E pluribus unum* – "Out of many, one," which was adopted after the War of Independence, reflects the composite nature of its constitution, with the individual states being incorporated into a single nation. It's a phrase which is also entirely applicable to the make-up of a nation in which many nationalities and cultures unite. No matter how they are hyphenated – African-American, Irish-American, Hispanic-American – there is a patriotic pride in the stars and stripes that seems uncomfortable and excessive to us British. The current motto *In God we trust* was adopted in 1956.

But France and America are republics – where all power is held by the citizens and their representatives. Strictly speaking we are not citizens of Britain but subjects. We have no succinct bill of rights, no written constitution. Our Royals have mottos a-plenty: *Honi soit qui mal y pense* (Shame upon him who thinks evil upon this), *Dieu et mon droit* (God and my right) – but there is no one phrase that stands for what the ordinary people of Britain believe in, that summarises the national character or that binds us together with a common purpose.

The idea of a national motto was introduced in 2007 as part of a debate about what it means to be British. The make up and character of the nation seemed, as so often, to be in flux, a 'statement of values' was needed which could become part of a future Bill of Rights. Newspapers took up the idea, inviting their readers to make their suggestions.

"Dipso, fatso, asbo, Tesco"

The serious and patriotic were in the minority: "Pride, passion, history, monarchy, exploration", "Courage, reason, humanity, democracy, monarchy", "A country so brave and true", "Fairness for all" and "For honour and for freedom". Some sounded like advertising slogans "Unity in individuality" or "Great people, great country, Great Britain".

Much more prominent were the humorous, and cynical, versions of our nation's present state such as "In America we trust" or "Once mighty Empire, slightly used". A little bitterness was also evident: "Smile. You're on CCTV" or "Land of yobs and morons". Many featured our drinking habits: "Drinking continues until morale improves", "Let's all go down the pub" and the wonderfully succinct "Dipso, fatso, asbo, Tesco" from a *Times* reader.

Another theme was the gently self-mocking: "Britain, a terribly nice place", "Less stuffy than we sound", "We apologise for the inconvenience". This was combined with a (typically British?) contempt for foreigners in one suggestion: "At least we're not France".

And perhaps that is the problem. We're not France, our identity has not been forged in the heat of revolutionary fervour. We're not America and didn't have to claw our way to independent nationhood by breaking away from an oppressive colonial power (Er, that's us, sorry!). Our national identity is not a suit of armour to defend us against others, but more like a familiar dressing gown that shows all the tears and stains of long use.

The response to this search for a motto suggests that our national characteristics include a taste for cynicism and subversion. Perhaps the nearest we can come to a statement that unites us is: we can't take anything seriously, especially not ourselves. In which case the national motto should be "Are you 'avin' a larf?"

Sources: Various

The Guardian 18 October 2007

As a British Muslim I find 'virginity repairs' on the NHS dangerous, demeaning... and utterly indefensible

By Saira Khan

Even by the standards of medical horror stories that have filled our papers of late, it's a tale that beggars belief. According to the latest figures, some 24 women have recently had their virginities 'restored', not by some divine miracle or act of magic, but by a surgical procedure paid for by our already hard-pressed National Health Service.

How ridiculous, how dangerous and how indefensible. At a time when cancer and Alzheimer's patients are routinely deprived of drugs, the idea that a single penny of NHS funding is spent on repairing something as fragile, ephemeral and medically useless as a woman's hymen is absurd.

Only where a young woman has been raped or violently sexually assaulted can there even be the slightest justification for the NHS to pay for such a procedure.

And yet in 2005-2006, the NHS clearly decided otherwise time and time again.

So who are these women who are seeking to have their virginities restored? According to the figures, they are 'immigrants and British women of ethnic origin'.

Well, speaking as a British woman of ethnic origin, let me make it clear. The British NHS should simply not be paying for a cosmetic procedure that is unnecessary, demeaning to women and totally at odds with modern British culture.

The report accompanying the figures is too politically correct to identify the religion of the women who have had the operation, but it's my informed guess that most of them – all of them, perhaps – will turn out to be Muslim.

As the daughter of parents who arrived in Britain from Pakistan in the mid-Sixties, I'm a Muslim myself but I'm appalled by the sort of cultural pressures these women must be under to seek such a procedure.

But I'm also angry that the NHS has agreed to carry them out. By paying for and performing such operations, the NHS isn't furthering the integration of the Muslim community into the British way of life; in fact, it's doing quite the opposite.

It's effectively condoning an increasingly fundamentalist Islamic culture that is patriarchal, regressive and increasingly demeaning to women. Surely that has no place in the Britain of today?

The prizing of a woman's virginity is a cultural tradition rather than a religious practice and it's an archaic one at that. True, the Koran does encourage both sexes to abstain from sex before marriage, but so do the religious texts that provide the basis for most of the world's religions.

Most, of course, are routinely ignored in modern Western societies, where both sexes are free to experiment or abstain as they choose. But not, increasingly, in Britain's Muslim communities today, where the differences between the sexes is in real danger of becoming a gulf.

Muslim young men in Britain are generally at liberty to live their lives as freely as any of their non-Muslim friends, with a blind eye being turned to their nights out and their sexual encounters with girls of all faiths or none.

Their sisters, by contrast, are having a far tougher time under mounting pressure to wear the veil, cover their bodies and not even to glance at a non-Muslim boy.

For them, sex before marriage could result in their being ostracised, beaten or even worse by their male relatives.

You can see why those who have strayed sexually might be desperate to restore their virginity, especially with so many young British Muslim women being sent abroad to enter into arranged marriages in parts of the world where their new in-laws will still expect to fly a blood-spotted sheet from the window of the wedding-night bedroom.

For a bride to fail to live up to these expectations of purity is to risk becoming a social pariah or, worse, another sad statistic in the shameful roll call of 'honour killings'.

But that doesn't mean the NHS should be helping them; indeed, it means quite the opposite.

What we desperately need now are British politicians to stand up and say this sort of practice is not compatible with the British way of life. But none of them will, terrified they'll be accused of being racist, anti-Islamic or politically incorrect.

Well, let me, as a British-Asian Muslim and a woman, say it for them: those of us who choose to live in Britain must follow and respect British values and the most precious of those is equality of the sexes.

Even my father, a devout Muslim from a Kashmiri village who read his Koran every day, understood that.

He knew and was profoundly grateful for the fact that it was the British taxpayer who paid for my free school lunches and my free school uniform and, until Mrs Thatcher enabled him to buy it, our Derbyshire council house.

He accepted that he had to adapt his religious beliefs accordingly, which is why my sister and I were educated every bit as well as our brothers, didn't have to go to mosque, and why we

> **For a bride to fail to live up to these expectations of purity is to risk becoming another sad statistic in the shameful roll call of 'honour killings'**

Under pressure: Muslim women can be ostracised for having sex before marriage

learned our Koran in English rather than Arabic.

And, although the minute I turned 17 unknown Muslim men would arrive on our doorstep asking for my hand in marriage, my father knew that nothing would happen without my agreement.

It was, he accepted, a more British way of doing things.

He understood then what so many immigrant communities seem to be struggling with today.

In Pakistan, you can live according to Pakistani values and customs, but once you come to Britain, you have to live according to British values.

The trouble is, too many of those who wield political influence in Britain today seem to lack the courage to stand up and say what those British values are.

And as such, they grant unwitting approval to practices that have no place in a modern, civilised nation such as ours.

No one in government would dream of condoning female circumcision – a barbaric practice still carried out in some Islamic communities in North Africa.

Yet the prizing of a woman's virginity is on the same oppressive continuum that subjugates women to men in a way that is totally unacceptable in Britain.

By offering 'virginity restoration' on the NHS, the State is effectively signalling its approval for such backward-looking attitudes. It is not only unacceptable, it is downright dangerous.

For what is the point in the Government spending millions on creating a 'Fortress Britain' to protect ourselves against terrorism when it is allowing the roots of Islamic extremism to spread into our hospital wards? Two decades on from my 17th birthday, I'm still living life by my father's enlightened approach to cultural integration.

On the one hand, I'm delighted that my mother is about to go to Hajj, the spiritual pilgrimage to Mecca that all Muslims must make once in their life.

But on the other hand, I'm pregnant, married to Steve, a lovely man from Essex and looking forward to celebrating Christmas as much as I am the festival of Eid ul-Adha that precedes it.

I'm delighted that, following my lead, three other British Muslim women I know have felt confident enough to marry white men without fear of reprisals from their own community.

But I'm also aware that we are in danger of becoming a fortunate minority among British Muslim women, a generation raised and educated before the fundamentalists got hold of Islam and before Britain became so politically correct it lost sight of the values that made this country such a great place to live.

For all our sakes, it's those values that need to be restored, not surrendered virginities.

Daily Mail 16 November 2007

Scandal of the schoolgirls vanishing into marriages of misery

With a wall of silence surrounding the kidnap and imprisonment of teenage girls in Yorkshire, Political Correspondent Tom Smithard reports on the forgotten victims of forced marriage

In the rarefied atmosphere of Committee Room 20 in the Palace of Westminster, surrounded by oak panels, green leather chairs and a marvellous view of the Thames, an influential group of 14 MPs has slowly been dissecting evidence.

The Home Affairs Select Committee launched an inquiry into domestic violence last July, and since then has had the difficult job of listening to some of the UK's most renowned experts describe in painful detail the distress and harm that can be caused

For years, schoolchildren in the UK have been quietly withdrawn from schools, many never to be heard of again

by husband to wife, father to daughter, brother to sister.

None more so than in the, until now, widely shielded topic of forced marriage.

For years, schoolchildren in the UK have been quietly withdrawn from schools, many never to be heard of again.

Mostly girls, mostly aged about 15 – though some as young as nine or 10 – mostly from towns and cities where the Asian community is largely segregated from the white; they disappear into home imprisonment or are flown to Pakistan and Bangladesh.

Their crime is to grow too close to Westerners in a community where people are still encouraged to marry their cousins. Encouraged? Often, they are forced.

Last week, Children's Minister Kevin Brennan, called before the committee to describe what the Government was doing to constrain forced marriages, admitted that Education Bradford, the private company that runs the district's schools, had lost track of 33 children in the 2006-7 academic year.

That the information was only divulged in public because of the select committee's intervention has raised eyebrows. That the police have not been informed may have meant that Education Bradford has neglected its statutory duty of care to its pupils.

But according to people familiar both with the vexed issue of forced marriage, and politics in Bradford, it is not surprising that the education authority has got itself in this position.

It all goes back to Ray Honeyford. In the early 1980s, the then-headteacher of Drummond Middle School, 90 per cent of whose pupils were Asian, wrote a series of articles criticising Bradford's policy of educating ethnic minority children according to their own culture, predicting that the move would create divisions between white and Asian communities.

He wanted to improve integration but was branded a racist and forced out of his job, taking early retirement in 1985 to protect his family. And since then, the argument goes, Bradford has been so scared of being seen as politically incorrect that it simply ignores the elephant in the room that is forced marriage.

Ann Cryer, MP for Keighley, has long been a lone voice in the wilderness campaigning for justice for victims of forced marriage – so much so that she faced expulsion by Bradford's Labour councillors for embarrassing the party.

She said: "Bradford has always been a hotbed of political correctness. Since Honeyford, it has been seen as unacceptable to criticise anyone from the Asian community. They've failed

Six years later, she was standing at her Bradford market stall when she learned her sister Robina, 24, had committed suicide to escape her abusive husband. Her sister had regularly complained of abuse to her family, but was told that leaving her husband would bring unacceptable shame on them. Ms Sanghera now runs the Karma Nirvana shelter in Derby and

He wanted to improve integration but was branded a racist and forced out of his job

acts as a political activist campaigning against forced marriages.

She said: "Part of the problem is that there has been a lot of denial. When we've tried to raise the issue of forced marriages with education authorities in the past there's been a reluctance to engage with us. They believe it's too politically and culturally sensitive a topic to deal with.

"They don't seem to understand this is about protecting children, this is about British-born subjects' human rights. It's not part of my culture to be abused."

West Yorkshire Police is the only force to collect statistics on forced marriages, and the only one to have a civilian worker dedicated to helping Asian women flee domestic violence. Because of its data, we now know that the force investigated 176 incidents of forced marriage in the last 12 months. But with much of that down to the proactive work of its community

workers, officers say the number would be even higher if social workers and education authorities always also reported their suspicions.

Salam Hafez, a researcher with the Centre for Social Cohesion, last month published a wide-ranging policy paper on violence within Asian communities, drawing upon research he conducted in Bradford. Yesterday he said: "Forced marriage is a real problem in Asian communities heavily segregated from white communities, and Bradford is one of those, where you get a real village mentality.

"I'm not at all shocked by these latest figures, indeed, from my research I wouldn't be surprised if the number was far higher. There is a real desire among the Asian communities in Bradford not to be westernised, so a lot of girls are pulled out of school and forced to marry relatives.

Attempting to be politically correct in all things means they're actually doing down the very children they think they're helping

to recognise that in order to protect vulnerable members of the community you have to take on the community leaders.

"We're now left with an apartheid situation with Bradford Council adopting the ostrich position. It's like being in the Dark Ages. Attempting to be politically correct in all things means they're actually doing down the very children they think they're helping."

Another woman branded racist for criticising forced marriages is the victim of one herself. Jasvinder Sanghera was 15 when she ran away in 1981 after her parents showed her a picture of the stranger she would have to marry.

Ms Sanghera compared the response to the missing Bradford girls to that of Shannon Matthews, the nine-year-old from Dewsbury, which more than 300 police officers were investigating.

"If 33 white girls went missing in Bradford, do you think that information would have to be wrestled out of an education authority by an MPs' Select Committee? What is the point of having child protection and education welfare officers if this is still allowed to happen?"

But while some authorities in Yorkshire are criticised for failing to deal with the problem, others are seen as national beacons.

"Education authorities don't want to deal with the problem because they're afraid of being seen as racist and they don't understand the Asian culture but really what they're doing is stopping human rights.

"I spoke to someone in Bradford whose job is to help vulnerable Asian women and he told me that if I come here in 20 years' time, I'll see exactly the same thing because people in the city are afraid to confront the issue."

His work has helped many in the political mainstream who previously had little idea of how widespread – and destructive – forced marriages are in the UK.

Authorities don't want to deal with the problem because they're afraid of being seen as racist... really what they're doing is stopping human rights

In his report, Honour-Based Violence in the UK, Mr Hafez wrote: "Many families believe that if their daughters become educated, men from the same ethnic or religious group, especially those brought up abroad, will become less willing to marry them.

"This fear of being unable to marry off their daughters can lead parents to withdraw their children from school when they approach a marriageable age."

He added: "Many women who are being forced into marriage suffer from physical and emotional violence.

Paul Hill, manager of Bradford Council's Safeguarding Children Board, said the authority is aware of its responsibilities and had measures in place to stop abuse: "Bradford Council and partner agencies, such as the police, take any suspected cases of forced marriage very seriously and we have a robust multi-agency system in place to support young people who face this prospect.

"We work closely with schools and other partner agencies, and staff are given special training, which we have developed with the Government's

who said they had no other option but to run away.

"What happens to these girls is quite horrific, and very varied as well," said one caseworker who did not want to be identified. "Girls are told who they must marry. If they refuse, they are locked in the house or are even kidnapped. If the girl runs away, the family will do everything they can to trace her, and if they find out she is somewhere like here, we get targeted as well."

She added: "So many people in the Pakistani community are behind the times. Probably about half the families in Bradford still think their daughters should marry their cousins.

"Everyone has got a mobile phone in their hand these days but when it comes to cultural values they remain very traditional, very tight to their heart. And it's us who have to pick up the pieces."

Yorkshire Post 11 March 2008

Probably about half the families in Bradford still think their daughters should marry their cousins

"In the period leading up to a forced marriage, young women are often withdrawn from school and can be imprisoned. This isolation from the outside world is often accompanied by physical violence and can lead to mental illness, self harm and suicide.

"In many cases, the only way young people at risk of a forced marriage – usually teenage girls – can escape is by running away. This can lead to other problems such as homelessness, poverty and dropping out of education as well as increasing the risk of violence from strangers."

Forced Marriage Unit, to help them spot a suspected forced marriage case.

"Young people are given advice of the options available, which can include working with the police and other relevant professionals to draw up an action plan. In some cases we may need to consider the need for immediate protection and placement away from the family."

But caseworkers at the city's Anah Project, an eight-bed shelter for Asian women fleeing domestic violence, said that they had to turn away girls daily

If you need help or advice on the issue of forced marriage, call the Karma Nirvana 'Honour Network' Hotline Free on 0800 5999247

Absent voices

Photo posed by model

Mixed race is the UK's fastest growing ethnic minority group, idealised by the media as the exotic, 'acceptable face' of diversity. But the reality, says **Laura Smith**, is rather different

There is a story my mother is fond of telling me and it goes like this. When I was three, a little friend of mine pointed at me and said with accusation in her voice: "You're black." My response was one that only a three-year-old could make. Puffing up my chest and probably sticking my nose in the air, I told her firmly: "No, I'm not. I'm pink and brown." It wasn't that being black was a bad thing. It was just that my skin was not literally the colour of my black crayons and so, logically, what she had said was nonsense.

Aged seven, I had the dubious distinction of being the only girl with one pink and one brown parent at my north London primary school. Although rarely intentionally unkind – apart from the little boy who called me poo in the school playground when the mood took him – my all-white classmates never let me forget that I was not like them. They asked me what it felt like to be black and

touched my hair uninvited. In turn, I cut off my curls as gifts to satisfy their curiosity and told them that where my mum came from they cleaned their teeth by chewing on sticks.

Nearly 25 years on, much has changed. The last national census counted 680,000 mixed race people, accounting for 1.2% of the overall population and nearly 15% of the ethnic minority population – and that is widely believed to be an underestimate. Suddenly, our image is everywhere, projected on posters selling Marks & Spencer's bikinis or sofas for DFS. Mixed-race people have become the acceptable face of ethnic minorities for advertisers and programme makers. We are sufficiently exotic for viewers and consumers to recognise as "other", and therefore a handy shorthand for diversity without the potential alienation associated with using somebody too black, too different, too dangerous.

And yet there is an inconsistency. Despite our growth in numbers and our incredible visibility, we are utterly absent from any public debate on race. We appear to be the elephant in the room: obvious to anybody living in a large British city yet invisible at a government level. Take the current discussion surrounding multiculturalism. The fact that people are increasingly falling in love, or simply in lust, and having children across a so-called racial divide is an inconvenient truth that challenges the government's notion of neat "communities" of black, white or Asian people.

It was only in the 2001 census that mixed-race people were finally given an ethnic category of their own – and then only in the face of opposition from black groups who feared it would reinforce a colour hierarchy that has its roots in slavery. Before 2001, mixed people, since they were not counted, were invisible in public sector policy making. The census showed that mixed is now a larger ethnic group than black Caribbean or black African, and is only slightly smaller than the Pakistani-origin group. The census also showed that more than 50% of mixed-race people are under 16, making mixed the fastest growing ethnic minority group in Britain. Research by the Institute of Education, which broke down the data by age, revealed that more than 3% of under-16s are mixed, and nearly 5% of under-fives. In some cities the proportions are even higher. Some 11% of schoolchildren in Lewisham, south London, for example, are mixed.

Ignored by curricula

As a group, mixed-race people have persistently underachieved in education. A report commissioned by the Department for Education and Skills in 2004 found that mixed children were ignored by school curricula and by school and local education authority policies on race.

The report concluded: "Their invisibility from policy makes it difficult for their underachievement to be challenged." The report highlighted a lack of awareness about mixedness among teaching staff and persistent negative stereotyping of mixed race families.

Anna Hassan, headteacher of Millfields primary school in Hackney, north-east London – where 30% of pupils are mixed – says teaching staff need to be aware of the issues facing these children at school. "[The concept of] race is supposed to be dead but unfortunately it's alive and kicking in schools, and I think mixed kids are beginning to face the next wave of racism," she says. "Up until now, mixed-race children have been neglected by people who weren't aware of that."

A former youth worker I spoke to agreed. "The black and white kids I worked with didn't seem to call each other racial names," she says. "But the mixed kids got it from both sides."

This can lead to problems finding friendship groups, especially among teenagers whose need to belong is acutely felt. "When they get to secondary school and children begin to sign up to certain groups, mixed children can find it difficult to fit in," says Mike Vance, consultant on Caribbean achievement to the Hackney Learning Trust. "Sometimes they are not accepted by black or white groups and they might be cussed about their skin colour or hair.

"Usually children access their heritage through family connections, but there can be problems where those are severed. Perhaps the mother or father is on their own and might have been ostracised by their own family because of their mixed relationship and brown child.

"Say you are a mixed boy growing up with your white mother who

The population of Great Britain
Non-white population 1951-2001

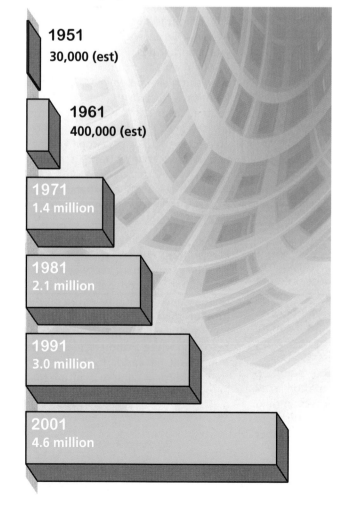

1951
30,000 (est)

1961
400,000 (est)

1971
1.4 million

1981
2.1 million

1991
3.0 million

2001
4.6 million

By ethnic group, 1991 & 2001, thousands

Ethnic group	1991	2001	% change
All ethnic groups	54,889	57,104	4.0
Whites	51,873	52,481	1.2
Mixed	*	674	*
Asian, Asian British/Scottish	1,677	2,329	38.9
Indian	840	1,052	25.2
Pakistani	477	747	56.6
Bangladeshi	163	283	73.6
Other Asian	197	247	25.4
Black, Black British/Scottish	890	1,148	29.0
Black Caribbean	500	566	13.2
Black African	212	485	128.8
Other Black	178	97	-45.5
Chinese, other ethnic group	447	473	5.8
Chinese	157	243	54.8
Any other ethnic group	290	229	-21.0
All non-White groups	3,014	4,623	53.4

*Mixed Ethnic group categories were not included in 1991 census
Source: 2001 Census, ONS, General Register for Scotland

doesn't know about the culture, and your hair's not plaited and your skin's not creamed. You are going to feel self-conscious and will probably be teased at school."

Clare Felix, national black and minority ethnic (BME) manager for the mental health charity Rethink, agrees.

"Mixed people can find it difficult to find cultural affiliations," she says. "They might be rejected by their black side because their skin's too light and their hair's too straight, and rejected by their white side because their skin's too dark and their hair's too frizzy."

Such challenges may, in part, account for the over-representation of mixed children in care. Last year, mixed children accounted for 8% of looked-after children, although only 3% of under-16s are mixed. One adoption worker I spoke to said more needed to be done to support white parents with mixed children. "As a white person you don't have to think about being white," she said. "It's the norm. But once you have a mixed child you are no longer white. Suddenly the privilege you have simply by being white is taken away. It's a hard lesson to learn."

There are other public policy issues. Those who work within underfunded sickle cell anaemia and thalassaemia services, for example, say the numbers with the conditions – which mainly affects people with origins in Africa, the Caribbean, the Middle East, the eastern Mediterranean and Asia – are expected to rise, in part due to greater mixing.

Despite the complex and particular needs of mixed people in education, social services or health, there is little evidence that public services have addressed how this might affect service priorities. One woman who works on tackling health inequalities for an inner-city borough told me: "If you're not black or Asian, you're not considered an ethnic minority with any particular needs."

Not all mixed people face the same issues. Our success negotiating our identity depends on a range of personal factors, some of which relate to our particular mix. A third of mixed people have one white and one black

Photo posed by models

Caribbean parent, but the number with white and Asian or white and black African parentage is growing.

As somebody with roots in both black and white culture (I have a white Scottish father and black Guyanese mother), with all the historical implications that come with that, I have sometimes felt as though I might buckle under the weight of other people's expectations. If you are not being eulogised by white liberals who believe you embody racial harmony – I have been told by more than one middle-aged white woman that they wished they had had a "brown baby" – you are being verbally abused by white racists terrified of the dilution of their genetic matter.

> 'If you are not being eulogised by white liberals... you are being verbally abused by white racists.'

If you are not being chatted up by black men – especially if you happen to be with a white man, whose presence is always ignored – you are being envied by black women who believe, probably with some justification, that you will get the jobs they want because your brownness is a non-threatening asset, a way to bump up the firm's "BME" representation. In all these cases, you represent something that someone else either wants or rejects. It can be difficult for either side to embrace you as their own.

Creating our garden

There were times as a young person when I wished I was either one or the other. Black, for what I imagined was the privilege of knowing who I was and not feeling somehow diluted, a "fake black". White, for the privilege of not having to think about it at all.

Being mixed does, however, have its advantages. While I am usually aware of my difference at all-black and all-white gatherings, I have the privilege of being able to fit in with both, and everything in between. My ethnic identity is not fixed, but fluid. My partner, who has a way with words, says it's a bit like being on the fence, able to see into both gardens – black and white – but without a garden of our own. All of us, with our families and friends, have had to create one.

Now, I see them everywhere. Mixed children being swung in the park between their differently-coloured parents; brown-skinned babies being balanced on the hips of their white mothers; frizzy-haired siblings shopping with their black and white grandmothers. I hope things will be easier for them than they were for me. But in a culture that still sees identity in terms of black, white or Asian, I'm not so sure.

The Guardian 6 September 2006

How immigrants are revitalising London

Darcus Howe

Not a day passes without a storm of anti-immigrant propaganda in the press. The leading exponent of this mischief is the Daily Mail. As I write, it announces a "Polish baby boom: fears for NHS and schools as a thousand Polish children are born every month". It goes on: "On current trends, there will be more than 13,000 such births this year," while "240,000 eastern European children have arrived in Britain's schools".

Yet the parents of these children pay taxes, too. And it takes no more than two months in their first class for them to catch up with local children and progressively bypass them.

I took a minicab from Waterloo to Camberwell last week. The driver apologised profusely because he had to pick up his daughter from school along the way. As soon as she got in, she started to read the billboards we passed. Here was an agile mind, a natural leader who will bring her English classmates in her wake. She is no burden, more an asset to her school. I confirmed as much from teachers in my community. The children of Polish immigrants overtake the locals in the twinkling of an eye.

These cries of crisis in British hospitals and schools have little material basis. They simply are attempts to get extra funds from the Treasury by exploiting anti-immigrant sentiment.

I live in a south London community, stretching from Streatham to Norbury, where many eastern Europeans have settled. The men are largely in the building trade; the women find work in the service sector. They live in houses bought for letting. "Buy to let" is an expanding business in these parts, and the rents are exorbitant. Neighbourhoods have been rescued from oblivion by the presence of eastern European immigrants, who have joined Indians, Pakistanis, Africans and West Indians.

Many of these eastern Europeans are single men. They work from sun-up to sun-down, whatever the weather, supplying skilled labour for roadworks and building sites. They have broken the monopoly not only of the British plumber, but of building trades from carpentry to decoration. The costs of refurbishing homes and building new ones have fallen spectacularly.

Many of the young women are domestic workers, with skills from child-minding to window cleaning, who lessen the burden of middle-class working women. Others have helped to reinvigorate the fading high streets of old England. The cheap labour provided by eastern European women can be seen in small restaurants, dry-cleaners, cosmetics shops and bars. This is a young, healthy population that costs the health service little. They are largely law-abiding, costing little by way of police, courts and prisons.

Their contribution to the revenue of the UK government far outstrips any cost to the Treasury. The Polish builder conceived in a Polish womb in Poland was delivered in a Polish hospital. He attended Polish primary and secondary schools. He was trained at technical colleges in Poland. All this costs the Treasury not one penny. The worker just turns up on our shores ready for exploitation.

Yet the one-sided view of immigrants as leeches that worm their way through the indigenous population is laying the basis for social conflict. And these half-truths are spread throughout the press for political ends. The Conservatives never let up and Labour is drawn along.

Mrs Howe and I, both of immigrant stock, go out of our way to embrace these new additions to our society. There is much to learn from the Poles, the Lithuanians, the Czechs, the Slovaks and the rest of them. And we must fend off that malign spirit which generates the xenophobia that is so native to the UK.

New Statesman 3 December 2008

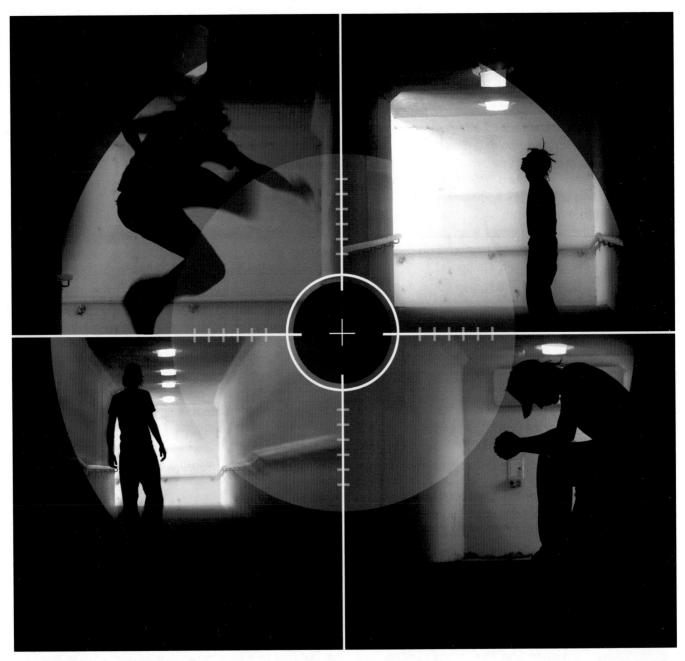

THE REAL QUESTION: WHY ARE OUR CHILDREN PREPARED TO KILL ONE ANOTHER?

**Camila Batmanghelidjh,
Founder of Kids Company**

We need to ask why so many young lives are being cut short by teenagers

There are two rates for renting a gun on the streets of Britain. If the weapon is returned unused, it can cost £50. If it is fired, the price is £250. That is the cost of shooting someone in the world's fourth richest country.

The harrowing and sad death of Rhys Jones brought home this week the unseen and sinister infrastructure for young people to use firearms that now exists in Britain's cities. The rage, bewilderment and hatred that have followed Rhys's murder while he walked home from playing football are understandable. Questions are being asked about whether we have a state of anarchy on our streets, whether a generation is being lost to violent lyrics, images that glorify murder and poor parenting.

But the question that needs to be asked is this: what brings a teenager to the point where he, or even she, could access the illegal gun infrastructure – either by loan, rental or direct order of a gang leader – and use it?

We are very strong in this country in showing condemnation. What we are not so good at is showing curiosity about what brings us to a situation where so many young lives have been taken with guns.

The answer is that Britain has created a society where vulnerable children are not being helped quickly enough. We have a society where it is the criminal justice system that is the first line of defence for dealing with the emotionally numbed individuals that lie behind these crimes.

This is a system every bit as psychologically flawed as the individuals it seeks to assist. We have youth recidivism rates of up to 80 per cent. Child custody does not work. We need to intervene long, long before the police, courts and prisons become involved. Kids Company has spent 11 years working in south London and we have learnt lessons about what creates the problems we face that do not appear in the textbooks.

Through the thousands of life stories of children who have passed through our doors, we have learnt what happens to make them capable of these acts.

It does not make easy reading. These are stories about very young children who suffer chronic abuse. Imagine a child who sees a bottle being broken over their mother's head within the notional safety of the home. Imagine a child who suffers verbal abuse and physical assault, whose early life is a montage of violent imagery.

They will initially react by trying to stop this abuse. But when they learn very quickly that this does not work they shut down their ability to feel. No one has stepped in to protect them and they have achieved a mindset which I describe as a kind of emotional and psychological death.

This is not what David Cameron refers to as anarchy; it is nihilism. It is an absence of values in which the notion of society, community and responsibility has been eradicated by violence. Every encounter with adults for these children has been toxic. Instead, the lives of these children and young people are about survival. They are, in their own words, "lone soldiers" who come into contact with those who will facilitate violence.

Their influence is viral. These young people gather around them imitators and hangers-on who want to copy the culture and accept the violence that goes with it in order not to be attacked. It is these imitators who are influenced by cultural factors such as music. In contrast, there are no robust structures within the community to redress the balance. There are no social facilities they can afford to use, there is no meaningful mental health provision and housing assistance for anyone over 18 consists of a list of private landlords who demand three months' rent in advance which they cannot pay. The under-16s are in bed and breakfasts and in unsupervised hostels.

There are never going to be enough surveillance cameras or police to counter the effects of profound emotional damage

---

Who steps into this void? Imagine three concentric circles. In the first stands the drug dealer and gangster, a remote-control businessman who leads a criminal network. In the second stand our lone children. They are recruited by the dealer, initially by riding around on their bicycles providing information. In the third circle are children who imitate the violence.

If the lone children prove trustworthy, they work as drug couriers. The gang that forms around them helps define them. They eventually get given their own drugs to sell or become someone who is told to go out and harm others. They access the infrastructure of firearms, provided by a central dealer or maybe a father, older brother or cousin. If you know the right people, they are simply for hire.

We do not yet know who killed Rhys Jones or where the weapon came from. But already the debate has been polarised into one about the "demon children" who are attacking the rest of us and the need for harsher punishments and more enforcement.

There are never going to be enough surveillance cameras or police to counter the effects of profound emotional damage.

Our society is not able to solve the problems of problem children. We do not invest enough in social care and mental health. One London borough we worked with last year received 7,165 formal referrals for assistance to its social work unit and child protection teams. They were able to give help to 215 of those cases. At the same time, referrals are going down because professionals in the system do not want to run the risk of formally recognising a child as vulnerable only for that child not to receive assistance.

There is a situation developing where some professionals are becoming as hardened to the dangers faced by these children as the children themselves. Into this growing deadlock, certain figures choose to pour criticism about music, film and television. These are solutions from their own point of view.

Just because they know about these influences, they are not the driving force and solutions based around them are shallow and trite.

Concerts in support of gun amnesties are great. But they do not solve the problem. The answers are long term and require dedication and resources. These children are not born criminals and we have the opportunity to divert them from what many increasingly consider their destiny.

The answer is to strengthen the influence of the parents and, where that is not possible, provide the structure of a family home.

There are not enough foster carers to deal with these children so organisations like ourselves provide a structure for seven days a week – a place to do homework or a college assignment; somewhere to eat or do laundry; a place where there is the doctor, nurse, therapist, musician. It is not enough to have a once-a-week hip hop lesson.

We have a cohort of 925 of these so-called "feral children" at Kids Company. Of these, two are in custody for gun crime, the others are far more likely to be victims of it rather than perpetrators.

It is time to get close to this problem. The fourth richest country in the world has a child mental health and protection system it should be ashamed of.

Let us not pretend we do not know who these youths with guns are. We know at the age of three or four who they are but we do not have the resources or infrastructure in place to help them.

The Independent 25 August 2007

Too much security makes us all a lot less secure

Ross Clark says that we will soon be the most counted and analysed people on earth – and the probability is that real threats will be lost in a fog of data

Here is a little paradox. For 30 years during the Troubles you have been taking the Belfast to Stranraer ferry. No one asked you for identification: you just bought your ticket and off you went, even though it is quite possible that among your fellow passengers on one of those journeys was a terrorist smuggling bomb-making equipment into mainland Britain. Eventually, peace is restored to Northern Ireland. And what happens? Suddenly you can't travel without a passport or ID card, and all your luggage is scanned. Once in Belfast you decide to take a train to Dublin, a journey you have been making unhindered for 30 years. When you book your ticket you are, for the first time, asked your name, address, credit card number and 50 other pieces of data, including the purpose of your visit and details of accommodation you have booked. When you ask a security officer why the sudden need for the formalities you are told it is all

because of the 'terrorist threat'. You want to ask him where he was for 30 years of the Troubles.

Last week the Prime Minister announced a huge increase in security measures at transport hubs. Passengers passing through 250 railway stations will routinely have their bags scanned and searched as if they were passing through an airport – and in the case of ferries, they will require ID to travel. On the same day the Home Office announced that it had signed a £650 million contract with a consortium, Trusted Borders, led by Raytheon Systems, to install and run the first phase of the £1.2 billion e-borders project. This will scan the passports of travellers entering the country, match their details against police databases and analyse 53 pieces of data collected about them when they booked the tickets. Like the Automated Targeting System already used to analyse travellers entering

the US, the information will be used to calculate a personal risk rating for each passenger. Woe betide anyone who attempts to travel on a single ticket without an organised travel itinerary: that is one of the markers which the system will use to pick out oddballs deemed to be a risk to national security.

For the moment few bother to question the government's passion for surveillance nor its fetish for databases. We swallow the government's argument that al-Qa'eda presents a new and sinister threat which justifies security measures never employed against Irish terrorists. Perhaps that might begin to change, however, with the leak of personal details of 20 million parents by Her Majesty's Revenue and Customs. I am one of those whose bank account details, national insurance numbers and everything else required to fake my identity are on a lost computer disc and might now be in the hands of criminals or terrorists. The perils of excessive data collection become clear: collect too much information from us and we become less, not more, secure.

Yet still the government ploughs on with numbering, classifying and examining us at every turn. In a couple of years' time, for example, criminals and weirdos will also have access to the proposed £241 million children's index, which will carry details of the health, education and social service records of the country's 15 million children. It won't be too hard for miscreants to gain entry to this database: it is to be made accessible to 330,000 doctors, teachers and social workers. The NHS's £12 billion database, Connecting for Health, will put all our health records online, with the result that any problem discussed with your GP will instantly be available to public servants nationwide. In a survey last week 38% of family doctors said they would refuse to upload patients' details on to the system without their consent – many of them citing fears that social workers cannot be trusted to keep information confidential.

To the old argument 'if you've nothing to hide, you've nothing to fear', the reply can be put into two words: hackers and errors. Connecting for Health had hardly got off the ground before one NHS practice manager discovered that the computer had somehow managed to classify her wrongly as an alcoholic. How are the rest of us supposed to find out that we are officially recorded as alcoholics until social services arrive on the doorstep to take away our children? The Police National Computer, first set up in the 1970s, hardly sets a good example: according to the Police Inspectorate, 2,700 of the people on it are wrongly connected with a crime. As for the US's Automated Targeting System, it has proved itself a hamfisted tool: at least one jumbo jet has been turned around mid-Atlantic because one passenger was wrongly connected with a terror group – at the very least, why can't the data be analysed before a plane takes off?

I wouldn't dissent from every security measure proposed by the Home Office: it seems evidently sensible, from the perspective of road safety as well as counter-terrorism, that public buildings should not be designed in such a way as to make it possible to drive cars loaded with explosives into them. But

> The reality is that in many cases surveillance is being used to fob us off, to give us the impression that the authorities are on top of their job when they are not

no matter what the government says, much surveillance has no counter-terrorism function whatsoever: the 7/7 bombers, like the 9/11 hijackers, did not seek to disguise their identities, only their intentions; therefore an ID card scheme would have had no role in stopping it.

The reality is that in many cases surveillance is being used to fob us off, to give us the impression that the authorities are on top of their job when they are not. Crime out of control and policemen confined to their stations under a mountain of paperwork? Put up some CCTV cameras instead and make citizens think we know what's going on – even though, as the Home Office admits, 80% of CCTV images prove to be useless in solving crimes. Local hospital just closed down? Put patients' health records online so they can more easily be stuffed in an ambulance and taken 100 miles away to the nearest free bed. Schools too large and impersonal? Sew a microchip into school uniforms, as one Doncaster school has just done, so that the teacher can take the register without knowing any of his pupils.

We will soon be the most counted and analysed people on earth, but don't expect it to make us safer. The evidence is that intelligence about genuine threats to security will quickly be lost in a fog of data. I will leave you with another puzzle: why in a country

with a quarter of the world's CCTV cameras, a police national computer, and facial and number-plate recognition software employed at every turn, were three terror suspects under control orders – Ibrahim Adam, Cerie Bullivant and Lamine Adam – somehow able to go missing in May, even though they were wearing electronic tags and supposedly under 24-hour surveillance? If anyone knows their whereabouts, please contact a uniformed officer. But don't be surprised if you don't get much response: the authorities will probably be too busy grilling your Auntie Doris about her coach excursion to Le Touquet.

The Road to Southend Pier: One Man's Struggle Against the Surveillance Society, by Ross Clark, is published by Harriman House.

The Spectator 1 December 2007

'Sorry, madam, I'm not trained to tell the time.'

The Spectator 17 November 2007

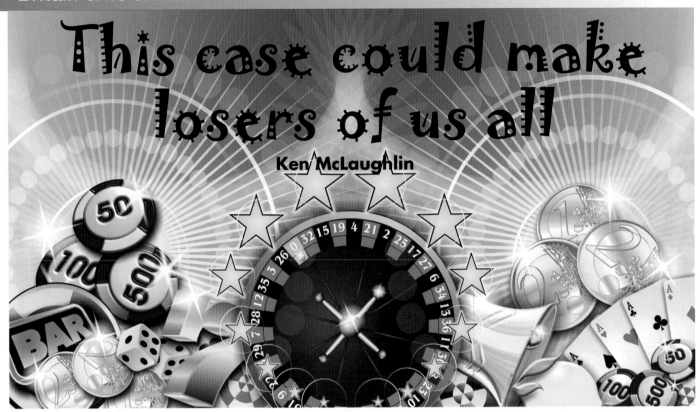

This case could make losers of us all

Ken McLaughlin

A British man is suing William Hill because they allowed him to gamble away £2.1million. But who is really responsible for what gamblers do?

Greyhound trainer Graham Calvert is suing William Hill bookmakers this week for the sum of £2.1million – the total amount he lost to them over a two-year period. The basis of Calvert's claim is that William Hill is in breach of the Gambling Act 2005, which requires bookmakers to promote 'socially responsible' gambling.

> **He had informed William Hill that he had an addiction and requested to be banned from placing any further bets**

Bookmakers are obliged to 'put in place procedures for self-exclusion and take all reasonable steps to refuse service or to otherwise prevent an individual who has entered a self-exclusion agreement from participating in gambling'. Calvert had requested such 'self-exclusion' but his bets were still accepted. He had informed William Hill that he had an addiction and requested to be banned from placing any further bets. According to his solicitor, this means the bookmakers are legally responsible for Calvert's losses, as they failed in their duty of care to him.

As someone who owns greyhounds and knows several trainers, owners and bookmakers, my own bank balance is testament to the fact that inside knowledge is no guarantee of success at the tracks. Nonetheless, by most accounts Calvert's losses are excessive. He was betting anything between £1,000 and £30,000 a time, and on one occasion he allegedly staked £347,000 on America to win golf's Ryder Cup. They lost.

I have no sympathy for the large bookmaking chains. If Calvert had been a shrewd gambler with a profitable account, instead of a 'problem gambler' who seems to have lost frequently, it is likely that his account would have been closed by William Hill or the size of his bets would have been severely limited. Bookmakers want gamblers, not winners. I know several shrewd punters who have had accounts shut down by money-hungry bookmakers (unfortunately, I am not one of them). It also seems to be true that Calvert's life has been ruined by gambling. Along with all that money,

he has lost his home and his marriage has broken up. He evidently has a gambling problem. However, a court victory for him would make losers of us all.

As many have pointed out on internet gambling forums, even if William Hill had refused Calvert any further bets, he could still have continued gambling. There are thousands of high street betting shops to choose from, as well as a plethora of online bookmakers and betting exchanges. It is easier to bet today than ever before, and betting is something that the vast majority of people enjoy without experiencing major problems. Also, increased competition between bookmakers and the introduction of betting exchanges (where punters bet with each other)

> **We are seen as victims unable to exercise control over our circumstances**

has led to greatly reduced profit margins for bookmakers. Their overall profits have increased, but this is due to the rise in turnover. And, contrary to Calvert's experience, punters have never had it so good: today, you have more chance of winning, or at least

We are told we can be addicted to everything... the internet, chocolate, shopping, sex and love

keeping your losses at a reasonable level, than at any time since betting shops were legalised.

However, my real concern is not for the technicalities of how and when bets can be struck, but rather for the fact that Calvert's case is symptomatic of a social climate in which we are increasingly seen as victims unable to exercise control over our circumstances. The concept of addiction is indicative of this trend, having expanded exponentially in recent years. It is a contemporary social phenomenon that is being used to describe an ever-increasing range of behaviours over which we are said to lack control. 'Addiction' used to refer, almost exclusively, to those with alcohol or drug problems – now, alongside gambling, we are told that we can be addicted to everything from nicotine to pornography, and to the internet, chocolate, shopping, sex and love. No wonder, then, that the British Advocacy group Action on Addiction can claim that 'one in three adults suffers from some form of addiction'.

The promiscuous use of the term addiction, and the spread of 'experts' who step in to cure our various addictions, reflects a profoundly fatalistic view of people and a belief that we lack the capacity to control our own lives. We are increasingly seen not as rational decision-making agents, but as irrational patients in need of control. Indeed, for some proponents of the idea that people need protecting from themselves, it is the very assumption of capacity that is the problem. For Paul Devlin,

director of the brain injuries association Headway, the problem is that the Gambling Commission's rules on self-exclusion assume that gamblers have 'sufficient decision-making capacity to exclude themselves'.

No doubt, in some cases steps need to be taken to minimise the dangers to those who really do lack mental capacity. For instance, there was the case of a 39-year-old man who suffered severe brain injuries as a child and who gambled away most of his compensation despite having signed several exclusion orders with bookmakers in his local town. However, such extreme cases do not justify the assumption that we are all brain damaged until we prove otherwise. Certain individuals no doubt should be afforded protection – but the notion that vast numbers of us lack the 'sufficient decision-making capacity' to exclude ourselves from gambling, much less to take part in it as we see fit, is patronising and dangerous.

A court victory for him would make losers of us all

Calvert, for his part, may not be brain damaged. But his lawyers, in seeking to blame his uncontrollable mind for his behaviour, may help pave the way to a situation where all of us are seen as irresponsible, dependent children trapped in adult bodies.

Spiked, 20 February 2008

Gambling facts

- 68% of the population, that is about 32 million adults, participated in some form of gambling within the past year.

- The money lost by British gamblers will exceed £10bn annually next year – a rise of 50% in nine years, and the biggest jump since the 1960s.

- The losses have been driven by abolition of betting duty, the emergence of online betting, poker and casino sites, and a steady unwinding of regulatory constraints. But the biggest single drain comes from a new type of slot machine, offering video roulette in betting shops.

- The most dramatic development due to the tax change was touch-screen roulette. It's estimated the 24,500 UK terminals take £650m a year.

- Just over half of all terminals belong to Ladbrokes and William Hill; together they take £420m a year.

- For around 10 million people, their only gambling activity in the past year had been participating in a National Lottery draw.

- 6% of people used the internet to gamble (3% did online gaming like playing poker or casino games and 4% placed bets with a bookmaker).

- The rate of problem gambling in the adult population was about 0.6%, which is about 284,000 adults.

Source: Gambling Commission

Enough is enough: it's time to stop buying and start being happy

John Naish

Visiting a local council tip, I met a busy crew of charity volunteers who monitor people throwing out their household goods, and who retrieve anything decent and re-sell it. The hoard of rescued items they showed me was astonishing. It included immaculate flat-pack furniture that had never been assembled, piles of new kitchen gadgets and sports gear, and even unridden bicycles.

Our hunter-gatherer brains are almost wired to buy

My tip is hardly unusual. A new study shows we throw away more new stuff than ever. A million tonnes of electrical and electronic gadgets alone get dumped every year in Britain, says a report by a Yorkshire-based recycling consultancy. All this stuff takes time and money to earn. Then we just bung it. Why?

Another new study offers an important clue: we're more prone to spend money on stuff when we're anxious or unhappy, claim American researchers in the journal Psychological Science. When we feel sad, we feel more needy, value the things we own less and are more likely to spree, the study reports. This adds to a growing body of research that shows how our buying behaviour is driven largely by primitive motivations in our brains; ancient acquisitive instincts prodded into a frenzy by modern culture.

Our hunter-gatherer brains are almost wired to buy. Scans performed at Emory University, Atlanta, show how the brain's "reward chemical", dopamine, is released as shoppers see a product and ponder buying it. But dopamine is all about the hunt, not the trophy. Anticipation, rather than buying, squirts it around our skulls. And the effect is only fleeting: once you've sealed the deal, the chemical high flattens in minutes, often leaving a sense of regret that some shop-owners call "buyer's remorse".

Anxiety plays a role, too. A study of students in the journal Behavioural Research Therapy reveals that anxious people are more likely to gather possessions. Getting gripped by the urge to stockpile stuff in times of threat would have helped our ancestors' survival chances. This old instinct helps to explain how advertising campaigns can prey on our deepest insecurities: you're not good enough, or popular enough, and other people are happier because they've got stuff you haven't.

But when we buy things we don't need, it proves disappointing. And in our throwaway society, we're then encouraged to bung them out, which is depressing. So we head back to the shops for more of that "retail

We need to declare that we generally have 'enough stuff'

therapy". It's a vicious, glum and planet-polluting cycle.

There's another problem, too: our primitive brains never evolved an "enough" button. In times of scarcity and famine, we never needed one. Now, despite the world of abundance surrounding us, an idea still haunts our heads that we can never have enough.

How can we break free? Two things that can help are often sidelined by our modern consumer experience: a sense of gratitude and a sense of value. We are encouraged to think that any consumer item we've just bought or already own is "so last year" and should be replaced by something newer and shinier, which would make our lives somehow better.

We need to change the way we own and value our things. We need to declare that we generally have "enough stuff". Instead of having a throwaway attitude to our possessions, we need to develop sustainable, rewarding relationships with them – by buying only items that are made to last for ages, which meet a real need and which we can grow to treasure. Tests by psychologists in Texas have suggested that people who show appreciation and gratitude tend to be significantly happier with their lot, so they need fewer retail kicks.

Most of all, we need to stop to consider what is "enough" for us in our lives, instead of exhausting ourselves by chasing after ever more wasteful, unrewarding things. Our throwaway habits don't just cause global warming, they cause personal overheating, too – more stress, more exhaustion, more burnout.

Despite our motivation to gather and hoard, this idea of sufficiency is an ancient and wise one. From the beginning of civilisation until the advent of consumerism, we created cultures that mitigated against

Our throwaway habits don't just cause global warming, they cause personal overheating too

our instinct for over-consumption. Aristotle, for example, invented the idea of the "golden mean", which pointed out how the path of happiness lay in the middle ground between having too little and too much. We have forgotten such lessons. But today, saying "enough" is our one hope of escape from the wrecking cycle.

John Naish is the author of: Breaking Free from the World of More.

Sunday Herald 26 February 2008

Does Britain need 100 more Starbucks?

Zoe Williams

I don't see how this works, but I am no businessman. Starbucks hopes to allay rumours that it is winding down in the US by scaling up in the UK. They will be opening 100 new stores here and in Ireland in 2008, bringing the total to 725 outlets of incredibly delicious hot, mainly brown milkshakes.

Now, where strong opinions are held about Starbucks, they are almost entirely negative. The creamy giant conjures forth every bad vibe anyone ever had about globalisation – they close down local businesses, homogenise city centres, exploit their workers and rape the developing world. But the truth is, tiny local shops used to sell horrible coffee, and the ones that survive only changed their Nescafé-in-polystyrene ways because Starbucks forced them to. High streets did, it's true, used to be more varied, but only because they were full of manky shops selling substandard drinks. If you don't believe me, go to a place where Starbucks hasn't arrived. Go to Dunstable, and order a coffee. And in fact Starbucks enjoys pretty high status as a fair-minded, benevolent employer, and they use Fairtrade coffee. People who rail against them might have a point, but only if

they object to all medium-to-large-scale commerce. You can't take the post-No Logo approach and hate Starbucks but cross the road to Pret a Manger (owned by McDonald's) because you like their tasty dry roast.

"High streets used to be more varied, but only because they were full of manky shops selling substandard drinks"

Besides which, Starbucks have lovely, tasty coffees, especially the seasonal ones, which embody the very spirit of Christmas. After you get back from Dunstable, go and have a gingerbread latte. You will forget about that horrible trip. They have babychanging units, they have toys, they have friendly people serving, they never stare at you if you have been in there for four hours because you have forgotten how to get your buggy through the door. They are so child-friendly, I bet this new wave will create its own baby-boom – thousands of cute babies, all ripped to the eyes on in utero caffeine. It warms my cockles, really it does.

The Guardian 24 November 2007
© Guardian News & Media Ltd. 2007

The end of the affair

Robert Llewellyn

I've just been shopping. I went to London, walked into shops and bought things. New things. Not many – in fact my little pile of shopping bags is tragically small. I rapidly got bored and tired, and came back home.

I found the brashness of the shops a little grating. I felt I was getting a headache from the lighting and the assistants asking me whether I needed any help. The whole experience was stressful.

All this might sound like it comes from someone who has been in prison or in a desert, when all I have done is not go into shops for a year. I should clarify that I've been into supermarkets and farm shops, chemists and post offices, but I haven't been in any consumer shops; not once in 12 months.

I also haven't done any online shopping, something I used to do quite a lot. Over the last month of my no-shopping experiment I admit I built up a list in my Amazon shopping basket. When my year was up I went to my list, scanned the collection of DVDs, computer peripherals and a new video camera, and hesitated. All it would take was a single mouse-click and all this stuff would be delivered in a couple of days. I couldn't do it. It made me nervous. Did I really need any of it? I went through the list again and removed about half. As I write this I still haven't clicked.

Something has changed and now I am worried it won't change back. I have found the experience of the past year very easy; it's been a massive get-out of all the stress of consuming. Over the past 12 months, whenever I have found myself tempted to buy I have had a simple default setting. Don't. End of problem.

When something broke, I fixed it (my watch took three months) and when something new came out, I ignored it. That was how I went along for 11 months. In the 12th I started wasting time on the internet, comparing the Panasonic HDC SD5 camcorder with the Sony HDR SR7E. I already have a camcorder but its lens is held together with superglue and gaffer tape. I dropped it just before my year started and it is something I use a great deal. It still just about works but the auto-focus is shot to bits and it's generally a bit knackered.

Then there's the iPhone. I went into the store and looked at it. I picked it up – I admit I was vain enough to watch myself on You Tube on it. It was really amazing, but I didn't buy it because I really don't need one. I have a mobile phone that came free with my contract; I make calls on it and people call me. It works. I don't need a new one.

> **How am I going to shake off this satisfaction with what I have already? How am I going to learn how to yearn?**

How am I going to shake off this satisfaction with what I have already? How am I going to learn to yearn? It was such a simple little step to make and it has utterly changed my life. I am still interested in working; I am still driven to earn money; I just don't want to buy things I don't really need. If it really is this simple, it could catch on. More people might do it and find it's not that hard; if they do, it could have devastating consequences for the economy. That's the problem: you say you're only going to give up buying new stuff for a year, but when the year's up you don't really want to go back. I feel a bit guilty. It's all my fault, I'm not doing my bit to support the economy – but then is it me that's wrong, or is it the economy?

Robert Llewellyn is an author, actor and television presenter

The Ecologist February 2008
www.theecologist.org

Save our Sundays – shut all the shops

Mariella Frostrup

In Bilbao recently for a weekend, it took me a little while to figure out why the atmosphere was so different to back home. Then I realised it was a Sunday and that all the shops were closed.

In this country, whether it's Chinese New Year or Christmas, Easter or Halloween, we're out there answering the call of the high street. And if M&S profits go down, it's a crisis in the economy. We've created a system in which our future depends on our ability to shop until we drop.

It makes our talk about global warming just hot air. I'm still not over the cost of Halloween and then Guy Fawkes Day. With pumpkins, fancy dress, fireworks and sweets, the nation's bill must be in the high millions.

When I was a kid in Ireland, Halloween meant snipping up an old sheet and wafting around the streets in search of pennies from the neighbours. Nowadays, even toddlers wouldn't be seen dead in a home-made ghoul costume. The streets were littered with children dolled up in the finest fancy dress that money can buy.

I can't help being impressed at how we embrace our civic responsibility to shop with such gusto. From the end of October until the January sales, it's impossible to be unaware of the fortunes that are bullied, seduced and downright blackmailed out of us in what's become our main leisure activity. Nominating the most destructive changes to our quality of life, I'd start with Sunday trading. The saddest manifestation of this buying imperative was the death of what, in my youth, was a 24-hour pause for reflection and relaxation. Now it is the second biggest shopping day of the week.

Argued for at the time on the basis that shift-workers struggled to find time to buy essentials, it has turned out as a cynical way to increase our levels of spending. Nowadays, with late-night shopping and the internet's 24-hour purchasing potential, there's little justification for a seven-day shopping cycle.

The streets and parks of Bilbao were full of families, parents and pushchairs, teenagers and grandparents all strolling about enjoying the sunny winter's day. If sharing quality time with those we love reduces the stress of modern life, a real day off makes perfect sense.

In the UK by midday on a Sunday, we're armed with plastic and ready for our next assault on the high street. Maybe it's time we asked why.

The Observer 11 November 2007
© Guardian News & Media Ltd. 2007

Consumers' revolt: power to the people

Consumers are fighting back against big business and the state. Here's how:

Banks

A mass revolt has left the high street banks facing thousands of claims from customers seeking to claw back some of the £4.75bn levied annually on charges for overdrafts and bounced cheques. More than one million forms demanding refunds have been downloaded from a number of consumer websites. The banks are settling out of court, often paying £1,000 a time.

Utilities

While average gas and electricity bills approached £1,000 last year, a record 4 million householders have dumped their supplier after an internet-led consumer campaign. British Gas admitted it lost 1.1m customers in just 12 months.

Road pricing

Plans for road pricing have faced massive public opposition spearheaded by an internet campaign. In just three months 1.8 million people have signed an online petition, linked to a new section of the Downing Street website, launched by a disgruntled motorist from Telford.

Supermarkets

From Devon to Inverness, planning applications for superstores are being thwarted by residents' campaigns orchestrated on the internet. Tesco scrapped a superstore plan in Darlington last year following opposition and this week residents sank a Tesco plan for a £130m retail development in Tolworth, Surrey. Friends of the Earth is co-ordinating the protests across the country.

Air travel

"Green" travellers are boycotting air travel because of climate change. Campaigners have staged sit-ins at airports while hundreds of people have signed up to an online pledge set up by a veteran environmental campaigner. An estimated 3% of people have stopped flying to help the environment, while 10% are cutting back on flights.

Packaging

A campaign launched by *The Independent* urging supermarkets to reduce excessive packaging has prompted a remarkable response. Supermarkets have had to defend their practices after thousands of readers emailed examples of environmentally damaging packaging. The campaign gained widespread public support – a day of action is planned later this year – and has been backed in an early day motion in the House of Commons.

Football tickets

Football fans fed up with paying £50 a time to watch games have joined forces online to put pressure on clubs to slash prices. Manchester City fans led a boycott of the club's match at Wigan in protest at the cost of tickets. Chelsea have announced a freeze on most ticket prices next year and Bolton promised a 10% cut.

Post Offices

Government proposals to axe 2,500 post offices have prompted an organised revolt from pensioners and consumer groups across Britain. The Federation of Subpostmasters and a number of other organisations have launched online petitions opposing the plan, and a rally was staged in London in February to increase the pressure on the Government to save the post offices from closure.

The Independent 23 February 2007

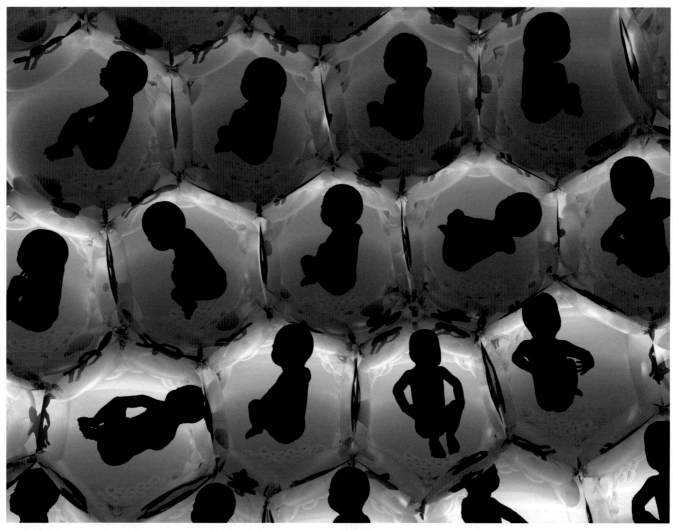

Of course a deaf couple want a deaf child

It is not as if the implantation of an embryo thought to be deaf is equivalent to mutilation

Dominic Lawson

Few broadcasters convey astonishment with an undertone of outrage as skilfully as the BBC's John Humphrys. Over the years the Today programme presenter has had a lot of practice. Yesterday, however, it was not an equivocating politician who got Humphrys to hit his top note. It was a bloke called Tomato – Mr Tomato Lichy, to be precise. The programme's listeners never actually heard Mr Lichy speak: he responded to John Humphrys' questions in sign language, and someone else turned his answers into spoken English for the interviewer's – and our – benefit.

Tomato Lichy and his partner Paula are both deaf. They have a deaf child, Molly. Now Paula is in her 40s and the couple believe they might require IVF treatment to produce a second child. They very much want such a child also to be deaf.

Here's where it gets political: the Government is whipping through a new Human Fertilisation and Embryology Bill. Clause 14/4/9 states that, "Persons or embryos that are known to have a gene, chromosome or mitochondrion abnormality involving a significant risk that a person with the abnormality will have or develop a serious physical or mental disability, a serious illness or any other serious medical condition must not be preferred to those that are not known to have such an abnormality."

This, Tomato Lichy signed to Mr Humphrys, means that he and his partner would be compelled by law to discard the very embryos that they wished to have implanted: "I couldn't participate in any procedure which forced me to reject a deaf embryo in favour of a hearing embryo." Mr Lichy argued that this legislation was specifically designed to discriminate against deafness. As a matter of fact, he's quite right.

The explanatory notes to the clause inform legislators: "Outside the UK, the positive selection of deaf donors in order deliberately to result in a deaf child has been reported. This provision would prevent (embryo) selection for a similar purpose." This all stems from a single case in the US six years ago, when a lesbian couple, Sharon Duchesneau and Candace McCullough, both of whom were deaf, selected a sperm donor on the basis of his family history of deafness. It caused outrage – outrage which clearly filtered through to the British Health ministry.

The most revealing account of this most unusual conception appeared in an email interview in the Lancet. Duchesneau and McCullough wrote: "Most of the ethical issues that have been raised in regard to our story centre on the idea that being deaf is a negative thing. From there, people surmise that it is unethical to want to create deaf children, who are, in their view, disabled.

"Our view, on the other hand, is that being deaf is a positive thing, with many wonderful aspects. We don't view being deaf along the same lines as being blind or mentally retarded; we see it as paralleling being Jewish or black. We don't see members of those minority groups wanting to eliminate themselves."

This is as clear an exposition as you will see of the concept of "cultural deafness". Adherents of this philosophy refer not just to "deaf culture" – Mr Lichy said he felt "sorry for" John Humphrys for not being able to appreciate "deaf plays" –

but to themselves as members of a "linguistic community". This idea of a separate language enables the proponents of cultural deafness to describe themselves as, in effect, an ethnic minority – and thus any legislative attempt to weed them out as embryos to be analogous with the most insidious racism.

Another deaf British couple, whose child is also deaf, told the BBC's disability magazine that "it is important that our culture is passed on from one generation to another ... the threat of losing our culture would be devastating because we have so much to show and to give."

In the most obvious sense, the argument that deafness is not a disability is self-evidently wrong. The absence of one of our most valuable senses brings with it many disadvantages on a purely practical level. So many careers are all but closed to the deaf – a deaf boy might

----

"We don't view being deaf along the same lines as being blind or mentally retarded; we see it as paralleling being Jewish or black"

----

well have fantasies about being a soldier or a fireman, but fantasies are what they will remain. Humphrys tasked Tomato Lichy with the fact that he would never be able to enjoy the music of Beethoven – a low blow, this, as Beethoven himself was vilely tormented by increasing deafness, which also put an end to his ability to conduct his own music.

Yet I don't share Humphrys's apparent incredulity at his interviewee's dismissal of the joys of music. If you have never been able to hear music, then you cannot be said to miss it, or suffer from its absence from your life. Indeed, I know one or two people who are completely tone deaf, who

are not in the least miserable about it: their only irritation is in occasionally having to hear what to them is just undifferentiated noise, when they would rather have silence. The idea that congenitally deaf people are "suffering" in some intrinsic sense, strikes me as mere presumption.

Moreover, it is not as if the implantation of an embryo which is thought likely to be deaf – and science at the moment would be very hard pushed to forecast such an outcome with any reliability at all – is equivalent to deliberate mutilation. What we are talking about is an already existing potential person; the choice isn't whether that embryo could be "made deaf" or not. The choice is whether to discard that already existing embryo for another one believed to be less at risk of turning out to be deaf.

Given that the fertilisation process within IVF generates many more test-tube embryos than are selected for implantation, there are always going to be vast quantities of 'normal' embryos which will be destroyed.

The real issue here, as Mr Lichy observed, is whether the state should be able to dictate to him and his partner which of their embryos they should be allowed to select, and which they should be compelled to reject. I am not surprised – still less, incredulous – that he can't understand why he and his partner should be prevented by law from choosing the embryo which might most turn out to resemble them.

John Humphrys argued that most people would regard his demands as profoundly selfish: Mr Lichy and his partner might want a deaf child, but what about the views of the child itself? I suspect that the child in question would be intelligent enough to be able to understand that the only alternative deal for him or her was never to have existed at all.

Nevertheless, if Clause 14 of the HFE Bill does pass into law, I do hope that Mr Lichy and his partner will find it in them to love and cherish a child who is not deaf. We hearing people are not so useless, when you get to know us properly.

The Independent 11 March 2008

Too many disabled people?

Simon Stephens

Because there does seem to be an awful lot of us. Mind you, an asthma attack is all it takes these days to swell our numbers.

When I was invited to write columns for Community Care it was hinted that I should be controversial and I think my previous articles have lived up to this. But, today, I am going to take a step further by arguing there are too many disabled people.

Despite just being 33 years of age, I feel like Victor Meldrew as I remember the good old days when disabled people were seen as freaks. Let me explain.

As a child, being disabled was a big thing. You had to look and act properly disabled to warrant the label and, as someone with cerebral palsy and a speech impairment, I was always safely defined as disabled. But nowadays the whole world and their dog seems to be labelled disabled as the range of impairments has grown. Even minor conditions like diabetes and asthma seem to count.

A perfect example of why there are too many disabled people is the blue badge system. In the old days, a town centre would have three disabled parking places. Nowadays, you can see "disabled car parks" with more than 200 cars and I wonder to myself, what is the point?

The problem is that disability is seen as an absolute in terms of the benefits given and the level of severity of impairment is not taken into account. While in terms of emotional experience, different impairments cannot be accurately compared like for like.

However, in terms of the physical environment and people's attitudes, I feel it is wrong to compare the experiences of someone who has diabetes or asthma to someone with severe cerebral palsy – the difference in terms of life experience and the level of daily discrimination experienced cannot be considered equal.

It concerns me that many people now find it easy to be termed disabled and enjoy the apparent benefits such as accessible parking and shopmobility scooters without understanding the history.

As a child and right up to my twenties, I was seen as a freak and it seemed I was the only disabled person within a 10-mile radius. As a young disabled man I pushed the boundaries of what could be achieved and opened the doors for others, and I continue to do this.

So the big question, is it my fault? Have I got what I've been asking for – and now have to come to terms with not being the lone ranger anymore?

Community Care 29 November 2007

> ❝ **I remember the good old days when disabled people were seen as freaks** ❞

"Strictly speaking, being unable to reach level six on Playstation 2 is not considered a disability."

Two little boys

Was passing on her impairment to her son a reason to feel guilty, asks:

Emma Bowler

I was recently asked if I thought I had been selfish having a baby, knowing I had a 50:50 chance of passing on my disability.

Whilst the disability activist in me might have argued that I have the right to have a baby, the maternal part of me now realises that the answer is not clear-cut.

I have Kniest Syndrome, which means I'm four feet tall and don't have the best mobility. Ultrasound scans indicated that our first baby, Archie, was going to have Kniest, but by the time he was due the initial guilt I felt had turned into protectiveness; at least I knew what I was in for, as I had the same disability.

When Archie was a few months old, I took him to my consultant and she said: "He's just a baby like any other baby, so go away and enjoy him." And that's exactly what we did. OK, he was smaller than other babies, he wasn't as boisterous as most, and it took him ages to walk solo; but to us he was normal.

I maintained that feeling of normality by not going out of my way to come into contact with children of the same age as Archie, therefore avoiding any cause to feel selfish or guilty about having passed on my disability because those situations would have involved comparing him to his peers and therefore highlighted his difference. Then I had Ben.

"He's just a baby like any other baby, so go away and enjoy him"

Ben is "Mr Normal Baby". Not even one, he's into everything: falling off the bed, climbing stairs, escaping into the garden – all normal things, but things Archie didn't do. He is also, despite the two-year gap between them, almost as big as

"He brings out the maternal side of little girls whose attentions he is more than happy to have!"

Archie. In fact, some people have mistaken them for twins, until Archie starts chatting away.

There's no avoiding comparing Archie with Ben, and the difference in their size, agility and mobility is stark.

When Archie started school a few weeks ago, there was finally no avoiding comparison with his peers. My original guilt reared its head once more: I worried about how Archie would be seen by his peers and whether he would now start to realise he was different.

As with most of my worries, they are already starting to come loose at the seams. Archie's classmates seem to have taken a shine to him; I think he brings out the maternal side of little girls whose attention he is more than happy to have! And rather than see himself as different, he seems to be thinking: "Why can't I do what they are doing?"

He now has a playmate who is always riding on his tractor, something he was scared of using before. After seeing her on it, he realised he wanted to try it; he's now quite happily freewheeling down slopes – so while before I was worried about him being timid, now I'm worried about him falling off!

Perhaps this is an analogy for the way things will go for him now he's with his peers. Once again, I will put my guilt to bed. Well, for the moment at least.

Disability Now February 2008

Mother's pride: Emma with her sons Ben and Archie

When seeing isn't believing!

When Belgian police officers are blinded with evidence, in step the visually impaired to solve the case

It's the 1930s and the police have numerous crimes to solve. In steps Hercule Poirot, the most famous – albeit fictional – Belgian private detective. He is meticulous in his work and exercises his 'little grey cells' to help solve crimes and murder mysteries. Wielding his mahogany cane, he cuts a fairly conventional private detective figure, assisting the police whether they require his services or not.

Now fast forward seven decades. Swap the cane for a white stick, the 'grey cells' for heightened senses, and the conventional detective for one that is anything but, and you've got the Belgian police force's new recruits. Brought in to help fight against terrorism, drug-trafficking and organised crime, the six blind or visually-impaired detectives are the country's newest weapon of choice. Forming a ground breaking unit within the Belgian police, they are dedicated to listening to phone-tapping evidence, bugged conversations and secret interviews.

You may wonder, why this can't be done by ordinary detectives. But it takes an extraordinary skill, one often possessed by visually impaired people, to pick up on the sounds, and therefore the clues, that 'ordinary' people miss. With the exceptional ability to distinguish between sounds that are hidden amongst noisy and busy recordings, the detectives can deduce whether a suspect is talking in a busy restaurant or a crowded supermarket, whether the caller is using a mobile phone or a landline and, in rarer cases, whether the hum from the car engine the suspect is driving is from a Mercedes, a Citroën or an Audi. Alain Thonet, one of the recruits working out of the federal police headquarters in Brussels explains that "being blind means you have to develop your other senses, so I hear things that for other people simply blend into the background".

While seeking to find ways of improving community outreach, the Belgian police heard reports about a blind police officer in the Netherlands and made the connection that blind people could prove more adept than the sighted at listening to and interpreting wiretaps. The scheme was given added impetus following a law passed by the Belgian government giving the police greater powers to use wiretaps and other bugging and recording equipment in investigations. However, part of the legislation also stated that every recording had to be fully transcribed. As the recordings can be taken anywhere that the suspect happened to be, from a noisy train station, to a party or football match, this process was both lengthy and very difficult. Now Mr Thonet and his colleagues, using adapted Braille keyboards and voice-activated software, are not only easing that burden, but enhancing its purpose and effectiveness. It is a situation that benefits all involved, except the criminals of course.

Born with only 10% vision, Mr Thonet was totally blind by the time he was just 12 years old. Despite being university educated he had enormous difficulty finding suitable work. While his credentials looked good enough on his CV to get him numerous interviews, once interviewers realised he was blind he would be refused the job, regardless of his abilities. For this task however, it is his inability to see, or rather the enhanced ability to hear, that is just the skill for the post.

However, while some blind and visually-impaired people may develop other skills to help compensate for their inability to see, like everyone else they have more routine skills they want to use in the ordinary workplace. "What needs to change is people's mentality" says Mr Thonet, "When people see blind people in a concrete work environment, it is easier for them to envisage a similar thing in their own workplace. Clearly, I'm not going to go to the airport and fly a 747 or turn up at the operating theatre and perform surgery. But there are lots of jobs where it is possible to hire a blind person with small adaptations like the Braille buttons we have in the elevator here."

Another member of the special branch is 36-year-old Sacha van Loo, an accomplished linguist who taught himself Serbo-Croat for fun. "People are afraid of employing blind people" says van Loo, "I want to knock down these kinds of prejudices and widen people's perspective, not just in the police force but in all fields." The fact that he has a mental catalogue of innumerable dialects and accents

"As a blind man I divide hearing into different channels. It is these details that can be the difference between solving and not solving a crime."

"People are afraid of employing blind people... I want to knock down these prejudices and widen people's perspectives."

in his head, and is also fluent in seven languages has already proven invaluable in obtaining vital clues.

Currently working on the latest batch of wiretap recordings which have come into the main police station in Antwerp, he has already extracted crucial evidence from recordings that are not only difficult to hear for most people, but difficult to recognise. In one investigation, police had identified from a poor quality recording that the drug smuggler in question was Moroccan. However, once Mr van Loo listened to it, he could tell immediately that the speaker was Albanian, (a fact which was confirmed after his arrest). Without this vital information the police would have continued with the incorrect line of investigation.

"I have had to train my ear to know where I am," explains Mr van Loo, "It is a matter of survival to cross the street or get on a train." A skill which he now uses to help other people survive.

"Some people can get lost in background noise, but as a blind man I divide hearing into different channels. It is these details that can be the difference between solving and not solving a crime." So for cases that need a little more than simply applying your 'little grey cells', Mr van Loo is working on adding another weapon to his wire-tapping arsenal. He is currently training himself to deduce what number is being called just from listening to the tones of telephone dialling pips, truly bringing detective work into the twenty-first century.

Although the first unit set up by the Belgian police, who were astounded by the response their adverts for blind applicants generated, could take only six people when it launched, there are plans to expand it next year. Non-seeing recruits are protected by a special status that grants them police powers but bars them from making arrests or carrying guns.

As with most things, this has not deterred Mr van Loo from trying. With the help of his sighted colleagues he was given some supervised, off-the-job weapons training. Behind his desk pinned up on a wall is a bullet-riddled practice target which tells the tale. "I did not see, but I definitely felt, my fellow officers go rather pale," he jokes, recalling his time on the shooting range with a trainer guiding his hands. "My instructor's verdict? There are colleagues that do a lot worse."

Sources: Various

Meet Leanne Grose
the girl who lost a leg...
& became a fitness expert!

When Leanne Grose lost her leg to cancer she was determined not to lose her lust for life. The first task she set herself was to find an amputee who had lost the other leg so they could buy shoes together!

As a teenager, Leanne was supremely fit, slim and sporty, playing netball and numerous other sports. Then her life changed when in September 2001 a tumour was discovered in her left foot. The tumour was removed and 3 months of radiotherapy and treatment followed. However the pain returned, and so did the tumour. In November 2002 she had to have her left leg amputated below the knee. Despite it all Leanne remained positive "I was fine with this and have always had the attitude that 'what doesn't kill you makes you stronger'!"

"It does indeed work you to a thorough sweat without ever standing up"

Unfortunately so much damage had occurred to the leg that by 2004 the tumour had returned again. "In 2006, I had the last of my operations, which meant removing some of my leg above the knee and five weeks more of radiotherapy," Grose says. "The first time it hit me as serious was when my mum and dad came in after talking to the surgeon and my dad began to cry. I couldn't bear for them to be upset and I found myself being positive to cheer them up."

And it continued from there. Despite now facing the sort of challenges that will make the rest of her life much harder she remains undaunted by her experiences. "I am a strong independent person who is passionate about life," Grose explains, "an individual who does not believe this disability will hold me back." And it certainly hasn't. With that same ambition and determination, Leanne carried on with her job, took her driving test for an automatic car and turned her attention to positive projects, such as

creating and launching both a fitness DVD and her autobiography (Just a Step). Her fiancé, accountant Paul Oxford, said: "Leanne's attitude has made it easier for everyone to cope."

"This disability will not hold me back"

Having always been a fit and sporty person, Leanne gained weight during her illness. Gyms and fitness classes were unable to accommodate her handicap. She wanted to find advice and enjoyable workouts for people in wheelchairs, but her search came to nothing. With typical determination she set about devising her own training programme, which she now sells as her Chair Workout DVD. More than 10% of the UK population has a registered disability but until recently, few fitness centres, gyms or workout DVDs provided for them. Although efforts are being made to ensure that more gyms will offer facilities for disabled people, Leanne has created something that is not only immediately available, but can be done in the comfort of your own home.

The routine is no easy option. It includes a warm-up, a fun disco section (with John Travolta moves), a combat workout with energetic punching moves and resistance work. Pilates exercises for core strength – important for preventing back pain in people who spend most of their time in a seated position – are also included. Despite finishing with a massage section, it does indeed work you to a thorough sweat without ever standing up. It has been so popular that Leanne has even taken her chair workout to the United States. Such is its appeal that elderly people and those who are overweight in general have also found the workout enjoyable and effective.

Leanne's positivity is infectious. She is determined to help others, as she says, "I am a somebody and want to get out there and be huge, helping others and ridding this country of a taboo. You can be young, sexy and feminine even if you are different, it simply makes you special!" Always a high heel girl, Leanne has now found a fellow amputee the same shoe size who had her right leg amputated, so they exchange shoes. So Leanne is not only special, but naturally stylish!

For more information go to:
www.leanneschairworkout.com

Shame of the middle class heroin addicts

By David Paul

There's a new breed of well-off white collar users dealing with their demons in the suburbs

HEROIN has become the fashionable drug of middle-class Britain, and it's thanks to bumper supplies of cheap opium flooding into the UK from the poppy fields of war-torn Afghanistan.

Drug charities are seeing a huge rise in the number of white-collar junkies, including doctors, lawyers and teachers, who are secretly hooked on the killer drug.

According to official estimates the UK already has 327,000 hard drug addicts, but charity officials believe the true figure could be nearer to half a million, and it's rising every day.

Until a recent crash in the street price for heroin, a typical addict needed £10,000 a year to fuel their habit. In some places in the UK heroin has been sold recently for as little as £2 a time, but that price is currently rising fast because experts say demand always goes up as Christmas approaches.

The cash needed to fund a heroin habit is no problem for many of those now smoking, snorting and injecting the drug every day.

Rock and pop stars like Amy Winehouse and Pete Doherty fight their addictions to heroin in the full glare of the media spotlight, but in well-heeled suburbs up and down the country many more addicts are dealing with their demons in privacy.

Drug counsellors told the Sunday Express this week how they are helping a criminal lawyer with a £600,000-a-year salary who has been a regular heroin user for 20 years, hiding the truth from his unsuspecting wife and children.

Another addict is a multi-millionaire property developer, who tells his family he has a minor liver complaint whenever they question why he looks unwell.

"Because of films like Trainspotting, starring Ewan McGregor, the public have become used to a certain stereotype image of a heroin user," said Elliot Elam of the drug treatment agency Addaction.

"This is normally someone who looks emaciated, with bad skin, needle marks on their arms, mugging old ladies to get the money for their next fix.

"But the new breed of white-collar user is well fed, looks after themselves, has a nice house and can easily afford the £100 to £200 a week it costs for five bags of heroin.

"They can usually smoke one joint a night without any serious repercussions and they tend not to progress to injecting because their professional lives give them a degree of control."

At the age of 40, Adam Slade had a smart home in a picturesque part of Cumbria, a loving wife Fiona and young son Josh, together with a £30,000-a-year manager's job with his local council.

But for three years Adam had been a secret heroin addict, hiding his habit from everyone he knew, and soon found himself on a downward spiral to a living hell.

"I was on a good wage and initially could easily afford the odd bag of heroin," said Adam. "I would buy it from a network of dealers in Carlisle. My family weren't aware, I was still able to do my job efficiently.

"My drug taking wasn't dirty and seedy as people expect. I wasn't injecting in a dirty room somewhere, I was simply smoking it at home and I wasn't the only one. I met several others who were getting their supplies from the same dealers as me. One was a GP. Another was a high-up executive in a leading business.

"They all had their reasons – stress, boredom, unhappiness at home. Some had started as teenagers and just kept going."

But soon Adam's secret habit forced him to take out loans. He borrowed cash from his parents and when he appeared ill told his family he simply had a cold.

"Money is always the problem in the end. Soon I was sucked into a spiral of drugs and debt," he said. "I could spend anything from £20 to £500 a day. I didn't do what a stereotypical drug user would do, like mugging a granny or shoplifting to fund their habit. That isn't me – I couldn't and wouldn't do that. I got the money another way, I took out loans. I was almost respectable but it was only a matter of time until my secret came out."

Christmas Eve 1999 saw Adam break down and confess to his family that he was an addict. "My parents stood by me but it was different with Fiona."

THE PAIR tried to save their marriage, for their son's sake, but then council bosses learned of Adam's addiction and he was suspended. "My employers made it clear they didn't want me around. My workmates seemed ashamed of me and almost embarrassed to know me. Some crossed the street to avoid me," he said.

After losing his job and his home, Adam took any work he could find, even painting the outside of the house that had until recently been his, so it looked smart for the new owners.

"That would have killed me if I hadn't been so out of it," admits Adam. Two years ago Fiona and Adam's 25-year marriage ended. Six months later Adam was homeless.

"I had to live on people's sofas and occasionally I slept rough. I even stayed in a tent in a park for a while. Things got so bad I begged on the streets of Carlisle to fund my next hit. Now I find it hard to walk down the street, I worry people might recognize me as the down-and-out who begged them for money."

Although he is now clean of drugs, Adam's life is in ruins. He is 47 and living in a hostel for homeless men in Carlisle, existing on state handouts. "I just fell off the tracks, yet I still see people in the street I know are addicts going about their business as normal," he said.

Nick Lockwood of the Promis Rehab Centre in Kent said: "We've certainly noticed an increase in the numbers of people with heroin dependency.

"Suddenly it's becoming incredibly fashionable among the middle classes again and because of the war in Afghanistan heroin is now far cheaper and far more freely available."

Additional reporting by Nick Brownlee

Sunday Express 9 December 2007

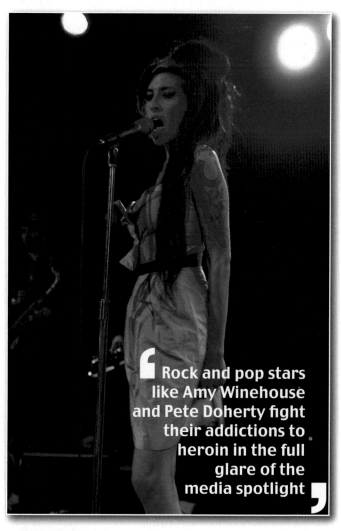

Rock and pop stars like Amy Winehouse and Pete Doherty fight their addictions to heroin in the full glare of the media spotlight

What is the truth about skunk, and have the dangers been overstated?

Jeremy Laurance

Why are we asking this now?

In February 2008, the Advisory Council on the Misuse of Drugs began reviewing scientific evidence on the classification of cannabis, amid widespread fears that Britain is in the grip of an epidemic of cannabis-induced psychosis. This view is based on the belief that cannabis sold on the streets is stronger than it was a generation ago and is tipping vulnerable people into mental illness, including schizophrenia.

The review, the second in two years, was ordered by Gordon Brown, who has indicated he is minded to reverse the decision of the former Home Secretary David Blunkett, who downgraded the drug from Class B to Class C in 2004. Mr Blunkett's aim was to free up police time squandered on prosecuting users, but the Prime Minister is concerned that the move sent the wrong message to young people, who are now confused about drug laws.

What is skunk?

It is the generic name given to potent strains of the cannabis plant containing the highest levels of the psychoactive ingredient tetrahydrocannabinol (THC). The original skunk, a cross between the fast-growing Indica and the potent Sativa strains, is believed to have originated in the US and was so called because of its pungent smell. Dutch growers have since refined and cross-bred the plants to produce a number of strains including super-skunk, Early Girl, Northern Lights and Jack Herer. They are normally grown indoors under lights, or in a greenhouse. The more intensive the cultivation, the higher the THC content.

How strong is skunk?

Traditional herbal cannabis contains 2% to 4% THC, according to the Drugscope charity. More potent varieties average 10% to 14% – three to four times as strong. Claims that skunk is 20 to 30 times as powerful as herbal cannabis are exaggerated. A European review of cannabis potency in June 2004 concluded that the overall potency of cannabis products on the market had not increased significantly because imported cannabis dominated the market in most countries. However, as home-grown cannabis has become more widely available, especially in the Netherlands and Britain, consumption of stronger varieties has increased. The Home Office yesterday claimed that 70% of cannabis sold on the streets of Britain was skunk.

Why is skunk so popular?

It offers a powerful high, similar for some users to that obtained with ecstasy or LSD but without the chemicals. Even in the world of recreational drugs, users prefer a "natural" high. It can be home-grown from legally obtainable seeds – many users grow a few plants on a windowsill for personal consumption. It is easy to identify, making it difficult to fake. Cannabis resin, by contrast, has been adulterated with everything from boot polish to the horse tranquilliser ketamine.

How dangerous is skunk?

This is an area of intense dispute. The greatest concern is over its effects on mental health. When the Advisory Council last reviewed cannabis in early 2006, it concluded that use of the drug by existing schizophrenia sufferers might worsen their symptoms and lead to a relapse in some. But on causation, it said: "The evidence suggests, at worst, that using cannabis increases the lifetime risk of developing schizophrenia by 1%."

Some scientists believe this underplays the risks. Professor Robin Murray, of the Institute of Psychiatry in London, says that in vulnerable individuals – those with an unsuspected genetic predisposition to schizophrenia – cannabis may be the trigger that starts a full-blown mental illness.

His research showed that up to 10% of the adult population – or about four million people – are prone to paranoid thoughts or grandiose ideas and, among those who smoke cannabis regularly, half may be tipped into psychotic delusions and end up needing treatment. The early age at which people start smoking the drug today, compared with two or three decades ago, is an additional concern, he says, because their brains may be more vulnerable.

Have the risks been overstated?

Yes. A recent report, printed in several newspapers last month, suggested that 500 people a week were being admitted to hospital for treatment for the effects of cannabis – a 50% increase since the drug was downgraded to Class C in 2004. The figure was repeated in reports this week. Drugscope said the figure, quoted by the Public Health minister Dawn Primarolo,

was actually related to the number of people consulting community drug treatment services for help or advice where "treatment" may amount to no more than an informal chat. The actual figure for hospital admissions was 14 per week in 2006-07 – and that was lower than the year before.

So why did the Advisory Council recommend that cannabis remains a Class C drug?

Because, despite the evidence of a link with schizophrenia, it concluded that cannabis remained "substantially" less harmful than the Class B drugs amphetamines and barbiturates. The classification of drugs is, in part, about proportionality. Experts have long argued that the current system for ranking drugs – Class A for the most dangerous to Class C for the least dangerous – is irrational. In terms of harm caused, alcohol and tobacco are more dangerous than cannabis, yet they are legal and cannabis is illegal. Defenders of the 2004 decision to downgrade cannabis to Class C say that it has not increased its use and it has freed police to tackle drug-dealers and other more serious crimes. Since 2004, consumption of cannabis has actually declined.

Are there other risks from skunk?

Yes – but they are small. Skunk is smoked like cannabis, contains carcinogenic substances and is often mixed with tobacco. The British Lung Foundation estimated that smoking three joints was equivalent to smoking 20 cigarettes but most users give up after a few years. Some experts also believe there is a risk of dependence among regular smokers. However, cannabis is not seen as a drug of addiction like heroin or tobacco.

Should the newer, more potent forms of cannabis be re-classified?

Yes...

* Vulnerable individuals with a predisposition to mental illness may be tipped into psychosis by the drug

* The younger age at which people start smoking means their brains are more vulnerable

* Skunk cannabis is three to four times stronger than herbal cannabis and has more potent effects

No...

* At worst, the experts say, the use of cannabis increases the lifetime risk of schizophrenia by only 1 per cent

* The chances that users of skunk will progress to harder drugs such as heroin are very small

* Skunk is safer than alcohol and tobacco, which are legal and cause more than 100,000 deaths a year

The greatest fear, alongside its effect on mental health, is that skunk may lead people on to use harder drugs. It is certainly true that many people who become heroin addicts have used cannabis in the past. But the vast majority of cannabis users never progress to heroin. Research by the Home Office concluded that the so-called "gateway effect" of cannabis – leading users on to harder drugs – was probably "very small".

The Independent 6 February 2008

STOP PRESS

Cannabis will return to being a class B drug from early 2009 against the advice of the Government's Advisory Council and less than five years after it was downgraded to class C.

Jacqui Smith, the Home Secretary, announced the change despite the Government's panel of drugs experts saying it would not deter millions from smoking the drug. Police officers also say it will be difficult to enforce.

Miss Smith said the move was needed to "protect the public". The planned changes will include a ban on the sale of cannabis seeds and paraphernalia such as pipes.

Miss Smith accepted all of the recommendations from the Government's Advisory Council on the misuse of drugs apart from its main proposal to keep cannabis at class C.

May 2008

BUSINESS AS USUAL IN THE DRUGS TRADE

Drug dealers generally have the same aim as all business people – to keep trading and making a profit. For a recent Home Office report, researchers interviewed 222 people in prison for high level drug dealing. They looked at the drugs trade using the model of a legitimate business – and found striking similarities.

MARKET FORCES

As in any trade, prices depend on three factors: demand, costs and competition.

The most reliable estimate of the value of the illegal drug market in the UK is £4bn to £6.6bn per year. That is about one third the size of the UK tobacco market and two fifths of the alcohol market. Demand has always remained high.

Comparing cocaine to a legal stimulant, coffee, which grows in similar conditions the researchers noted that the mark up on coffee from the stage at which it is produced to the point at which it reaches the UK consumer is 223%. For cocaine that mark up is about 1,600%, from £325 per kilo in production to £51,850 per kilo on the street.

Prices can be affected by law enforcement 'purges' and by seasonal peaks in demand, with prices for a kilogram of heroin increasing by as much as £1,000 around Christmas.

Some dealers add extra to their prices when they do not know the buyer or if they think the buyer has little idea about the going rate. Some charge less to regular users as 'loyalty bonuses'. Some of those interviewed did not pass on price increases for reasons such as keeping customers or only needing enough to finance their own drug habit.

Although dealers were aware of the prices charged by their 'competitors' there is little evidence of them getting together to fix prices (except among importers and national distributors). Dividing up geographical areas or customers is more common, with big towns often having several dealers but smaller ones only one.

THE 'CAREER' PATH

As with many legitimate businesses drug dealing is often a family affair – for rather special reasons.

Most people enter the drug trade through having friends or relatives already involved and, not surprisingly, money is their motivation. It is important to be regarded as trustworthy by those already trading, so family connections or having been known since childhood are important assets. Having served time in prison and not 'grassed' might help to establish someone as trustworthy. (While prison was not the place where most drug dealers started their career, it was certainly a good place to network and develop helpful contacts). There are few barriers to entry – no need for any special skills or qualifications other than a willingness to break the law. It does not require a great deal of money to get started and the amount is easily obtained through credit or crime. As with many careers - it's not what you know but who you know!

At the bottom end of the business are the street dealers, selling small amounts to users. They have lots of customers (10 to 100s), usually found through networks of other users. They are nearly all drug users themselves and most deal simply to feed their habit. The move from user to dealer is an easy one – they already know where to go for the drug and for customers. Most stay at this level in the 'business' – some over long 'careers'. They are often involved in petty crime and have frequently been in prison.

Then there are 'wholesalers', who buy and sell drugs in bulk within a small region or town. They mostly operate alone, as 'sole traders', and deal with a variety of drugs. Above them in the business hierarchy are national dealers who buy and sell in different UK cities and often have long careers, dealing in a variety of drugs. They have to be very adaptable, moving on to new drugs and new methods to meet the market. At this level, they work with people in many different roles within the trade and may even have salaried employees. This means that even if the 'boss' is put into prison the business can continue.

International dealers use sophisticated operations and professional services and some use legitimate trade to aid business. Some dealers have long and complex careers involving both legitimate and criminal activities and many see prison as an everyday hazard of their line of work.

PROFIT AND RISKS

Legitimate businesses always have to be aware of profit margins but for street dealers in the drug trade revenues are so large in comparison to costs that they have no need for a detailed analysis. Two international dealers did mention that the exchange rate was a factor in their profit and loss.

Cutting the drug by adding other, cheaper substances was one way of maintaining profit margins, but dealers, like legitimate businesses, were conscious of the need to balance customer satisfaction and profit.

Some of the dealers interviewed said that cash flow became a problem when drugs or money were stolen. One national-level dealer commented that the risk of drugs being stolen by competitors tended to increase when there was a shortfall.

However, the theft of money seemed to concern dealers more. One dealer said that after all the planning and getting it right and succeeding in getting the drugs through and sold, "it would be catastrophic to lose the money".

Ethnic ties, selling to friends who were users, having contacts within legitimate businesses that could facilitate dealing operations, and meeting contacts in prison were key factors that helped the business to grow.

LEGALISATION

So, given that the drugs business operates in a generally conventional way, would it be a simple strategy to legalise drugs, legitimise the trade and remove the criminal element? The Executive Director of the United Nations Office on Drugs and Crime, Antonio Maria Costa, thinks not. He argues, 'Legalisation may reduce the profits to organised crime, but it will also increase the damage done to the health of individuals and society. Evidence shows a strong correlation between drug availability and drug abuse." Pointing to the controls now being placed on the sales of tobacco and alcohol, he asks why we would allow a new threat in the form of legal drugs. He also points out the damage done to whole economies in Africa – corruption, violence and instability – by the European drugs trade which passes through them. He has a further suggestion: celebrity users should stop making cocaine look cool thereby undoing millions of pounds of prevention and education. The media too should stop, in effect, advertising drugs by acting as "a cheerleader or a megaphone for celebrity junkies".

> **How the drug market is shared out:**
>
> **Crack 28%**
>
> **Heroin 23%**
>
> **Cannabis 20%**
>
> **Powder cocaine 18%**
>
> **Amphetamines 6%**
>
> **Ecstasy 5%**

> **The breakdown of wages and profits per transaction for a cocaine importation and distribution 'business', based on a typical 10kg transaction of cocaine (in an average week 50-60kg of cocaine was shipped):**
>
> * **Cost: £180,000**
> * **Revenue: £220,000**
> * **Wage bill: £1,750 (including main courier, money collector, money counter, money deliverer and driver)**
> * **Gross profit: £40,000 (Revenue minus Cost)**
> * **Wages accounted for 0.8% of revenue and 4% of profit**
>
> **Salaries can be estimated as follows:**
>
> * **Main courier annual salary: £188,000 (weekly salary of £4,000 over 47 weeks, including expenses)**
> * **Money collector annual salary: £58,750 (weekly salary of £1,250 over 47 weeks)**

> **One strategy not available in the conventional business world was violence or the threat of violence**

The need for secrecy and to avoid the law brings extra costs for drug dealers, in the same way that legislation and regulations (such as health and safety or employment laws) have an impact on legitimate business. One strategy not available in the conventional business world was violence or the threat of violence. This was used to protect the customer base, enforce contracts, defend the reputation of the business and protect against the risk of being 'grassed up'.

GROWTH

Three-quarters of dealers had attempted to develop their operations by finding alternative sources of supply to protect them from fluctuation. The most successful ones were able to adapt to new circumstances and exploit new opportunities which often came about through chance meetings with others involved in the drug market.

A BUSINESS SOLUTION?

If the drugs trade operates like a legitimate trade then perhaps it can be controlled with a strategy that hits the profits. Asset recovery – the confiscation of goods from convicted dealers – has been particularly effective, given that most dealers had spent their money on themselves, on lavish lifestyles or just paying the mortgage. Confiscation orders mean that dealers lose significant sums of money and goods – even if those items were not acquired directly via the drugs trade. From the interviews with those involved in the trade, it seems likely then that the best way to counter the drugs trade is to hit it where it hurts – in the money.

Source: The illicit drug trade in the United Kingdom, 2007

HOW HEROIN CREATES TERRORISTS

RAGEH OMAAR

Hundreds of young British Asians and Somalis in cities throughout the UK have become vulnerable and isolated within their own communities as a result of dealing in and using drugs. They form a critical recruiting ground for militant organisations.

Heroin's grip on inner city estates used to be described through the phrase "King Heroin" – but a much better phrase to describe the role the drug has played in helping militant groups reach out to young British Muslims is "Sergeant Heroin". It is a real and important recruiting officer for militant groups.

I've spent much of the past month exploring the meteoric rise in the dealing of hard drugs among young Somali, Pakistani and Bangladeshi boys in London – in Hounslow, Woolwich and Tower Hamlets. Most of them belong to gangs, but only in the loosest sense of the word. They describe themselves as "crews" – often nothing more than a group of young boys who have all grown up together, and are tightly knit around their families, culture and skin colour.

Brick Lane has changed enormously over the past decade; regeneration has transformed it into one of the capital's tourist highlights. You're as likely to meet young tourists from Denmark and Holland as young Somalis and Bengalis. But step away from the glitz and buzzing restaurants of Brick Lane, down any of the side streets that lead to the estates three minutes away from the celebrated road, and you find some of the most deprived wards in the UK.

Down one such side street is a small fenced-in five-a-side football pitch and patch of green. The area is notorious for the sale and use of heroin. At 11pm on a cold Friday, I was taken here by volunteers from the Brick Lane Youth Development Association. Muhammad Rabbani and his co-workers counsel and mentor hundreds of boys as young as 14 and 15 who find themselves in a world of drugs, academic failure, racism and much more.

As we walked through the estates behind Brick Lane, Muhammad and his colleagues were recognised by respectful young teenagers, both Asian and Somali. Irham, 16, and his Somali friend, Abdallah, spoke calmly of how dealers offered users a combination called "Black and White" – a wrap of heroin (black) along with a wrap of crack (white). Around the corner, in one dealing hotspot – completely in the open – were older Bengali lads selling the heroin wraps, while users sat around smoking the drug. Even here, Muhammad and his colleagues have access and sufficient respect to approach dealers and urge them to stop what they are doing, offering support to help them do so.

Drugs play an important role in radicalisation. Everyone knows who is dealing. It is when these young men have been ostracised or go to prison – in other words when they've hit rock bottom – that they are ripe for targeting by proselytisers. At first, it is a way out of drugs. Families are overjoyed at seeing lads who were once dealing drugs going to the mosque, studying in madrasa groups – even asking to go to Pakistan or Somalia to study the Koran. It is a far more radical version of how the Nation of Islam spread among black Americans whose lives were blighted by drugs, poverty, crime and alienation.

When the government speaks of concentrating on combating radicalism in cyberspace, they betray how ill-equipped they are to reach out to those young men most vulnerable to al-Qaeda's message. Organisations such as BLYDA need support. The men in these organisations have respect and legitimacy among young British Muslims. Many have gone through what these 14- and 15-year-olds are facing and many others have gone through radical "first point of contact" organisations such as Hizb ut-Tahrir.

Many British Muslims do heroic but utterly unsupported work with youngsters to keep them from being disenchanted, hopeless and radicalised. I call them the Thin Brown Line. The battle will be lost without them.

New Statesman 12 November 2007

Absorbing scenes from a class struggle

Photo posed by model

By Thomas Sutcliffe

Anyone uncertain about China's future standing in the world should take a look at the standard school day at Xiuning high school, as revealed in BBC4's engrossing series Chinese School. The pupils get up at 5.45am and are in the classroom by 6am for 45 minutes of "self-study". After that, they break for 30 minutes of

As tears rolled down the boy's cheeks, the teacher beamed approvingly

aerobics and breakfast at 7.30am, heading back to the classroom at 8am. Lessons run through to 11.30am, when they get lunch and 90 minutes of free time, and then it's back to the classroom from 1pm till 5pm. Another break for supper and then they squeeze in another two-and-quarter hours of schoolwork before finally shutting their books at 10.15pm. At that point, the indolent

slackers call it a day, though really dedicated bookworms, such as Wu Yufei, a 17-year-old who is aiming at exam gold, will add a couple more hours of revision before grabbing a few hours' sleep and starting all over again.

Granted, Xiuning high school is for high performers, and they are

cramming for the Gao Kao, a dreaded public examination that will determine whether they get a university place or not. It's true, too, that the headmaster murmured some unconvincing noises to the assembled parents about not putting too much pressure on their children. But it was advice he didn't appear to believe applied to himself. "You must shoulder your parents'

expectations, the great trust of your school and the hope of our Motherland," he told the students. And the parents hadn't been listening, anyway. "He carries all our family's hopes and dreams," said the mother of another boy, during a trip to the family grave to plead with her ancestors to do their bit in boosting him up the results tables. Meanwhile, Wu Yufei's mother had given up work for a year, in order to take her daughter home-cooked meals twice a day and nutritionally bolster her academic chances. The overwhelming impression was of a society almost fanatically dedicated to maximising its potential.

The discipline starts early, if Ping Min primary is at all representative. A kind of Chinese Montessori school, run as a charity for disadvantaged children, Ping Min expects its pupils not only to behave perfectly in class but

also to clean the school and work in vegetable gardens fertilised with their own night soil. I wouldn't have been at all surprised if it had been revealed that they put in an eight-hour shift at a television factory as well, such was the regimen. Not that they don't have the odd problem. One small boy found himself hauled up for a bit of self-criticism after his pencil eraser was voted the most ill-used in the class. "Do you think the eraser's happy to be full of holes?" he was asked, before being forced to put on a shabby jumper as a badge of his eraser-torturing shame. As tears rolled down the boy's cheeks, the teacher beamed approvingly at the way his fellow pupils had helped to bring this antisocial element to his senses before his stationery-abusing tendencies had got out of hand.

The Independent 9 April 2008

Can the Swedish style sway English Education?

Photo: Kunskapsskolan

Imagine a school in which pupils decide their own timetable, choose their own lessons and can use their iPods and mobile phones in lesson time. It sounds like the worst excesses of 'permissive' education, yet it is a system being championed by people from all sides of the political spectrum as an answer to Britain's educational problems

In the early 1990s, Sweden introduced a system which allowed anyone to set up a 'free' school, however small, and claim an allowance from the state for each pupil. This meant that parents who were opposed to the closure of a local school could counter it by opening one of their own. Religious groups could also have their own schools, as could advocates of various alternative educational systems. This variety meant that parents had a choice in the way they 'spent' the allowance made for their child's education. There are now about 900 of these 'free' schools in Sweden and one organisation is about to bring the concept to Britain.

The biggest for-profit company – Kunskapsskolan – is about to open two academies in Richmond and is hoping to open 30 more in the next ten years. Kunskapsskolan means 'knowledge school' and their website says: "The main task of the school is to impart knowledge. In addition to this, it is the aim of Kunskapsskolan to provide each pupil with additional skills – methods of acquiring and using a variety of knowledge, as well as personal development – to be able to meet a future world of vast flows of information and a rapid rate of change. The fundamental principle behind our method of learning is the conviction that all pupils are different and that they

learn in different ways and at different rates, and that it is the school's task to meet these differences"

It is this philosophy which dictates the unique structure of the schools – the learning is personalised. Each student can negotiate an individual timetable each week, in co-operation with teachers and parents. There is a weekly target in every subject but the student has the freedom to decide how to reach it. A personal tutor oversees progress at a weekly meeting and parents can follow it online. British students don't have this level of responsibility for their own learning until at least AS level or more probably university. As one student said, "You

shouldn't go to this school if you can't take your own responsibility. You can slack off whenever you like, sure you have to make up for it later, but if you feel tired one day you can slack off and fix it another day. A lot of people do find that very difficult."

The two British schools will maintain their current size, buildings and facilities. In Sweden the schools are small, averaging about 180 pupils and do not, therefore, require purpose-built premises. Some are located in empty offices which have been remodelled. They are often not well endowed with playing fields (sport does not feature as strongly in the Swedish curriculum as the British) or the latest educational technology and the internet features more strongly as a learning tool than do books.

In Kunskapsskolan there is no fixed timetable and no bells. The business plan was to be deliberately different, to offer a choice. Parents who opt for this system often feel that their children were being stifled in the more rigid state system. Although the equivalent schools in Britain will be obliged to follow the National Curriculum in English, Maths and IT they will still be allowed to offer personalised education. Anders Hultins, who co-founded Kunskapsskolan says, "We are popular in Sweden as an alternative to the teacher-led factory model

Photo: Kunskapsskolan

In contrast, chances of educational success in Britain are heavily skewed towards those with an advantageous start and a good school. Our

high spending on education. One further significant difference is that the Swedish Kunskapsskolan are run as profit-making ventures – something not permitted in Britain.

It is too early to pass judgement on their academic success, though recent results

show that Kunskapsskolan students have performed better than the national average in Swedish and English. The claim made by some supporters that by introducing competition between schools, they drive up standards all round, will take longer to assess.

In any case, can a freer and more equal system be imported into our culture? Even if it can, is it a solution to Britain's education problems? British schools are often heavily criticised and yet repeatedly loaded with responsibility to solve many of society's problems, from knife crime to unemployment. Would smaller schools, which treat pupils as individuals, help? Looking at the wider issues, do better schools make a better society – or would a better society result in better schools.

Sources: Various

> **Each student can negotiate an individual timetable each week, in co-operation with teachers and parents**

of education. When you see a normal school you will find classrooms of equal sizes and a bell ringing; there is factory thinking behind that." It is, perhaps, ironic that what is a commercial enterprise in Sweden is offering an alternative to a factory model of learning in the UK.

One reason for the British interest in the Swedish system is that Sweden scores highly on international measures of educational achievement. But schools don't exist in a vacuum. Swedish society is less divided by class than ours. Although middle class parents can still work the system to their advantage to some extent, there is a more equal playing field for Swedish children. The education system is centred more on the child and less on standards. Children start later and are under less pressure. Those in favour of the free school model hope that by importing it they can import some of the wider advantages too.

education system is based on competition. There is a contest to get children into the best places and schools compete with one another for bright pupils. Children are tested throughout their education and the results are used to assess both the youngsters and their schools.

In addition, in Britain there is already an alternative to the state system in the form of the independent sector. Here, high fees and selection are the norm. One of the benefits that parents are prepared to pay for is a traditional style of teaching and curriculum.

In Sweden the 'voucher' with which the state pays for the child's education cannot be topped up – every pupil in every school is worth the same amount of money. In addition, the 'free' schools must take their pupils on a first-come, first-served basis. Selection, by whatever means, is not allowed. Swedes also accept high taxation to allow for

"He's been very naughty – he's hacked into our bank account and won't tell me where he's transferred the money."

Saga April 2008
www.saga.co.uk

ONLY SNOBS SNEER AT McDIPLOMA GRADUATES

By Paul Taylor

'D 'YOU want fries with that A Level?' First we had McJobs and now we have McDiplomas, with news that the burger giant has been accredited to give out qualifications.

Cue a welter of jokes about BScs in burger-flipping, and accusations that the Qualifications and Curriculum Authority is dumbing down our education system. But all this hilarity has exposed a rich vein of snobbery in British society, not just about fast food and American business values but also about the lower reaches of the service industry.

What McDonald's will offer is a basic shift manager's course – a qualification which shows that the young person has learned what needs to be known about the day to day running of a restaurant. Is this any different from the old idea of the butcher's or baker's apprentice learning the shop trade?

Now, some may say McDonald's may not be the most wholesome of eateries, and there may be nutritional and ethical qualms about their products. But no one can argue that McDonald's is not a phenomenally successful business which has got that way by giving people something they want in the most efficient and cost-effective manner.

Anyone who has stood in a queue at a busy McD's – and I'm not ashamed to say I've scoffed my share of Big Macs – will have witnessed a hustle and bustle which simply did not exist in the catering industry before the Yanks arrived. I am pretty sure that if you can be taught to marshal that kind of frenetic activity, you are equipped to run just about any small retail enterprise.

Those who deride the idea of McQualifications would presumably prefer these wannabe burger bar managers to be in a classroom studying a "proper" academic subject. That, I'm afraid, is one of the great conceits of our over-qualified age.

New Labour long ago declared an aspiration that, by 2010, 50% of all young people would go into higher education. As low-wage jobs, in the global economy, bleed inexorably towards Asia, Britain has only its knowledge capital to offer, so the reasoning goes.

Fine in theory. But in practice, a good proportion of those graduates are being set up for disappointment. Too many of the jobs available do not need a graduate to do them. So thousands of young people will emerge, saddled with student debt, holding less than prestigious degrees and absurdly raised expectations, to find that years of study have prepared them only to read a script in a call centre.

As we have become a brainier nation in recent decades, the old apprenticeships which would onc have been taken up by 16-year schoo leavers have shrunk away, which is ho we have had the bizarre situation i recent years of white collar workers r training as plumbers to meet a critic national shortage. Some of thos school-leavers for whom there wer no apprenticeships have grown up i a world of near-worklessness, not ju because they do not have specific skil but because they do not even have th basic discipline to get in to work o time and do as instructed. It doesn take much imagination to guess wh contribution these people make t crime and other social problems.

Now here's a strange statistic. spring 2004, unemployment stood 1.43m. In autumn 2007, it was pret similar at 1.65m. But, in between time expansion of the EU meant we had least 690,000, possibly over a millic east Europeans arriving here lookin for work. All those Polish, Slovakian ar Czech migrants found work which o own unemployed couldn't or wouldr do. Presumably that also include flipping burgers.

What we should be doing is involvir everyone possible in the world of wor If that means dishing out qualificatio for running burger bars, selling mobi phones or even sweeping the stree then so be it.

Manchester Evening Ne *30 January 20*

Can Science Really Save the World?

Endless treaties to cut carbon emissions and halt global warming have failed to turn the tide of pollution. Now scientists want to intervene on a planetary scale, changing the very nature of our seas and skies. Ahead of a major report on 'geo-engineering' we reveal the six big ideas that could change the face of the Earth

Robin McKie and Juliette Jowit

They are the ultimate technological fixes: schemes that will span our planet and involve scientists in reshaping our world to save it from global warming. Yet only a few years ago, such projects – giant space mirrors, flotillas of artificial cloud makers and ocean fertilisation programmes – were dismissed as the stuff of science fiction.

Today many engineers and researchers – fearful of the rate at which our planet is warming – say geo-engineering projects are now mankind's only hope of saving itself from the impact of climate change. A major report and a new exhibition at the Science Museum starting next week will resurrect the debate.

Despite 10 years of international negotiations aimed at reducing carbon dioxide levels by between 60-80%, global emissions are still rising. The only hope, say geo-engineers, is to change the planet, alter its oceans and reshape its cloud cover.

It is a point highlighted by Brian Launder, professor of mechanical engineering at Manchester University, who was once 'neutral' about these great geo-engineering projects but who has come to believe that current attempts to reduce CO2 emissions are doomed to failure.

'As time has gone on I have become increasingly concerned about the lack of progress on climate change and [although] they once seemed a last resort, I have to say we're going to need to do this.'

Launder is now editing a forthcoming issue of the Philosophical Transactions of the Royal Society which will be devoted to the subject of geo-engineering schemes. 'We're moving, but I think we need to go a lot further.'

An exhibition – Can Algae Save The World? – opening at the Science Museum will also focus on hi-tech projects aimed at saving the planet.

The latest assessment report by the Intergovernmental Panel on Climate Change, published earlier this year, considered three major techniques to reduce sunlight reaching the Earth: orbiting mirrors, sulphur particle schemes and projects for enhancing cloud cover.

The ideas 'could have beneficial consequences' by increasing agricultural productivity and forestry, the panel concluded. Carbon dioxide would be left in the atmosphere, stimulating plant growth, while reductions in sunlight would stop temperatures from rising even as CO2 levels continued to increase.

> **These ideas were our last resort. But now we're going to have to try them**

'Geo-engineering is one of the types of thing that are worth investigating,' says Ken Caldeira, of the Carnegie Institution of Washington. 'If we can generate 100 ideas, and 97 are bad and we land up with three good ones, then the whole thing will have been worthwhile.'

Opponents to such schemes point out that it is technology that got mankind in its current fix. An even bigger dose of technology is therefore the last thing the planet needs. Schemes for fertilising the oceans with iron compounds pose immense risks to marine life, for example. Geo-engineers defend their schemes by pointing out that emissions of greenhouse gases are already bringing huge changes to natural ecosystems.

It is a point stressed by the distinguished ecologist James Lovelock: there are dangers in intervening but the risks posed by doing nothing are worse. 'There may be all sorts of ecological consequences,' he said. 'But then the stakes are terribly high.'

Ocean pumps

Two of Britain's leading environmental thinkers, Chris Rapley, head of the Science Museum, and James Lovelock, creator of the Gaia concept, suggest vertical pipes could pump deep cold water to the sea surface. Cold ocean water is considered to be more 'productive' than warmer water because it contains more lifeforms. And these lifeforms are vital for absorbing CO_2.

Using special valves, cold water would be made to flow up floating pipes and out on to the ocean surface, bringing increased numbers of lifeforms into contact with the atmosphere and its carbon dioxide. These lifeforms would absorb CO_2, die and then sink to the ocean floor, storing the carbon away for millennia.

Marine biologists point out that the scheme could pose major problems for sea life, in particular for creatures such as whales and porpoises.

Chance of success: 3/5 Impact on marine life could count against the scheme

Sulphur blanket

During major volcanic eruptions, the Earth often undergoes significant cooling. For example, when Mount Pinatubo in the Philippines erupted in 1991 the average temperature across the Earth decreased by 0.6C. Scientists pointed the finger of blame at the 10 million tonnes of sulphur that the volcano ejected into the stratosphere. So why not copy Pinatubo? That is the suggestion of Professor Paul Crutzen who won a Nobel prize in 1995 for his work on the ozone layer.

He has proposed creating a 'blanket' of sulphur that would block the Sun's rays from reaching Earth; to do this, he envisages hundreds of rockets filled with sulphur being blasted into the stratosphere. About one million tonnes of sulphur would be enough to create his cooling blanket, he says.

The idea alarms other scientists, who fear such a massive input of sulphur into the upper atmosphere could increase acid rain or damage the ozone layer. Crutzen believes his idea may still be necessary if Earth continues to warm up at its current rate. 'I am prepared to lose some bit of ozone if we can prevent major increases of temperature, say beyond two degrees or three degrees,' he says.

Chance of success: 1/5 Risks of acid rain and ozone depletion will provoke opposition

Forests of the seas

Blooms of plankton and algae are the grasslands and prairies of the oceans. They absorb carbon dioxide, die and then sink to the seabed carrying the carbon dioxide they absorbed during their lifetimes. Increase such blooms and you could take out more and more carbon dioxide from the atmosphere, scientists argue – an idea that formed the core of a recent meeting of experts at the Woods Hole Oceanographic Institution in the US.

The favoured method for stimulating plankton growth is to use iron fertilisers. It is known that tiny amounts of iron are critical in stimulating phytoplankton growth in seas. However, in many parts of the world iron in seawater is virtually non-existent and plankton levels correspondingly low.

Several groups of US entrepreneurs have begun experiments aimed at correcting this problem by pumping tonnes of soluble iron compounds into sea areas. Several trial schemes are now under way. But some critics warn that very little carbon dioxide would be removed from the atmosphere this way, while there is a danger such schemes could cause dangerous pollution.

Chance of success: 2/5 Method already in trials, but faces considerable opposition over potential damage to marine life

Mirrors

Radiation from the Sun heats our planet and sustains life here. But as Earth warms up, scientists want to cut that radiation and one of the most ambitious ideas involves firing giant mirrors into its orbit.

Physicist Lowell Wood, at the Lawrence Livermore National Laboratory in California, has put forward the idea of using a mesh of aluminium threads, a millionth of an inch in diameter. 'It would be like a window screen made of exceedingly fine metal wire,' he explains. The screen wouldn't completely block sunlight but would filter infra-red radiation.

However, such mirrors would be expensive to make and put into orbit. To produce a 1% cut in solar radiation would require mirrors with surface areas of 600,000 square miles. But once in space such mirrors would be extremely cheap to operate.

'It's very hi-tech,' said John Shepherd, professor of marine science at the National Oceanographic Centre at Southampton University. 'Who knows whether they can really do it? And it's going to cost a lot of money to find out.'

Chance of success: 1/5 Incredibly expensive

Cloud shield

John Latham, at the National Centre for Atmospheric Research in Colorado, and Stephen Salter, of Edinburgh University estimate that increasing cloud cover using a seawater spray 'seeding' process could increase cloud cover by 4% – enough to counter a doubling of carbon dioxide in the atmosphere by shielding Earth from solar radiation.

Their plan is one of the cheaper ideas for countering rising carbon dioxide levels and is relatively low-tech, leading to hopes that, if computer simulations give good results, a field trial could start in five years.

Latham acknowledges there are dangers in changing weather patterns. 'We certainly shouldn't implement [it] in any global sense until we've done our best to examine what implications it might have,' he says.

'But if one felt that there are unlikely to be any implications that are more severe than the damage global warming is causing, then I think we'd begin.'

Chance of success: 2/5 Will need major global commitment to succeed

Synthetic trees

Planting trees that absorb carbon dioxide has become a major eco-industry. But now scientists are proposing a surprise technological variant: synthetic trees. These trees would not grow or flower or leaf – but they would absorb carbon dioxide.

This startling concept is the brainchild of Klaus Lackner of Columbia University who first outlined his proposal at an annual meeting of the American Association for the Advancement of Science. He describes his synthetic trees as looking like 'goal posts with Venetian blinds'.

Lackner has calculated that one of his synthetic trees could remove about 90,000 tonnes of carbon dioxide in a year – the output of more than 15,000 cars and a thousandfold improvement on the natural behaviour of a real, living tree.

Lackner's concept is a variant of carbon sequestration technology which involves the seizing of carbon and storing it underground. Already schemes exist for removing carbon dioxide produced by burning coal, gas or oil at power plants before it reaches the atmosphere. Other projects are investigating ways to liquefy this carbon dioxide and store it in old mines or oilfields.

However, the process does not work for all polluters, in particular cars and lorries – hence Lackner's synthetic trees which would act like filters, removing carbon dioxide from the atmosphere. An absorbent coating, such as limewater, on slats would capture carbon dioxide so that it could be removed and then buried. However, critics say the scheme suffers from the fact that engineers could end up expending more energy in capturing carbon dioxide than they would save.

Chance of success: 4/5 Carbon sequestration is likely to play a major role in the world's battle against climate change, though perhaps not in the form of synthetic trees

The Observer 7 October 2007
© Guardian News & Media Ltd. 2007

Stop trying to save the planet

In this extract from his new book, George Marshall challenges us to think differently about climate change before we take the "Carbon Detox"

I have to make a confession. When I hear people talk about climate change I often find myself alternating between despair and boredom. Most of what I see in the newspapers, in scientific presentations and in the information leaflets of government or green groups leaves me unmoved and unmotivated. I have dedicated my life to this issue, but only because I have worked hard to use my own imagination and create my own storyline. And if the standard communication leaves me cold, it can't be doing much for anyone else.

I want to encourage you to abandon the usual messages about the things you can do to prevent climate change. I don't ask you to 'save the planet'. I don't pretend that small, easy steps will 'make a difference'. I want you to be true to what you know and believe and to change the way you think before you change the way you live.

Counting carbon

Consider your contribution to climate change as weight, as something that can be measured precisely and down to the last gramme. You can shift it around from one activity to another and choose which bit you want to drop first, but your objective must be to drop as much of it as you can.

No other problem can be measured in this way. You could never measure your personal contribution to the torture of political prisoners, land mines in Cambodia or stockpiles of nuclear weapons. With climate change you can consider your results and make direct and completely valid comparisons. You can say, 'this year I made half the contribution to climate change that I made last year'.

Why "small steps" make little difference

Last month my local council posted a green magazine through my door that asks householders to 'do your bit to save the planet'. It lists a standard set of actions, all of which are phrased as sacrifices – giving things up, doing with less and turning things down – and then assures us that these small personal actions can really 'make a difference'.

Local residents also offered their own tips for low-carbon living. First prize goes to Mrs Roberts who suggests that we turn off the lights when we watch television, as we already have enough light from the TV. Great idea, Mrs Roberts. Sitting in the dark will inspire a lot of people.

And you can find similar things all over the place: on the television, in magazines, in a plethora of new books full of green lifestyle tips. All of these articles have the same formulae. First, they state that there is a huge global problem. Then they tell people that they have a moral responsibility to take personal actions to stop it. And then they give a list of such actions that are so small and trivial as to appear largely pointless.

I don't doubt the sincerity and good intentions that lie behind them, but I have come to the conclusion that these lists of tips are ineffective and often counterproductive.

First of all, telling people that very small measures can resolve a huge problem is neither honest nor plausible. This trivialises the overall problem and makes us think that maybe it is not such a big deal after all. Putting trivial measures alongside alarmist warnings – headlines such as 'Twenty things you can do to save the planet from destruction' – can lead people to mock and reject the very notion of climate change.

Second, these lists are misleading because they encourage you to think of different actions as being equally important. A typical list will suggest that you never use a new plastic bag and fly less, even though the comparative impact of each is hugely different. Clearly there is something very wrong with a list of personal action that lumps together actions that have a one thousand-fold variation in effectiveness.

This is highly misleading and encourages people to adopt a trivial behaviour change and believe that they are being effective.

The truth is that there may be lots of good reasons for recycling your plastic bags – but they make doodly squat difference to climate change. An average plastic bag produces 31 grammes of carbon dioxide, about the same as comes from driving my car 300 feet. Once put within the context of our overall emissions, plastic bags are virtually irrelevant. I'm sorry to tell you, but adopting some diversionary good behaviour is a classic psychological strategy of people who don't want to face up to facts. In the case of climate change, this innate tendency is actively encouraged by all those articles that outline some catastrophic climate impacts and then provide a box of 'small easy things you can do now to make a difference'.

Organisations are also prone to absurd token activity. My favourite example is Virgin Airlines. In 2006 they announced the first step towards reducing the climate impacts of their transatlantic flights: planting trees to soak up the emissions of the limousines that pick up their first-class air passengers.

Although they smell like cynical publicity stunts, I suspect that the real intended audience is the company's own employees. After all, most people want to believe their work is worthwhile and making a positive contribution to the world.

The lesson is that you need to keep everything in perspective. There are strong and accurate objective measures of our climate impacts and it is these that should guide our actions. The only thing that counts is the carbon bottom line.

Say no to sackcloth

Dropping the carbon is not a penance. First of all, let's be clear – light living is not about becoming a climate saint: it is about doing things differently. People who are living light will choose very different ways to live, and nowhere is this more evident than in the area of treats. Treats are those occasional splurges that are fun, memorable and give you pleasure. Who would ever want to live in a world without them?

Treats may be extravagant, wasteful and decadent – that is what makes them treats, after all. It is the habitual 'heavy' behaviour that racks up the emissions, not the rare treat.

Driving around the corner to buy a sandwich because it's raining and you don't want to get wet is not good for you or the world, but easy and handy once in a while. Green literature is scathing about unnecessary local car trips. They create congestion and urban pollution and make roads unsafe for children. I agree, and I recommend that you ditch

Typical 'tips' with their actual savings

Tip	Kgs of CO2 saved per year
Never use a new plastic bag	5
Change one standard lightbulb to a low-energy lightbulb	17
Never leave your TV on standby	25
Turn down heating by one degree	230 (average house)
Commute to work by bus	400 (average UK car commute in average car)
Become a vegetarian	500
Make one less flight	500-12,000 (depending on the flight)

the car. But in terms of the carbon bottom line it is habitual, long-distance driving that is the problem, so let's get our priorities right.

Even if I ran a Ferrari Testarossa round a racetrack at full whack for 20 minutes I would still only have burned as much petrol as I would driving our sluggish Volvo estate to visit my mum. Come on kids, which one would you rather do?

Stop trying to 'save the planet'

Finally, you should not believe that it is your responsibility to 'save the planet' or 'stop climate change'. These are slogans to put on banners, not arguments for individuals. I want to say this to everyone, including the most dedicated greens: "Please don't do this to 'save the planet'". Of course, your actions contribute to the huge shift we will all make; you will be a positive role model; your purchases will send a signal through the markets. But you need to do it for the right reasons. If you are changing the way you live out of guilt or fear, then you are setting yourself up for a fall. Your reasons for changing must be more personal.

You are not going to give anything up. This is not a loss, it's a gain. As we detox, we are not going to give anything up: we are going to do things differently. Do it because you don't want to contribute any more to a major problem that will hurt people. Do it because it is the smart 21st-century thing to do. Do it because you want to do it.

George Marshall is Director of the Climate Outreach and Information Network (www.coinet.org.uk)

Ethical Consumer March/April 2008
www.ethicalconsumer.org

Keeping critical data on ice

Secret probes beneath the Arctic ice fields have unearthed some disturbing data about the course of climate change.

Mad Scientist reports

A working scientist often gets phone calls at all hours. Calls in the small hours of the night are not uncommon, usually another scientist with something important and interesting, across thousands of kilometres and several time zones. Excitement makes them forget the time difference. Pilots get jet-lag. Scientists get phone-lag. So the distant call from America was not unusual.

It was my friend 'Dr X', out on the West coast, still at work in his lab; early evening there, but 2am here. But his subject – Greenland and Arctic ice wilderness – instantly grabbed my attention. 'Also,' he asked, 'what do you know about a certain mysterious mission of a British nuclear submarine deep beneath the Arctic ice fields?' Not a lot. But an hour of highly technical discussion later, I hung up, feeling intrigued. I went back to bed, but not to sleep. A restless night then a day of intense activity, emails, phone calls and faxes. Dr X's nocturnal call started to make sense. I scanned pages of notes over supper that night, truth sinking in, wondering what to do.

The wall above my desk now held huge blow-ups of marine charts of the North Atlantic, showing winds and ocean currents, vast white masses of Arctic ice running right across the top. Covered in scribbled comments and yellow post-it notes, I was looking at a future disaster of gigantic proportions.

Staring me in the face was the planet's first big climate change disaster, an environmental apocalypse that might eventually engulf most of the northern hemisphere. Not in a hundred years, but perhaps in as many months. Possibly even less. Beginning, say, 2020, to roughly 2030. It sounded like a Hollywood disaster movie script; I thought of the blockbuster film, *The Day After Tomorrow*, with America and Europe overwhelmed by ice-catastrophe. But it only sounded like fiction until you checked the meticulous work of the scientists involved, listened to the urgent way they were speaking. Put simply, although most would not go so far in public, they were absolutely dire in their private predictions.

The nuclear sub had been on a critical scientific expedition. The Commander's briefing was that this is 'The most important British naval mission ever, peacetime or war.' So HMS Tireless set out last spring from her UK base, heading out into the vastness of the North Atlantic, scientists and instruments on board, diving deep under the sea-ice, then south, very deep, back-tracking along and underneath the massive northwards flow of the Gulf Stream.

Taking dangerous risks, the sub nearly sank during a massive fire to oxygen generators, crashing through sea-ice to the surface with two dead, many injured and crew half gassed. The Navy nearly lost the sub, but, with true grit, brought scientists and precious data back to Britain.

Tracking this tale of secret nuclear sub expeditions, disaster and Arctic danger, was pure B-movie script. But the cold reality involved serious scientific discussions with experts.

Experts like Professor Peter Wadhams, senior oceanographer at Cambridge University, who had been chief scientist on the sub expedition. I listened, fascinated, to his explanations of what it all meant. Or might mean.

The problem is, he explained, that Arctic and Atlantic climate change is reaching a critical tipping point. Scientists could make predictions, all of which sounded absolutely frightening, but when it came to timelines, or accurate estimates, all computer models went wobbly, or simply didn't exist.

> **Temperature rises like this meant huge droughts, searing heat, agricultural collapse, waves of desperate refugees – all headed North**

Science, and the planet, would be entering unknown seas. I thought of ancient sea-charts, with drawings of mythical sea-monsters in vast gaps of ocean where mediaeval geographers could only guess at future voyages and discoveries. Except this time, there were real monsters, called climate-disaster.

Pressed for explanations, the professor was only certain of the sheer scale of future events. Basically, sometime between 2020 and 2030, all of the Arctic Ocean pack-ice cover was going to melt, leaving a vast bare expanse of open ocean, where before there had been only solid white ice. Winters would see limited ice re-forming, melting away again like fog in the spring. The ice, now gone, had been vital to the stability of the entire northern hemisphere weather system and climate.

Without it, solar heat, reflected back into space by the expanse of white ice, acting like a giant mirror, would relentlessly heat up Arctic seas. Extra heat would be pure fuel for the polar weather system. It would spawn storms and highly disturbed weather patterns sweeping down on Europe and North America with unprecedented violence. Atlantic Ocean weather would change radically. The great storm tracks that now swept up the central Atlantic, striking the Arctic in Spitsbergen, would curve further south, hitting the British Isles instead. Everything, from rainfall to floods, would be affected. All this starting possibly as early as 15 years from now, perhaps no more than 20 years in the future? 'Yes', was the grim answer. The changes would be huge, dramatic. The problem was, right now, we could not accurately predict these events. Only pure luck had given us this warning of things to come.

The Royal Navy is now the only one still doing submarine science expeditions beneath the polar ice, charting the relentless collapse of ice-floes and their thickness. Professor Wadhams had watched his research funding being ruthlessly slashed by NERC (The UK Natural Environment Research Council); the submarine's expedition was nearly cancelled. Just in time, last-minute alternative funds were found. Pure luck, or we would have been walking blind to future disaster. Even with future Royal Navy expeditions, we would have only about 60 months' warning before the tipping point.

There is, apparently, very little that can be done to avert this. Climate change feedback loops have been triggered, and will run their course, until the wildly fluctuating climate of our planet finally settles, perhaps in 150 years' time. This forthcoming Arctic ice-disaster is not just a climate catastrophe; it is an advance warning signal, one we had nearly missed completely.

There was, surprisingly, some good news in the form of a 'cooling effect'. Apparently, climate changes would see European temperatures soar in the next few decades – by at least four degrees centigrade, perhaps more. Mark Lynas's book, *Six Degrees*, with its dire predictions, came to mind. Temperature rises like this meant that Southern Europe would become like North Africa. Huge droughts, searing heat, agricultural collapse, and waves of desperate refugees, all headed north.

And in Britain? The Gulf Stream was failing, slowly, as the ice vanished. It would slow down by perhaps at least 20 per cent or more. As that vast invisible river in the sea lost its flow of heat, a strong chill would descend on Northern Europe. Temperatures would go up, but by only one and a half degrees.

This 'good news' meant that Britain would probably escape the heatwaves and droughts destroying Southern Europe – for a time. And after that? The computer predictions did not exist. Things became dark and uncertain. Probably, possibly, things might get worse.

I went for a late-night walk on the beach to clear my head. When I came back, the phone was ringing – again. It was an old friend, prominent in British environmental journalism. He was, he announced, off to Greenland. With the head of the Orthodox Christian Church. Plus assorted Coptic Popes, ayatollahs, cardinals, archbishops and a mass-media circus.

Why? Because religious leaders were convinced that climate disaster was now certain in our lifetime. The key was the Arctic changes. They were going to assemble, out on the Arctic ice, and pray, fervently, for the safety of the world.

The Ecologist October 2007
www.theecologist.org

Toxic chemicals blamed for the disappearance of Arctic boys

By Daniel Howden

Twice as many girls as boys are being born in remote communities north of the Arctic Circle. Across much of the northern hemisphere, particularly in the US and Japan, the gender ratio has skewed towards girls for the first time.

Now scientists working with Inuit villages in Arctic Russia and Greenland have found the first direct evidence that this trend is linked to widespread chemical pollutants. Despite the Arctic's pristine environment, the area functions as a pollution sink for much of the industrialised world. Winds and rivers deliver a toxic tide from the northern hemisphere into the polar food chain.

Scientists have traced flame-retardant chemicals used in everything from industrial products to furniture, phones and laptops to the food chain, finding high levels of these pollutants in seabirds, seals and polar bears. The Inuit have traditionally relied on a hunter-gatherer's diet almost exclusively made up of marine animals, making them especially vulnerable to toxic pollutants.

Historically in large populations, it is considered normal for the number of baby boys slightly to outnumber girls in a trend believed to compensate naturally for greater male mortality rates.

> **'We heard that our heavy metal consumption is dangerous. If you ate me, you would die'**

But a peer-reviewed US study found an unexpected drop in the proportion of boys born in much of the northern hemisphere. The missing boys would number more than 250,000 in the US and Japan, using the gender ratio at the levels recorded up until 1970.

The researchers suspected that this linked widespread exposure among pregnant women to hormone-mimicking pollutants. But Danish scientists examined 480 families in the Russian Arctic and found high levels of the hormone-mimicking pollutants in the blood of pregnant women, and twice as many girls being born as boys.

They are now studying similar communities in Greenland and Canada and although full results will be published next year, their initial findings exactly match those in Russia.

Lars Otto Riersen, a marine biologist, pollution expert and an executive with the Arctic Monitoring and Assessment Programme (AMAP), says: "When you see such things happening in the Arctic, it may happen here first, in the same way as climate change did."

Although the nature of the Inuit diet is believed to have triggered

Photo: CANADIAN PRESS/Canada Press/PA Photos

the disturbing ratios in the Arctic, a similar pattern may be emerging further south. Until now, the only evidence of the impact of these toxins was circumstantial. The most skewed ratio had been in Canada, where a First Nation community in Sarnia lives amid Ontario's petrochemical industry, and the number of boys born has plunged since the 1990s. The fallout from the toxic cloud in Seveso in Italy in 1976 allowed scientists to monitor dramatic impacts on both the gender ratios and numbers of babies born.

Every year in the industrialised world, household fires cause billions of pounds worth of damage, and chemical flame retardants designed to curb this are big business. They contain a host of chemicals some of which mimic human hormones. These chemicals became notorious in the 1960s and a worldwide ban on one category, PCBs, was introduced after tests showed they had entered the food chain with potentially lethal consequences for humans and animals. But the chemicals industry continues to produce variations of the retardants, which scientists claim are not subject to the long-range testing required.

The Inuit are hunter-gatherers whose food derives from an area that has become a pollution sink for the world

Dr Jens Hansen, leader of AMAP research, said they were finding incredibly high levels of banned PCBs among a cocktail of other hormone-mimicking chemicals in pre-natal mothers. Pregnant mothers, he said were ingesting these hormone-mimicking chemicals in their diet and passing them through the placenta where they influenced the gender of the foetus or killed male foetuses.

Aleqa Hammond, Greenland's Foreign Minister, says: "We heard from scientists four years ago that our heavy metal consumption is dangerous." She adds wryly: "If you ate me, you would die."

Aqqaluk Lynge, head of the Inuit Circumpolar Council, said they were trying to raise the alarm internationally but nobody was listening. "People don't want to talk about such a critical question. We are talking about our people's survival which is very alarming."

Greenland, the world's largest island and still a dependency of Denmark, now has the highest proportion of women in the world.

The Independent 12 September 2007

CHINESE WORKERS?
Let them pick up litter

Declaring war on the "white pollution" choking its cities, farms and waterways, China is banning free plastic shopping bags and calling for a return to the cloth bags of old – steps largely welcomed by merchants and shoppers.

Angus Kennedy

The hysterical campaign against plastic bags in the West is causing massive job losses in the East, and leaving people on the scrap heap.

The banning of plastic bags was exposed at the weekend as plain 'bad' science, yet no apology is forthcoming. Instead, environmental one-upmanship escalates, Chinese workers are left on the smug rubbish heaps of green conceit, economic growth goes discredited, and we all kow-tow to the new eco-authoritarianism.

Rebecca Hosking, the British campaigner against plastic carrier bags, preached to us 'how plastic is lethal in the marine environment, killing at least 100,000 birds, whales, seals and turtles every year, and how, even after the animal dies, its body decomposes so that the plastic is released back into the environment where it can kill again; how an estimated one million seabirds choke or get tangled in plastic nets and debris every year. And so the horror goes on.' Sickened to her core by a vision of a world where only plastic would survive, she banished the carriers of evil from her sleepy town of Modbury, England, and looked set to free the whole nation from the Curse Of The Bag That Could Not Die. Yet now it turns out that plastic bags can't really kill whales after all.

They may be brilliant for carrying fish home, but they turn out to be rubbish at strangling seals. According to scientific reports discussed in the British media at the weekend: 'There is no scientific evidence to support the claim that 100,000 marine mammals have been killed by plastic bags...

marine biologists say their effect is minimal.'

It seems the bags are not killers, and nor are they immortal. 'Bags are unlikely to survive longer than 10-20 years. Biodegradable bags take months. More research is needed', said scientists. Greenpeace's marine biologist, David Santillo, said: 'It is very unlikely that many animals are killed by plastic bags. The evidence shows just the opposite.' The claim that carrier bags are killing thousands of animals a year seems to have emerged from a 1987 report titled Incidental Catch of Marine Birds and Mammals in Fishing Nets off Newfoundland, Canada. It was an easy mistake for eager environmentalists looking for a convenient truth to misread 'fishing nets' for 'plastic bags', and to spread this green counterknowledge into everyday life. The British government is now seriously considering banning plastic bags. The Chinese government has already done it in some cities.

For trend-setting eco-souls in the West, the very height of self-regard is to look down at those Asian arrivistes in consumerist-Communist China in horror. As one writer put it: 'The hope that fuels the pursuit of endless economic growth – that billions of customers in India and China will one day enjoy the lifestyles of Europeans and Americans – is an absurd and dangerous fantasy.'

Western narcissistic fears of pollution and killer plastics may be more fantasy than fact, but there is no doubting the reality of the effect it is having in the East. Plastic bags may not kill seals, but banning them is putting people on the scrap heap. China's largest plastics factory closed after China announced

that it was banning production of super-thin bags from June this year. In January, 20,000 people lost their jobs when Suiping Huaqiang Plastic closed its doors. The Chinese government has taken British prime minister Gordon Brown's identification of the plastic bag as 'one of the most visible symbols of environmental waste' to a higher level than even his support of the Daily Mail campaign to have them banned. The Chinese are now campaigning 'against "white pollution" – the term used to describe the visual eyesores caused by Styrofoam trays and carrier bags, which snag on trees and get blown far and wide by the wind'. Expect more job losses as the Chinese economy is made to respond to the aesthetic niceties of Western environmentalists, politicians and media pundits.

The Chinese government is denying its people free bags as a cheap way of keeping the West happy. In Beijing, according to one report, 'a foreigner-friendly chain called Jenny Lou's has introduced a charge on plastic bags, to the delight of Western Europeans and to the bafflement and occasional irritation of the many Russian and Chinese customers'.

For many Chinese consumers, it is only in recent years that they have had the luxury of being able to throw things away. China has lifted 300 million people from poverty in the past 30 years: without economic growth, many of them would be making a living as rag-pickers, scavenging plastic and metal out of landfill. It seems that many in the West think it would be better if they were doing that: on the environmentalist discussion website greendaily.com, contributors have been remarkably cavalier about carrier bag-related job losses in China. 'Sad

Plastic bags are seen littered among other items at a market in Beijing

Photo: Andy Wong, AP/PA Photos

ENVIRONMENTALISM IS A ROD THAT WESTERN GOVERNMENTS USE TO SMASH CHINA, THE GREAT POLLUTER

for the workers but great for the rest of the 6.6 billion people that live on this earth', says one. 'You could give those 10,000 people jobs picking up all of the plastic bag litter that was produced while they were in business. More jobs, less litter', says another.

Factories closed in Bangladesh when plastic bags were banned in 2002. Maybe Bangladeshis could come to Britain to clear up the mess they have made? Taiwan has banned plastic cutlery as well as bags. As a result, 'the local plastics industry, which has been producing 20 billion bags a year, says it expects to see 50,000 jobs lost'. As a result of the hysterical war on the plastic bag, there have been serious impacts across the Asian plastics industry: in Vietnam, Nepal, Malaysia, Singapore and Thailand. All of these countries employ many low-skilled workers in the plastics sectors.

Western pressure on China to open up and liberalise has had some ironic and unexpected effects. The closest thing the West has to a credo worth exporting these days is environmentalism. It is a rod that Western governments use to smash China, the Great Polluter. It is the one area in which the West can lay claim to some real moral authority: the smug satisfaction of not producing enough to do any serious environmental damage anymore.

So it should be no surprise that it is in the area of the environment that China feels a need to react. This will not lead to more freedoms for the Chinese people. As well as losing recently created jobs, they can expect the same bans and restrictions that we in the West now labour under in the name of protecting the environment. Allowing the red of Stalinist authoritarianism to be repackaged as the green of austerity economics may make the growth sceptics and environmentalists at home feel good, but it is rubbish for those of us in the West and the East who still believe in progress.

Angus Kennedy is a member of the organising committee of the Battle of Ideas.

Spiked 10 March 2008

Why plastic is the scourge of sea life

Steve Connor

One cigarette lighter, a toothbrush, a toy robot and a tampon applicator. The list of plastic items recovered from the stomach of a Laysan albatross chick that died on a remote Pacific island reads like a random assortment of everyday household objects.

It is now clear this chick is among many thousands of seabirds that have died from ingesting plastic debris, and nowhere in the world seems to be too isolated for this deadly form of marine pollution.

Dutch scientists have found that more than nine out of 10 European fulmars – seabirds that eat at sea – die with plastic rubbish in their stomachs. A study of 560 fulmars from eight countries revealed they had ingested an average of 44 plastic items. The stomach of one fulmar that died in Belgium contained 1,603 separate scraps of plastic.

Birds are not the only ones to suffer. Turtles, whales, seals and sea lions have all eaten plastic. But the most sinister problem may be a hidden one at the other end of the food chain.

Small sand-hoppers, barnacles and lugworms have also been found to have ingested tiny fragments of plastic, some of which are thinner than a human hair. Apart from the physical damage these particles cause, they may also transfer toxic chemicals to creatures at the base of the marine food web.

It is fairly well established that certain toxins in the ocean, such as polychlorinated biphenyls (PCBs), the pesticide DDT and other potentially dangerous substances, can become concentrated on the surface of plastic debris.

The reason why plastic is so ubiquitous in our homes and offices, of course, is the same reason why it builds up in the wider environment: it is resilient and takes years to break down into its constituent molecules.

This is even more so in the marine environment, where the sea tends to protect plastic from the ultraviolet light that helps to break it down.

In fact, it is estimated that much of the plastic rubbish that fell into the sea 50 years ago is still there today, either floating in the huge circulating "gyres" of the Pacific or sitting on the seabed waiting to be gobbled up by a passing sea creature.

It is estimated that the amount of plastic we are consuming will continue to grow substantially, by as much as a third in the space of a single decade in the case of each American consumer.

The only way to deal with the growing threat plastic poses to wildlife and the environment is to curb our consumption and to no longer treat plastic as an innocuous disposable commodity. Indeed, there is now a case for it to be treated as a potentially toxic waste product with the stiffest sanctions for its desultory disposal.

The Independent 5 February 2008

The bag habit we can't seem to kick

By Oliver Pritchett

> **"There's such an incredible buzz in walking down the street knowing that any moment the handle could break and I'll be humiliated"**

'Hi everybody, my name is Judy and I'd like to welcome you all to our little support group. There are plenty of free seats in the front here, so don't be shy. That's right move forward; we're all friends here and we're all here to help each other. Let's introduce ourselves and I'll kick off. As I said, I'm Judy and I am a PCB addict.

"I realised I had a problem when I noticed people were giving me looks in the street, sometimes whispering and pointing. I looked down and saw I was actually holding six plastic carrier bags of shopping. That's when I acknowledged that I had to do something.

"And that's the most important first step. I took a look at myself and saw somebody who was not just plastic-bag dependent, but was addicted to those tempting, gaudy and flimsy receptacles. So let's go round the room and introduce ourselves."

"Hi, I'm Geoff. I've been trying to come off plastic carrier bags for three months. It's been hard. Sometimes I can't resist and I have to start all over again. I do it for kicks, mostly.

"There's such an incredible buzz in walking down the street with a heavy load of groceries and knowing that any moment the handle could break and I'll be humiliated, standing in the street with broken lager bottles and tins of pineapple chunks rolling into the gutter.

"Nothing can beat that excitement. I know I'm letting the planet down, letting future generations down and, above all, letting myself down, but I can't help it."

"OK, a round of applause for Geoff. Somebody help him back to his seat. You see, Geoff, we're all feeling a bit weepy after that. It's not just you. That was so lovely, so brave. Who's next?"

"Good evening everybody. My name is Diane and I haven't had a single plastic carrier bag for 23 days and 16 hours. The trouble is, it's making me put on weight. Because I don't want to carry too much out of the supermarket I eat a lot of the stuff, like biscuits, while I'm still in there.

"And I also put things in my pockets. My fiancé says I'm not a real shoplifter, I'm just an eco-shoplifter. He says a few nicked chocolate bars are nothing compared with the cubic metres of landfill I have saved. Is he right?"

"We're not here to judge you, Diane. Just to give our loving support. Everybody give Diane a hug, but take care, she's got custard tarts in her coat pockets. OK, somebody else now."

"My problem is that since I gave up PCBs I've been ostracised by my mates. Sorry, I should have said, I'm Doug. You see, a group of us goes rambling at weekends, then, when we stop at a pub for a half of lager shandy, we put plastic bags over our muddy boots before going in. Now I don't have any bags my fellow ramblers have rejected me. I feel so dreadfully alone in the car park."

"Doug, you've got us. We're your real mates and we know what it is like to suffer rejection for our beliefs. Maybe we could organise our own ramble and all go into the pub with our muddy boots as a gesture of solidarity. Next, the lady in the red headscarf."

"Sorry, only I feel so guilty and embarrassed. Is it all right if I remain anonymous? I hoard plastic bags. I've got several hundred of them under the sink. Each one of them is linked to some happy memory.

"There's the Selfridges bag I was carrying when I met my second husband, and the M&S bag I kept my knitting wool in when on a nice holiday in Sorrento. I'm afraid one day the environment police will break down the door and find my collection and I'll be sent to prison."

"Don't worry dear. We won't let that happen. Somebody give her a bit of bubble wrap to pop to calm her nerves. Time for one more introduction before we break for coffee."

"I'm Philip. I think there's been a mistake. I thought this was the group helping people overcome their fear of asking for tap water in restaurants."

"No, Philip, that's the room next door. But go with all our love."

Daily Telegraph 5 March 2008
© Telegraph Group Limited 2008

This is NOT a plastic bag!!

Ecological

Neil McCormick

I went to Margate for a break. It was cold and it rained. Nothing unusual about that, you might think, but this was Margate in South Africa.

It is a seaside resort on the Eastern Cape and I went at the height of their summer holiday season, when it was packed with families and beach paraphernalia. Hawkers stood in the drizzle, selling buckets, spades and surfboards, but you couldn't buy a raincoat for 100 miles in either direction. I know, because I tried.

Before the environmental police arrest me for excessive air miles, let me stress that I wasn't actually on holiday. In this era of transcontinental travel and communication, we may call Earth a global village. But, when a much-loved relative becomes ill, the fallacy of that notion is cruelly exposed.

Popping next door for tea and sympathy can be a very complicated business. So we paid our carbon offset levy and flew 6,000 miles to do our bit. And, since we had to go all that way, we thought we might as well treat our four-year-old to some sun, sea and sand, only without the sun.

South Africans are becoming like us – talking of the weather all the time

It was an interesting lesson in the micro-economic effects of climate change. Street vendors, mostly from poorer, outlying African communities, were having a disastrous time. One fellow told me that if he couldn't get rid of his cheap tat (well, not in those exact words), his family wouldn't eat.

All right, it might have been a plaintive (and not particularly effective) sales pitch, but further down the coast they were still recovering from severe flooding, which had displaced almost 40,000 people (mostly from squatter camps). Meanwhile, inland in KwaZulu Natal and Mpumalanga, unexpectedly dry conditions had caused bush fires which had destroyed 30,000 acres.

One unexpected consequence is that South Africans are becoming more like the British: they talk about the weather all the time. Formerly, this would have been a very brief conversation. The outlook was sunny, with more sun to follow. Now they are in the same unpredictable stew as us.

My visit was like a glimpse into a possible future. A meter showing the drainage on the national electricity grid pops up during live television programmes with a message asking viewers to turn off unnecessary appliances (though presumably not the TV). Five minutes later, a thank-you message appears, with the dial graphically demonstrating how much electricity has been saved.

It is a highly effective method of inspiring mass action and one we could easily adopt in Britain. But the African example is not so much Green politics in action as a national emergency.

Electricity supplies are so low that the Government has resorted to "load shedding" – turning the power off, apparently at random. It can be a case of one block on, one block off. A clue to which blocks are out is found in the number of car crashes at intersections where the traffic lights have been extinguished without warning.

But, of course, not everyone uses power equally. Post-apartheid South Africa is still split between the First and Third worlds. The middle class may live in air-conditioned homes with all mod cons, but every conurbation features shanty towns apparently assembled from cardboard and corrugated iron, with no electricity or running water. It is a very graphic metaphor for the global village where we all share diminishing resources, but some shares are more equal than others.

Driving past one such settlement, I was struck by a huge sign declaring it to be an eco-village. Intrigued, I drove down a muddy track, past wandering goats and cows, to where an ancient, weatherbeaten woman was showing children how to use a newly installed well. She cheerfully admitted the "eco" designation was just creative relabelling.

"We are trying to uplift the community by giving them a sense of their own worth," she said, smiling. But she also pointed out that such communities have lessons for us all.

"The carbon footprint here is non-existent," she cackled. "If we all lived like this, the world wouldn't have a problem."

The Daily Telegraph 12 January 2008
©Telegraph Group Ltd 2008

I had no choice but to give away my baby...

The teenage heroine of the film Juno chooses to have her baby and give it up for adoption. But, asks David Harrison, how common is it for young women to make the same decision today?

Catherine Murray was having the time of her life. Eighteen years old, intelligent and attractive, she was revelling in her new-found freedom at university after being brought up in a strict but loving middle-class Catholic home in an affluent London suburb.

She met Michael, a fellow English student, in the university bar during the first week of her course. Ten days later, they met again at a party, got on well, laughed, flirted and got very drunk. "We went back to my room," she says, her voice trembling. "I was so stupid... Michael was only the second guy I'd slept with."

Weeks later, Catherine sat in disbelief as her doctor told her calmly that she was pregnant.

"I was in total shock," she says. "My first thought was that my parents would be devastated. My second was that my life was over." She told Michael. "He was

in an awful state. He kept saying it was a terrible mistake and I should get rid of it, for both our sakes."

But abortion, the solution for many today, was not an option for Catherine, who is a practising Catholic.

Her parents were distraught, but they insisted that Catherine have the baby. After many long, tearful conversations, she came to an agonising decision – the baby would be given away for adoption. "I was immature, I had my life in front of me. It sounds selfish but I didn't see any other way."

Catherine's tale is unusual in 21st-century Britain. The contraceptive pill, the morning-after pill and easy access to abortions have ensured that only a small number of women, those opposed to terminations for religious or other reasons, resort to giving away their babies.

Her story mirrors that in Juno. In the film, directed by Jason Reitman and produced by John Malkovich, Ellen Page plays Juno, a middle-class 16-year-old who, on discovering she is nine weeks pregnant to an old friend and admirer, decides to have the baby and put it up for adoption. She finds a suitable, wealthy young couple and, supported by her parents, makes the adoption arrangements.

But the grim reality is that the vast majority of children offered for adoption in Britain today are removed from their families because they are suffering – or are likely to suffer – physical, sexual or mental abuse from alcoholic, drug-addicted or violent parents. Others are taken into care if their parents are disabled, have mental health issues or, for some other reason, simply cannot cope.

More than 60,000 children are in care on any one day and few have a realistic chance of being adopted.

Babies are easy to place: there is a constant demand from couples unable to have children. Many children in care will return to their families, but thousands – especially those who are over 11, disabled or in a sibling group – face being shunted from one foster home to another, or languishing in care homes until they are 18.

"There are thousands of children who desperately need to be adopted," says David Holmes, the chief executive of the British Association for Adoption and Fostering. "They need the stability of a secure, supportive family."

The face of adoption in Britain has changed dramatically in the past few decades – and particularly in the past few years. In the 1950s and 1960s, it was much more common: the number of adopted children peaked at 28,000 in 1968; last year there were 3,300. Adoption is now seen as a last resort and every effort is made to keep children with their birth parents.

Decades ago, the numbers were high because of social pressure. Young women who became pregnant were sent away to "mother-and-baby homes", where they would give birth before being forced to hand their babies over to adoption agents. Unlike Catherine – and Juno – most of these young mothers-to-be did not want to give their children away.

The mother-and-baby homes were run strictly and moralistically, along the lines of old-fashioned boarding schools, by nuns and other charities. One home in Liverpool was even called the House for Fallen Women. The pregnant women were treated as "sinners" and were expected to show repentance. They came from all backgrounds. Records of assessments made by adoption agencies describe one woman as: "A better class of girl. Wears gloves." Another is: "A pathetic-looking creature from Eire. She even has red hair."

'I thought about my daughter all the time, especially on her birthday'

The hand-over rituals were heart-breaking. At a country house used as a mother-and-baby home in the Midlands, the girls would wheel their newborn baby in a pram to the gatehouse where the adoption agency was housed. The girl would wait in a back room until the adoptive parents arrived and took away the baby. She would then have to push the empty pram back to the main house.

The formidable women who ran the homes were proud of their work as guardians of the nation's morality. One matron at the Midlands home is recorded as saying: "The system worked very well. I never had the same girl back twice."

Today, those same young women are part of another dramatic social change, as legal reforms allow them to make contact with the children they handed over in such wretched circumstances. Pressure from campaigners – including many of the mothers – has led to adopted children and birth parents being given the right to be reunited, through approved intermediaries, if that is the wish of both parties.

90% of birth mothers and up to 80% of adopted children respond positively to requests for reunions and the vast majority of those who do meet remain in contact, according to Pam Hodgkins, the chief executive of the adoption charity Norcap, who fought for years for the law to be changed. "We have seen so much happiness as parents are reunited with children they never wanted to lose," she said.

Maureen Fox had to give up her daughter at a mother-and-baby home in Sutton, Surrey, when she was 18 and unmarried in the 1960s. "I didn't want to give her up, but I accepted that every child should have two parents and I didn't want my child to suffer because she didn't."

Her daughter was never far from her thoughts. "I thought about her all the time, especially on her birthday or whenever I read stories about children in the newspapers," she says.

They were reunited in 1992, after 28 years apart. "It was very emotional. And I discovered I was a grandmother," she adds, with glee. The daughter's adoptive parents have since become friends. "We've spent Christmases together. They're lovely people and we are all part of the same family."

The first significant legal change came in 1975, when adopted children were given the right to have copies of their birth certificates, so they could trace their parents. But it was not until December 2005, after nearly 30 years of campaigning, that birth parents won the right to make contact with children who had been adopted.

Most reunions are sought by parents who had to give up their babies in the 1950s, 1960s and early 1970s. But others go back even farther: one woman in her eighties is trying to find her brother, who was adopted in 1932.

No attempt can be made to contact an adopted child until he or she is 18 – and the children have a veto over contact.

"The changes have had a huge impact on society," Ms Hodgkins adds. "They have changed the nature of thousands of families and allowed that strong bond between children and their parents to be renewed when it is wanted by both sides."

Catherine, now 22, has not seen her son, Henry, since he was handed over to adoptive parents in the summer of 2004. She does not know if she will ever see him again.

After dropping out of university while she was pregnant, she has resumed her studies with the full support of her parents. "After what happened, I don't like to plan too much for the future," she says. "Of course I think about Henry and I feel guilty about what I did. But I did the right thing."

Some names have been changed
The Sunday Telegraph 10 February 2008
© Telegraph Group Ltd 2008

My mother deserted me

My neighbour has come to take me to school with her daughter. Mother asks if I can go to their house afterwards because she is "going to the pictures". I don't remember what happened after school, except that my mother didn't come home. She didn't go to the pictures. She left home and I didn't see or hear from her again for almost 10 years.

My father, brother, sister and myself are eating at the kitchen table. My father is saying that he is no oil painting. Who is no oil painting? What is an oil painting?

The dog is ill. My father has taken him to the vet. My sister is in charge now. I am eight and she is 18. She has made me egg and chips for lunch. I make a mistake and shake sugar on my chips instead of salt. The dog is OK.

I am out with my father and he takes my hand to cross the road. It feels strange; I feel uncomfortable holding his hand.

These are snapshot memories of the time immediately afterwards. During the years after my mother's departure, I don't remember thinking about her much. I suppose, like many children, I just accepted what had happened. My sister got married the following March. When she and her husband bought their first home, I moved there with them. A new school: when the other children asked about my mother, I learned it was easier to say she was dead.

When I was 14, I moved back to live with my father and changed school again. When I was 17 he died: hit by a drunk driver.

Shortly afterwards, our mother entered our lives again: a friend had told her about our father. She

I do not judge her for leaving her husband, but I judge her and find her guilty for deserting her children

died three years later, and for me it meant nothing; I concluded that you can't grieve twice for the same person.

That was all a long time ago. I am 59 now, and in the intervening years I have thought very little about my mother. During the past year, however, I have found myself thinking a great deal about what happened and pondering on how her desertion affected my sister and myself.

My sister's memories tend to be good ones. She remembers never coming home to an empty house after school. She could tell our mother "anything". Our mother was "gentle and soft", always the one wanting to be friends after an argument, even when it wasn't her fault.

My memories are different. After returning to live with my father, there was rarely anyone in the house when I came home. Meal times did not exist and we lived mainly on fruit, fish and chips and Birds Eye.

When my mother reappeared, I can remember thinking I was glad she had left. To me, she seemed a selfish individual and she made no secret of the fact that she didn't want me "messing things up" for her and her partner, the man she had left with all those years before.

Thinking about the past has induced an anger I have never acknowledged during the past 50 years. I cannot forgive my mother for what she did. I do not judge her for leaving her husband, but I judge her and find her guilty for deserting her children so completely that she never even acknowledged any of us with so much as a birthday card.

My sister feels no anger, but I feel it for her. At a time when she should have been enjoying the carefree time between leaving full-time education and settling down, she had to leave work to look after a home and a younger sibling. She has been my substitute mother, and it is only in recent years that we have become sisters in the true sense of the word.

Sometimes when I think about it all, it is as if I am trying to analyse the life of somebody else, as my work over many years has caused me to do. I find attachment of any kind difficult. My few friends have had to wait several years before I "let them in". I have never managed to sustain a relationship with a man. My catchphrase is, "Nothing lasts for ever". This is the legacy my mother gave me: a fear of loss that prevents me becoming too close to people.

The most difficult realisation the past year has brought is that my mother did not love me. Perhaps she once did but, like me, I think the years apart severed any love there had been. Despite my mother's desertion, I have had a fulfilling life, with little of it spent thinking about her, but perhaps she has always been there in the shadows. These past 12 months, she has been brought into view, examined and put finally to rest.

The Guardian 19 April 2008
© Guardian News & Media Ltd. 2008

What exactly are family values? What exactly is a family?

Gabrielle Carey considers the issues

'We had another one of those family dinners," wrote author Jane Smiley in an article some years ago, "you know, me, my boyfriend, his daughter and son by his second wife, my daughters by my second husband, and my seven-year-old son by my third husband."

But being upfront about coming from a not-quite-normal family isn't always so easy. For years I didn't bother explaining. I just watched as people looked at me, then looked at my son (white), then looked at my daughter (brown) and then looked back at me, utterly befuddled. (Hey, if Angelina and Brad can have children of various colours, why can't I?)

I'm the kind of wife and mother loathed by advocates of traditional family values. I'm so adept at losing husbands that even my daughter thinks I need chastising. "Two husbands, that's normal, but three! That's just stupid!"

As you can imagine, being a chronic husband-loser can have its complications. Labels can become particularly difficult. The daughter of my ex-partner's sister by her first marriage used to be my step-niece, but now that he's re-partnered (as they say in the relationships business) and so have I, (twice), what do I call her?

Not an ideal scenario perhaps but let's be honest, how many of us have ideal families? In any case, I am advised by relationship experts that the important thing

Hey, if Angelina and Brad can have children of various colours, why can't I?

these days is not whether you're part of an "intact" family or not. The important part is whether you're functional or dysfunctional.

"I find this phrase 'dysfunctional family' very curious," said Jonathan Franzen when interviewed about his hugely successful family saga, The Corrections. "It seems to imply that there is such a thing as a functional family."

How do we measure a functional family anyway? Aren't we all sometimes functional, sometimes dysfunctional? Sometimes loving and generous, sometimes hateful and mean? Isn't that the whole problem with Christmas — the fact that we're supposed to be nice to our families — not just for a moment, but for the whole day.

Every December my mother cheerily reminds me that the last month of the year is the most popular period for suicide. The lead-up to the festive season and the get-togethers with family creates phenomenal levels of tension, not to mention moments of self-destructive madness.

It seems to imply that there's such a thing as a functional family

From the outside, my family may not look normal — we're not a matching set, we're all different colours, and there's a certain — how can I put it? — a certain fluidity to the position of the father figure. But from the inside I don't think it's all that different from any other family. My ex-step-niece is still part of the extended family. These days she's nursing Grandma in the mornings and tutoring my ex-partner's girlfriend's children in the afternoon. She's friendly with her father, tolerates her stepfather, goes fishing with her half-brother and babysits my youngest (that's her cousin, I think). Oh, and she recently won a scholarship for Latin at Sydney University.

It's a complicated life, yes, and she's had her fair share of suffering. But as a graduating doctor, the difficulties she's had to negotiate in life might actually serve her well. You could even argue that her family history has prepared her far better for a career dealing with people's problems than a medical graduate from an upper North Shore private school with a neurosurgeon for a father and a mother utterly devoted to the family except for Thursday afternoon tennis. What doesn't kill you only makes you stronger, said Nietzsche. And he learnt that from experience, not just through philosophical theorising.

Defenders of "family values" would have us believe that everyone outside the sanctity of the nuclear family is doomed to penury, psychotherapy, failure and forever ending their sentences with "but". It's true that non-traditional family structures can be difficult. But so is learning Latin or writing a Pulitzer Prize-winning novel (as in the case of marriage recidivist Jane Smiley), or anything else that involves desire, persistence and imagination — qualities that are sometimes nurtured from within the nuclear family and sometimes, maybe even more often than we care to recognise, cultivated from without.

The Age 21 December 2007

'You have three children. How lovely. And what are they – obese or drunk?

Daily Telegraph, 22 February 2008
© Telegraph Group Ltd. 2008

To My brother... who I never see

They say you never appreciate what your parents did for you until you become a parent yourself. Well, I've heard you now have a girl and a boy. Not that I have met them. And not that Mum and Dad have met them. And I can't help wonder if it has dawned on you yet what Mum and Dad did for you; indeed what they did without for you – the sleepless nights when you were a baby (and a teenager). The hard work and long hours to give us both a happy and secure start in life. Their worries for you as you grew into a young man making your own way in the world. Passing your driving test. Getting a job. Finding a wife and starting your own family.

But although I have had no interest in contacting you myself (you've been out of my life for so long now that it feels like you were never a part of it), I do wonder why you have not considered the fact that you have walked away from your parents and their unconditional love for you. You know, I never understood my mother's love until I became a mother myself. Did you know I have a five-year-old daughter and a two-year-old son? I scan my boy's face hoping there's no trace of you to upset Mum and Dad.

And now that you have children, there is also another layer: the love and support they would have for your children. If only they knew them.

For to see your parents as grandparents is to see their very reason for being. They live and breathe for news of my children's latest triumphs and milestones. They visit often and my son's face lights up at the sound of Grandad's voice on the phone. He says "goodnight" to his grandparents every night as he passes the room where they sleep when they come to stay. It's a relationship free of the complications of parenthood. This is a relationship built purely on the good times; the carefree times. But it's also more than that. It's about a love that flows down through the years. That intertwines family history and stories. And it's part of who you are. And who your children are.

I could never deny them that relationship with my children and I wouldn't want to deny my children their grandparents. And that's what I find so hard to think about when on the odd occasion you flicker into my thoughts as I watch our father lift my son on to his shoulders. Why would you deny your children the chance to know their grandparents?

I know you aren't making this decision to cut Mum and Dad out of your life on your own. Your wife forced your hand. A more insecure person I have never met. So insecure about her relationship with you that she couldn't share you with any other woman, not even your mother or your sister. (Not to mention your friends, who no longer hear from you.) How sad that she too has denied her own children the right to know their father's history, his roots and his connections. But have you noticed that she hasn't severed the connection with her own family?

But will there be a point when maybe you will think about all these things? A moment when you realise what you have lost and what your children have never had? Maybe that moment will come when you become a grandparent yourself.

Maybe one day your wife will see what a one-dimensional family she has constructed for her children. Or maybe your children will want to seek out what is missing in their life? But I hope it's not left too late and their connection with their grandparents and every generation before them is gone for ever.

Name and address supplied

The Guardian 16 February 2008
© Guardian News & Media Ltd. 2008

Scarlett Keeling died at the roll of a dice. It's a perilous game

Sarah Sands

Each human tragedy has its socio-economic dimension. The terrifying abduction of Shannon Matthews is coolly discussed as a portrait of a debased white working class, with its multiplicity of fathers and attendant social workers. When Madeleine McCann went missing we rapidly absorbed the context. The parents were doctors, ambitious, gym conscious, dressed in high street chic. The holiday destination, Mark Warner in Portugal, was family minded and middle class. The McCanns felt safe to leave their children in the room, because they were among their own people.

Fiona MacKeown was as trusting of her own way of life. Goa was the geographical affirmation of her identity. Gentle, free, non materialist, non judgmental. True to her beliefs, she has rejected the conventions of work, family structure and social aspiration. She has nine children by five fathers.

One person's small holding is another person's squalor. The shack that she calls home looks wretched to me, but I was not very shocked by the interior shots of Scarlett's bedroom. My daughter's room is just as untidy. Similarly, I do not share the distaste of many journalists for Fiona MacKeown's hippy appearance. She has a calm beauty and resembles Charlotte Rampling in some photographs. Scrubbed up a bit, the whole family could appear in a Calvin Klein advertisement. The children with their tousled hair and burnished bodies laughing on a beach with their carefree mother. It would be an alpha ideal if they had a few million in the bank and a Bryanston education.

Perhaps it was negligent to pull children out of school for six months to go travelling, but Fiona MacKeown was only following the advice of Times columnist Mary Ann Sieghart. The gap-year students I know have animated debates about whether their lives should be "on or off road." They are pouring into African orphanages and Indian villages in search of different values and meanings. They find little to condemn in Fiona MacKeown's way of life. She has flawless green credentials and is a loving mother.

Yet those same students are aghast at her decision to leave a troubled 15-year-old girl to fend for herself among strangers. Her hippy ideology destroyed her common sense. Although she had been a victim of a knife attack herself she persisted in her belief in unerring global citizenship. It is either saintliness or egotism. She judges no one, not even herself. There are official suggestions of parental negligence yet she can find no fault with herself beyond being "trusting." Only agents of institutional authority (ie the police) must be blamed.

You would not do it in London, so why would you do it on a drug-strewn beach?

Freedom without maturity can be a terribly dangerous thing. I remember once dropping off my 13-year-old daughter

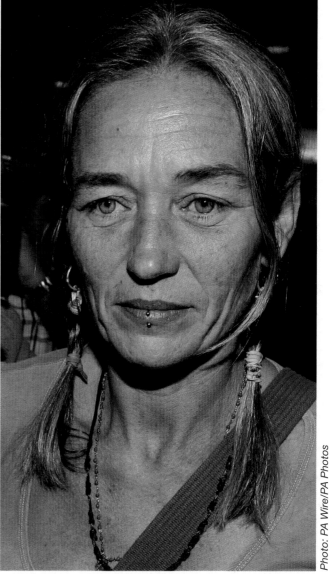

Fiona McKeown: negligent or trusting?

Photo: PA Wire/PA Photos

You would not do it in London, so why would you do it on a drug-strewn beach?

at a peer group party in a local hall. A couple of hours later, the manager of a B&B some miles away rang to say he had a girl with him in tears. I was so grateful for his kindness. Any parent hopes that the stranger who approaches their daughter has good intentions and dreads the consequences if not. It is the ghastly roll of the dice.

The fragmentary final hours of Scarlett's life are utterly bleak. A stoned, drunken, frightened girl tottering about the beach. A man lying on top of her. Her pitiful confidence to a friend that she was sleeping with the tour guide to ensure a roof over her head. Finally, her lifeless young body washed up by the waves.

She may have been a free spirit, but Scarlett was also a child. Fiona MacKeown put ideology before humanity.

Independent on Sunday, 16 March 2008

YOUNG FATHERS: FACTS AND FABLES

The UK has the highest rate of teenage pregnancy in Western Europe, yet there are no official statistics on how many young fathers there are. **Sue Learner** meets three fathers who are challenging negative perceptions of young dads

Jason Parrott

"If I hadn't become a dad I would have ended up in prison," admits Jason Parrott, who was excluded from school at the age of 15 and has been in and out of Borstal-type institutions most of his life.

Jason, who works as a parking attendant, lives with his wife Gemma and two-year-old son Samuel, in Loughton, Essex. He says: "I had a bad background and upbringing. I have never seen my dad regularly and because of that it has made me more determined to be there for Samuel."

When the couple found out that Gemma was pregnant, they were in shock. "We were thinking of having children but Gemma was only 17. She had been on the pill but when she came off we were told that it could take six months for her to get pregnant because of the pill. But she got pregnant straightaway," he says.

Jason always wanted to have children young. "I felt that after they grew up I would still be young enough to get on with my life and do the things I wanted to do. I will still be young when Samuel is having kids," he says.

Life has changed since having Samuel. "I just want to be happy and be a family. Instead of going down the pub with my mates, I go for a walk down the river with my son and my dog. I walk along holding his hand and I feel so proud. He is so clever. Just waking up every day and seeing him and knowing he is yours is amazing," says Jason.

The couple recently got married and Gemma, aged 20, is pregnant with their second baby due in March.

Jason believes there is not enough support for young dads. "Young mums get funding to do courses, but there is nothing like that for young dads. The emphasis is always on getting young mums back into work," he says. He finds that people are quite negative towards young fathers and assume "they are on the dole and are having an easy ride".

"If your child misbehaves, I do feel the older generation is looking at you, saying those are young parents and they can't control their child," he says.

Jason has been in and out of work since leaving school at 15. However, since having Samuel he is determined to support his family and challenge people's perceptions.

"I want to make sure I have a well paid job to support my wife and son. I want Samuel to have a good life," he says.

Michael Tanner

Michael Tanner is 23-years-old and he already has three daughters under the age of four.

There's Lily, aged three, Ruby, aged one and May who is six-months-old. He is engaged to Marie McNulty, 22 but the couple cannot afford to live together. If they lived together, Marie would be forced to give up her benefits and they would have to live on Michael's wages, which would not be enough for five of them. So Michael is forced to rent a room in a shared house until he can earn enough to support his family.

Marie lives with her daughters in Bradwell village just outside Milton Keynes. She is currently doing a hairdressing and counselling course. She says: "There is all this criticism in the newspaper asking why there are all these single mothers, but there seems like there is no support for young parents who do want to live together."

Michael was 20 when he found out Marie was pregnant. "I was scared but I was more worried about what my parents would say," he says. Being a father was "strange" at first. "I was so tired but it felt good. It took about a year to get used to it. It has been hard," he admits.

When Marie first got pregnant, Michael found there was a lack of support for young dads. "None of my mates had any children. I think there should be somewhere for people to go and chat with somebody about how they feel. You can't tell your partner you are feeling uncomfortable as she wants your full support."

Michael has found that many of his friends "don't want to know now I have kids". He doesn't miss going out and says: "I think my time should be spent with my family. It is more fun being with them and bringing them up properly. If I wasn't happy I wouldn't be with Marie."

Michael believes he has changed since becoming a father and says: "It has matured me. I have more time for people and I am more patient. I don't let stresses get to me, as I know that when I walk through the door Lily comes running up to me and gives me a kiss and a cuddle."

Since meeting Marie, Michael has continually worked and is currently training in his spare time to be a plumber. He started a plumbing course four months ago and hopes to be fully qualified in a year. "So far I have got 100 per cent in all three tests, which I am really pleased about," he says.

He currently works for a kitchen company on the trade counter. Michael says: "For people like me there should be help to retrain. I have had to get out a loan of £5,000 to train to be a plumber. A little bit of help with training would go a long way. Perhaps the government could give a loan like university students get where you don't pay it back until you can afford to. There is this view that if you are silly enough to have kids at this age, then you have to deal with it."

FACT FILE

- The UK has the highest rate of teenage pregnancies in Western Europe
- Young fathers are largely absent from statistics
- In the study *The Transition to Fatherhood in Young Men* (2002), David Quinton found young fathers were "mostly ignored, marginalised or made uncomfortable by services"
- Quinton also found that by ignoring young fathers, services were ignoring mothers' wishes

Karl Edwards

Being a father is tough, but being a young father is even harder. Karl Edwards is only 20 but he already has a one-year-old son. He admits: "My teenage life has been cut short because I have a son. I miss going out and being with my friends."

It has been a turbulent time for Karl and his girlfriend Emily Finn since she found she was pregnant at the age of 16. "We split up a hell of a lot while Emily was pregnant because I didn't have a job and because of the hormonal changes that Emily was going through. It took me a while to come to terms with the fact that Emily was pregnant. I was being supportive but not to the extent I should have been as a father," reveals Karl, who found out his son was born after he received a text from Emily.

"The text said she had given birth to a baby boy and called him Liam Joseph. I was very shocked. I cried. My son had just been born," says Karl who lives with Emily and Liam in Milton Keynes.

Emily refused to let Karl see his son for three and a half months. "I got a job at Argos and I contacted her again. We talked for two hours on the phone. When we met up after that, it was as if we had never been apart."

Life is now very different for Karl who says: "My friends laugh about Liam and tease me, calling me the big daddy. But I wouldn't change Liam for the world. So many people judge young parents but teenage parents are still human beings. I think all the Asbo stuff and all the stuff on antisocial behaviour in the papers makes everyone think all teenagers are the same."

Karl would like the government to provide a lot more funding for young parents. "They need to build more houses so we get more help with housing. It would help if the government paid for young fathers to have time off work so they can bond with their children more," he says. He would also like there to be more dads' groups and a rise in benefits.

Karl believes that Liam has made him change for the better. "I was really immature before I had Liam. But Liam has made me think I have to better myself. I want Liam to have a happy family. I never had that and I don't want Liam to grow up as I grew up. I want him to be with his mum and dad," he says. ●

CASE STUDY UK Youth's Fable and Fact Project

There are a lot of stereotypes and misconceptions about young parents, according to Andrew Cummings, the project worker who runs UK Youth's Fable and Fact, which is currently project funded for 18 months by the Camelot Foundation.

"When people see young parents they always assume the child was a mistake," he says. He has also found that many young couples are forced to live apart because if they live together they lose benefits. "Yet young couples are under enough pressure as it is without this adding to it," he says.

Fable and Fact was set up to examine issues young parents face and what services they need. Its aim was also to challenge some of the misconceptions held by people who work directly with young parents, such as social workers, health workers and youth workers.

Cummings found 10 parent champions to lead the project and give presentations to people training to be social workers and youth workers. They hope that about 500 social workers and health workers will take part in the workshops.

Karl Edwards, Michael Tanner and Jason Parrott and their partners, are all parent champions. Jason says: "It is more about saying we are young parents and if you want to help us you need to approach us in this way."

PHIL ADAMS

Karl believes that having his son Liam has made him want to better himself and give Liam a good life

9-15 January 2008

Why we need a dad's army

Tony Sewell

IT'S A funny old world. I grew up during the time when black youths were terrorised by the infamous 'sus' law. The law allowed police to stop and search anyone they suspected was planning to commit a crime.

In reality, it gave police the licence to stop black males in the street, throw them in their vans and kick the living daylights out of them. The result was the 1980s uprisings in Brixton and Tottenham.

Now, the Government wants to increase its powers of stop and search in order to protect black youths from killing each other. Personally, I find this embarrassing and those who fought so hard in the eighties must feel bitter at this sad irony.

What is interesting is the lack of outcry from any community agency. It is clear that our community has lost the battle, literally, on the home front, where black and white single mothers are waving their SOS flags.

The consequences of wider stop and search will be innocent black young males being made to feel that they are living in a police state. It has been evident to me for some time that we should stop listening to the madness that comes from some community leaders, particularly the ones that have conferences which blame white teachers for our predicament.

We need to ignore researchers who come out saying that teachers are picking on students because they wear hoodies. Of course I am going to pick on you if you come to school looking like you're going to rob a post office. Boys should come to school looking smart, they should open doors for women, they should wear a tie, and when adults come in the classroom they should stand up and say 'good afternoon'.

...for too many young people the streets remain as unsafe as their homes

What we need is a campaign on the home front. We need to have the equivalent of the sus law not on the street but in the home. The reality is that too many boys are a law unto themselves, and they really can't cope.

For me, the media that pumps out the most negativity about black men, is not MTV or even the BNP, it is black women and their bitterness against men who may have disrespected them in the past.

When his father is rarely or never seen, the child depends on his mother or other relatives to inform him. If a boy with no contact with his father hears from his mother only that he is a bad man (perhaps along with all other men), he will feel that he is descended from someone who not only could not stay at home to care for him, but also does not love him. This, though not necessarily wholly true, is painful and can damage the child's self esteem (whether a girl or a boy).

If the mother says good things about the absent father, that when they were together there were some good times, and that the father loved his baby or his partner, or both, then the child is likely to grow up with a positive image of his father, and of himself.

This requires brave and active mental work on the mother's part. She may despise the father of her child, or feel nothing for him, but it is possible for a mother to make sense of their broken relationship, just as parents can make sense of their own parents' deficiencies. A bad father can still be understood, and not just rejected out of hand.

The police may well get their new powers unopposed, but for too many young people the streets remain as unsafe as their homes.

The Voice 4-10 February 2008

Dads enforcing their daughters' purity

SUE CONLEY

is just not right

FORGIVE me for drawing this to your attention, because it's creepy and weird. It may, in fact, sound like a joke, but it's thoroughly unfunny.

Recently, in Colorado, a ball was held, much like a debs ball here. The girls had their hair done and wore pretty gowns that they had probably spent weeks searching for and agonising over. And their dates brought them flowers.

Thing is, their dates were their dads. Or their stepdads. Or their future fathers-in-law.

The ages of the girls ranged from nine to university age, and they all were there to enjoy each other's company, to dance the night away, and to make a pledge to ensure each girl remained pure.

Following the meal, each of the fathers read aloud a covenant promising "before God to cover my daughter as her authority and protection in the area of purity".

Their dates brought them flowers. Thing is, their dates were their dads

Then, the fathers and daughters gathered in a bare ballroom, its only decoration a seven-foot wooden cross standing at one end. Someone made a speech, and two men moved to the front of the cross, holding up swords to make an arch.

The 'couples' then walked through this arch to the cross and knelt down. Dad might pray if he liked; daughter, dumb, laid a white rose, representing the purity she was placing in the care of her dad and her Saviour, at the foot of the cross.

Such so-called Purity Balls are sweeping the States, and are a direct result of the Abstinence Movement. What started as a disparate group of adults keen to address the problems of teenage pregnancy has grown into a fully funded non-profit corporation that preaches the virtues of virginity. Sex before marriage is no longer the only sin: education is, too. Some states have scrapped their sex education courses in schools, claiming that talking about birth control encourages teens to use it, and that condoms and such don't really work anyway, so just say no.

Now, let's be truthful: no one wants more young girls to fall pregnant if it can be helped. No one wants young ones to contract sexually transmitted diseases. And more truth: if dads were better at their job, we'd have a generation of daughters who possessed confidence, self-esteem, and the ability to think for themselves in all situations, not merely the sexual ones. If we had strong fathers, we'd have strong daughters, girls who would place their own safety first, in all ways.

However, the notion that these girls are essentially placing themselves under their father's authority in this fashion is positively Biblical. Saving themselves for marriage means they are only transferring their caretaker, from father to husband.

ENFORCING

In enforcing their purity, the fathers are not actually doing anything useful to encourage their daughters to be adults. By insisting they adhere to their dads' dominance, they are little more than passive ciphers, waiting for the day that they can let loose and do the deed.

And it is creepy and borderline sexually suspect to get all dressed up and go out dancing with your dad.

The notion that these young women are being dolled up and trotted out solely to ensure that their fathers can sleep at night is enraging. What 14-year-old girl has the backbone to say no to dad? And in turn, not being able to stand up to dad makes it tougher to stand up to the young fella that wants to get in her knickers.

And what about the young fellas? Are these girls getting pregnant all by themselves? What's being done about those randy teenage boys? While the abstainers claim a significant number of boys amongst their members, are they having purity balls for mums and sons?

A 15-year-old lad agreeing to go out on the town with mother, and in turn allowing her to pledge to be the defender of his purity?

Don't make me laugh.

Evening Herald (Ireland)
26 May 2008

I felt like an informer

Katherine Clarke moved to a new house, with bright and happy children next door. Then their mother got a new boyfriend, the children stopped smiling and Katherine had to contact social services

As soon as we moved in, the children who lived next door jumped over the wall and started playing with my son and daughter, who were similar ages. Together they would climb our tree and dig to Australia in our tiny garden, then come in and run up and down the stairs, leaving black smears of mud everywhere. Clare and Nick's mother, Margaret, seemed happy that they spent most of their time with us. I would hear her telling them to "go round Kath's and see what the kids are up to" when she wanted some peace or to clean and they would appear at the back door, Clare usually wearing her sparkly pink wellies and pink towelling shorts.

Clare was a beautiful, skinny, blond-haired child, bright but with a nervous energy that meant that she seemed to find it hard to concentrate on anything. She would bombard me with questions and not wait for the answer before she asked another. She was wildly daring and would often try to climb up the houses using the grey plastic drainpipes or walk on our kitchen roof, inspiring admiration and adoration from my children.

Margaret's husband, Mike, brought home a decent amount of money as a civil engineer but there was a sense of frugality about their lives, with no car, no foreign holidays and shopping at the £1 stores in the high street. Then Margaret started salsa dancing: she met a new man and everything changed. She got a job in an office, Mike moved out and the new dancing man moved in. Margaret stopped being the neat-as-a-pin housewife, and started wearing tight jeans, cropped tops and blue eye-shadow. Clare was in the second year of secondary school and was unimpressed by her mother's new image ("What does she think she looks like in them teenager clothes?") and her mother telling her that now it was time for her to have a bit of fun and that she should try to be nice to her new stepdad.

My children, meanwhile, told me that Clare had changed and that they had seen her hanging out with boys and smoking and swearing on the street. She never came round to play any more. I started to see her sitting on her doorstep in the early evening and she told me that her mother had taken her key away.

I would invite her in for tea and she would sit and chat or watch television with my children. It became a routine. When I asked Margaret why she didn't let her daughter go in the house, she said she "couldn't be trusted" and that I shouldn't let her in my house either as she would "nick stuff". I told her I was prepared to take that risk and thought how odd it was that she spoke about her own daughter like that. Clare started to talk to us about her mum's new boyfriend and told us that he had a temper and would hit them. She claimed he had held her upside down when she had been rude to her mother. Another time she showed me bruises on her arm where she said he had held it behind her back.

I talked it over endlessly. I felt vile judging someone else's parenting

Then one evening Clare dragged her old Wendy house out on to her roof terrace and told me that she was going to live there from now on. She didn't want to be in the same house as "that man". Her old mutilated dolls sat like deranged guards around the house. She wrote graffiti on the terrace walls protesting at her mother's treatment of her and spent two nights folded into the small house in a sleeping bag. I lay awake all night worrying about her and begged her to come into our house. She refused because she was so determined to make her protest.

It was a desperate situation. Then one day the neighbour who lived on the other side of Clare's house came and told me she had contacted the social services and that I should too. She said that she was desperately worried about Clare, who was being locked out of her house more and more frequently in the evenings and was left walking the streets. She said she had heard screaming dozens of times from inside the house. She told me we would both regret it if we turned a blind eye and that we would never forgive ourselves if something terrible happened to Clare. She gave me the name and number of the woman at social services. We had both tried to contact Clare's father but he was so bitter about what Margaret had done that he said he was taking a long breather from the lot of them.

I put off phoning and talked it over endlessly with my husband. I felt vile judging someone else's parenting, particularly as Margaret had heard enough shouting and arguing coming from our far from perfect family through the walls. I thought how furious I would have been if Margaret had called the social services on me.

We decided to talk to Margaret and her new boyfriend first. We knocked on the door and asked them if everything was all right with Clare. They answered with a barrage of complaints about her attitude, her language, handing in her homework late – all normal teenage stuff. We sympathised, as we knew from our son how infuriating teenagers can be, but then the boyfriend started shouting and saying that Clare was ruining their lives together and that she was making it impossible for them because she refused to accept that they were in love. I told them that she seemed very vulnerable and too young at 13 to be wandering around the streets on her own and that it was unlikely that Clare was just going to fall in line with living with a new man. The boyfriend said that he thought she was "disgusting" and "evil" and that compared to her, the boy was no trouble.

I called the social worker the next morning. She said that they were already aware of the situation because more than one person had phoned up to express their concern. She asked me for my name and I gave it. I had agreed with the neighbour on the other side that we didn't want to hide behind anonymity and that it might be a wake-up call for Margaret if she knew how worried we all were.

A few days later Clare came to our house, crying, to tell me social services had been round.

Her mother had told the social worker that it was a choice between her daughter and her boyfriend and that she chose the boyfriend. Clare went to stay with a friend nearby, and my husband and I agonised over whether we should take her in. We told ourselves it would be too strange for her to be next door to the family that had rejected her but probably the real reason was that we thought she would be too much for us to take on.

After a few days Margaret dumped all Clare's stuff on to the pavement for the rubbish collectors to take – her bed, her toys, books and the Wendy house. I went outside and asked her what she was doing and we had a huge argument, with her telling me that I should keep my nose out of it for once and me telling her that she was cruel, that she couldn't just give up on her own daughter like that. I will never forget the sight of Clare walking past all her stuff and picking out as much as she could so that her arms were full. Two weeks later Clare was moved to a children's home and we didn't see her any more.

Margaret, her boyfriend and her son moved out of the area, telling the couple that ran the corner shop that they had been driven out by the interfering attitude of me and the neighbour on the other side. I saw Clare a few times by chance, on the train and in the West End and she seemed too thin and even more nervy although she said she was "all right. Better off without them".

I felt awkward and guilty both times I bumped into her, and so I think it was me that stopped her being able to speak about how she really was. I still feel guilty that we didn't take Clare in because I think that if you believe that every child's welfare is everyone's responsibility then we should have followed through our concerns about how she was being treated by her own family by offering her shelter in ours. The worst feeling comes from being able to remember how disgusting it made me feel calling the social services on a family I had known for years – it didn't just make me feel like a curtain-twitching, judgmental busy-body, it made me feel like an informer.

All names have been changed

*The Guardian
12 January 2008
© Guardian News &
Media Ltd. 2008*

Muscovites count the cost of Valentine's Day

Duncan Bartlett

You could almost feel the love in the Coffee House cafe in Moscow's university district.

Most tables were occupied by young couples smooching over frothy cappuccinos and fancy cakes. It was there I met Katya Kuznetsova, a beautiful and confident advertising executive with a weakness for strawberry ice cream, although you would hardly know it from her slim figure.

Katya, who's 22, is dating Sasha, a drummer in a heavy metal band. This will be their second Valentine's Day together. Last year he took her to see a romantic foreign film, which was rather more her cup of tea than his.

> **Valentine's Day: an economic burden grudgingly borne by men**

She also likes watching the TV comedy series "Sex & The City" about the seductive antics of some very liberated New York women. There's a Russian equivalent, in which Katya says the characters want more than hot dates and casual sex. They're looking for marriage. It's a silly programme, she says, but in a way very Russian.

Speaking of her parents' courtship back in the days of the USSR, Katya says: "They took everything very seriously back then. If you met someone, marriage was the main aim." It seems that's changed. According to Katya, young women in Russia have a lot more power and independence than their mothers. "We know what we want," she explains. "We don't need to find a man to earn money for us and get us a home and a family. We have relationships just for fun."

Costly fun

Having fun can be expensive, though, especially in Moscow which has one of the highest costs of living in the world. It also has a soaring 10% inflation rate although that's nothing in comparison to the hyper inflation in the flower business, which occurs in the run up to Valentine's Day: an economic burden grudgingly borne by men.

However, it makes Nadezhda, who owns a little florist's stall in the underground station near the coffee shop, a fan of the free market economy. She's expecting 2008 to be her most lucrative year. "In Russia we have a saying: every flower has its buyer," she says.

Some men have even asked her to put rings and jewels in the bouquets. "It certainly wasn't like this under Communism," says Nadezhda, who's been in the business 20 years. "Back then, hardly anyone seemed to buy flowers. Now we have to work from seven in the morning until 11 at night just to keep up."

She would like to buy a store in a more glamorous district, but at 49, she thinks she's too old to move upmarket to somewhere chic. "You'd have to be young and thin and beautiful to work in a place like that," she laughs.

Birth incentives

For romantic Russian men, the next few weeks will involve a great deal of additional expense and bother. Women's Day falls on 8 March and men are expected not just to buy gifts but to do housework and cooking. In theory, it sounds like a chance for their partners to relax, but many women dread the idea of having to eat burnt sausages made by men who haven't been near the cooker for a year.

But has all this romance brought about the thing Russia badly needs – babies? The birth rate has fallen drastically since the demise of the Soviet Union. And abortion rates are the highest in the world. Many women choose to terminate their pregnancy rather than bear the expense of bringing up children without much financial help from the state.

The child care allowance is 200 roubles (£4) a month – about the same as the money it costs to buy a single orchid from Nadezhda's flower stall. The government has become so worried about the falling birth rate that it's come up with a scheme. When a woman's second child reaches three years of age, she receives a payment of 200,000 roubles (£4,000) and, if she manages to bring more three-year-olds into the world, she'll get a payment for each one.

All very well, say the mothers, but the first three years of a child's life are very expensive and it is hard to go out and earn money with two more young children to look after.

Thriving families

Back in the coffee shop, Katya and Sasha aren't thinking about babies just yet although they reckon they'll move in together soon and Katya makes it clear that if she were to become pregnant, she is against abortion and would like to keep the child. Such a heavy responsibility seems a long way off.

But if the Russian motherland is going to have a thriving family, women like Katya may have to consider letting go of a few of their precious new freedoms to care for its children.

*From Our Own Correspondent,
BBC Radio 4,
14 February 2008*

A marriage of convenience

Letter from Cairo

Maria Golia observes the wheeling and dealing behind a Cairo wedding

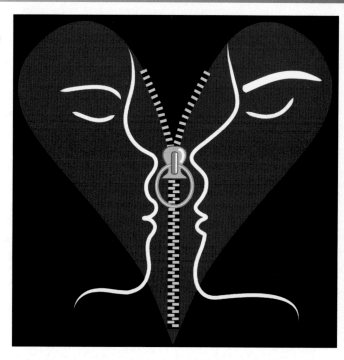

My neighbour Selwa is a jovial young woman, hefty and assertive, but when she visited the other day she was upset. She and her family live on the roof. Her father used to be the building's guardian, but he died recently, and Selwa assumed the role of her mother's right hand. She told me the family was in crisis, because of her brother Ahmed's prospective marriage. Ahmed, the eldest of six siblings, is 33. He left school at 10 and has since helped support his family. He too became a building guardian, earning around $50 per month.

Recently, Ahmed's mother arranged his engagement to Karima, a second cousin from their hometown in Upper Egypt. Since Karima's father is also dead, her brother negotiated the marriage contract, as is customary, on her behalf. Ahmed would supply the apartment, and certain furnishings. Karima's family would provide other household items, in addition to supplying Karima.

Selwa and her sisters were thrilled to have found Ahmed an affordable apartment ($35 per month) in a shantytown on the outskirts of Imbaba, a relatively central quarter. They secured the required furnishings with cash deposits, and organised the wedding celebration, paying in advance for a band and an outdoor space to hold the party not far from the couple's future home.

Then, just a week before the wedding, Karima's brother raised an issue. How could his sister live in a flat with no electricity? Unless a more suitable dwelling was found, the deal was off. Selwa's distress was equally distributed between her brother's thwarted chance for happiness and the cash they'd lose if the marriage fell through.

The family gathered, she told me, to examine their options – things like gas-operated generators, which were expensive. Kerosene lamps and candles were more typical solutions, but unsatisfactory to Karima's brother. They tried to explain that the Imbaba neighbourhood would one day be embraced by the municipal grid and, if not, people would pirate nearby electricity wires. Meanwhile, god had seen fit to position the flat in such a way as to profit from his light throughout the day. The brother remained obdurate and Selwa's mother, who suffers from diabetes and high-blood pressure, had, in the local parlance, 'blue genies dancing in front of her eyes'.

'What can we do?' Selwa asked. I suggested she tell Karima's brother once more exactly what she'd told me: that they'd done their best and it wasn't easy, and if he didn't like it, he could help pay to solve the problem himself. Otherwise they should drop the engagement. Better to lose money than for Ahmed to marry into a family of unreasonable ingrates. Selwa sighed. I wished her luck and gave her some money that she refused, as is expected, several times before accepting it.

I'd nearly forgotten about her visit when two days later I heard ululations coming from the roof. I figured they'd reached an agreement and Ahmed and Karima would marry after all. I was half right.

Selwa's mother came by to make sure I'd go to the wedding. I told her I was glad they'd settled things with Karima's brother.

'We didn't,' she said.

'What do you mean?'

'We found another one.'

'Another apartment?'

The wedding took place on an empty lot in a garbage-dogged maze of informal housing blocks.

'No,' she laughed, 'another bride'. This was a third cousin by the name of Hind, who showed up moments later to introduce herself; a sturdy woman wearing jeans and a headscarf, who had known Ahmed for years and was apparently game.

I figured what the marriage lacked in romance it gained in practicality. Both parties were well past marriageable age, poor, uneducated and unlikely to find a better match, especially considering that their families' rapport was evidently longstanding and harmonious. Life is a difficult enterprise, requiring reliable partners. It was that simple.

The wedding party took place on an empty lot in a garbage-clogged maze of informal housing blocks. The band played beside a crude brick wall, with a swathe of printed fabric as backdrop. Several hundred people filled the surrounding benches, wooden planks that bobbed up and down as we sat or stood. Men were on one side of the stage, women on the other, with kids swarming back and forth in between. People danced, particularly Selwa, who moved with robust innuendo, as if her whole body was winking.

I slipped away after midnight, following a tight alley to something resembling a street, walking ankle-deep in the ghostly sun-dried shreds of plastic bags, like the skins of moulting snakes. This is Cairo in pursuit of renewal: heroically defiant of the odds, hopelessly romantic after all.

New Internationalist November 2007

FEED THE WORLD

Photographer Peter Menzel and his author wife Faith D'Aluisio had a simple idea – to find out more about one of our most basic and essential activities, eating. They invited themselves for dinner with families from 24 different countries around the world. By picturing each family with a week's worth of food shopping, they give a visual insight into the hugely varied global diet, revealing wider social, financial and health issues.

USA Weekly spend £170.71
The Revis family, from North Carolina, clearly enjoy the convenience of prepared and fast food. It accounts for more than a third of their budget. Fresh fruit and veg are hard to find among their purchases.

Japan Weekly spend £158.37
A balanced diet of meat, fish, fruit and veg makes up the bulk of the Ukita family's shopping in Kodaira City. Dairy products, snacks and desserts, comprising 5% of the budget, hardly feature at all.

Kuwait Weekly spend £110.57
A surprising number of UK brands comprise part of the weekly diet of the Al Haggan family of Kuwait City – names such as Liptons and Vimto. Their snacks include Ritz crackers, Mars bars and Pringles.

India Weekly spend £19.60
Dairy products comprise the largest single part of the diet of the Patkar family from Ujjain in the central state of Madhya Pradesh. More than a quarter of the family's budget goes on milk, yoghurt curds and ghee.

Britain Weekly spend £126.37
The Bainton family, from Wiltshire, have plenty of favourite British staples on display, including tomato ketchup and salad cream – but where's the Marmite and HP sauce?

Mongolia Weekly spend £19.98
They like their meat in the land of Genghis Khan. The Batsuuri family, from Ulaanbaatar, had more than 14lb of beef, mutton and dried sausage in the photograph – less than their usual weekly supply.

Chad Weekly spend £0.61
Neither quantity nor variety enriches the diet of the Aboubaker family in Chad. The only luxury is 9oz of dried goat meat and a few small limes.

Ecuador Weekly spend £15.72
The Ayme family's gleaming smiles testify to a diet rich in grains, fruit and veg (including a bunch of stinging nettles from which they make tea) but there is no meat, fish or eggs. Milk comes from the family cow.

Greenland Weekly spend £138.25
The food bill of the Madsen family includes the nominal value of fresh meat from hunted musk ox, walrus, arctic geese and polar bear. Much of the remainder of their diet comes from tins and packets.

Germany Weekly spend £249.64
Confounding the stereotypical image of German dietary habits, the Melander family of Bargteheide have no room for sauerkraut or bratwurst but £45 of their food bill is spent on vitamins and supplements.

Bhutan Weekly spend £2.51
More than 66lb of red rice fortifies the Namgay family in the Himalayan village of Shingkhey every week. Red and green chillis are treated as vegetables rather than condiments and are eaten at almost every meal.

Egypt Weekly spend £34.21
There's plenty of vitamin C in the Ahmeds' diet. More than 80lbs of fresh fruit and vegetables help to satisfy the large Cairo family's appetite. Meals are prepared from scratch; they hardly eat any convenience foods.

FOODIE BOY

VEGETARIAN?
With a flock of trigger-happy friends and woods stuffed with partridge, fat chance,
SAYS ALEX JAMES

I remember hearing Paul McCartney explain how he stopped eating meat when he moved to a farm. Exactly the opposite thing happened to me. I had been a vegetarian for almost 20 years when Claire and I bought our farm on our honeymoon, but soon after we arrived in the country I completely changed my mind.

When we took over the farm, there was a flock of sheep in residence and it was clear it is rather nice being a sheep while it lasts. I'm not sure if the same is true for the majority of chickens, but sheep don't have it too bad at all. To have been a lamb and be roasted is better than never to have been a lamb at all, I began to think, and it wasn't long before I was tucking in.

When I was a vegetarian I used to get quite riled by the sight of groups of people with guns in the countryside. It was the last thing the sublime pastoral scenario needed, nobby types with guns tramping around shooting stuff.

In the first few months we lived here, I received letters from various people asking if they could come and shoot on our land, the thought of which appalled me. Then I realised I had to get a gun myself, a 12-bore, for the rooks that were beginning to take over the woodland, and pretty soon I was eyeing up the game birds that were straying on to our land and wondering what they'd taste like.

The idea of taking pleasure in killing things is iffy ground, but there's something wonderfully holistic about bagging dinner with your shotgun: the 'pack-your-own' approach. Buying organic, ethical, biodynamic, rare-breed meat is definitely a step in the right direction, but at some point death comes into the equation and who better to pull the trigger than the consumer? The shooting isn't the horrible bit. That's pretty much the same feeling as lining up a long red on a snooker table. But everyone should try plucking a bird. That's a really nasty business. For the last couple of years, around this time, I've spent a day wandering about the farm with friends picking off the stray pheasants, but until last week I'd never been on a proper driven shoot.

Shooting is about the poshest, nobbiest, most expensive way of pleasantly wasting time anyone has ever dreamed up. It requires vast swathes of countryside, huge numbers of beaters, keepers, loaders and dog handlers, and the amount of gear involved – togs, guns, sticks, bags and cartridges – is apparently endless. Like a dinner party, a shooting party is only as much fun as the other people that will be there, and this was a good one.

At some point death comes into the equation and who better to pull the trigger than the consumer?

There were eight of us, ranging from a minor royal to a major celebrity: all richer than King Croesus and just as tired of everything. I was the only one who was a rubbish shot. There were discussions about other shoots in the area. At Overbury, apparently, they pluck the birds during lunch for you and vacuum-pack them with bacon on their backs.

It was an absolutely brilliant day. I'm used to seeing a couple of pheasants fly up when the dogs go in but there were hundreds of birds. The partridge rise first. It's heart-stopping stuff, particularly for the birds. Partridge is absolutely delicious, but butchers have trouble selling them, I guess because people are nervous about cooking them. They're just small chickens, right? It's no more complicated than that. Chickens live in cages and taste a bit like chicken. Game birds taste wonderful and live on fantastic, historic country estates and get finished off by members of the royal family and oligarchs. Not a bad way to go. If you see game, grab it. It's a good bargain.

Observer Food Monthly
27 January 2008
© Guardian News &
Media Ltd. 2008

Faking the flavour

Flavouring is a frequently over-looked ingredient which crops up in much of our food and drink. But, why does our food need extra flavourings and what are they made from?
Ian Tokelove investigates

There are approximately 2,700 different flavourings currently allowed into our food, but few are ever identified on ingredients lists, other than by the description 'flavouring(s)'. Unlike food additives they do not need to be identified by their name or a number, so it is impossible to know exactly what is being added to our food and drink.

Safety testing is largely dependent on the companies that make the flavourings, but can we trust them? As flavourings remain unidentified on food products, how could we tell if they did cause problems?

What are flavourings?

Flavourings are purely cosmetic food ingredients with no nutritive value of their own. They are used in processed foods to replace flavours lost during processing or to 'bump up' the taste of such foodstuffs.

They can also be used to mask unpleasant flavours caused by other ingredients or additives. Some are artificial and others are derived from natural sources. In their pure, concentrated state they tend to be fairly unpleasant, necessitating the use of protective clothing, goggles and even respirators. However, once diluted sufficiently, they produce a flavour or aroma which encourages consumption of foods and drinks.

Flavourings are used in so many food and drink products that they can be hard to avoid.

Labelling and the law

Specific legislation (and associated guidelines) regarding the use of flavourings are confusing and hard to access, although their use does have to conform with general food law (ie they should not be harmful to health). Where guidelines exist, they are haphazard and vary from country to country. Even now, a flavouring that is approved in one country may be unapproved or banned in another.

Back in 1996, the European Parliament ruled that an EU-wide 'positive list' of approved flavouring substances should be created. The evaluation process was supposed to take five years but it is still ongoing and is unlikely to be completed until 2009 or 2010.

As a consequence, there is still no positive list of approved flavourings. Even when such a list is published there will be no need to identify flavourings on food products as specific, named ingredients.

The ongoing EU evaluation of flavourings is reliant on the industry providing accurate testing and usage data. In a significant number of incidences the industry has been unable to provide sufficient testing data for evaluation, but in such cases the flavourings have remained on the market until further data is forthcoming.

The Scientific Committee on Food has reported that intake estimates of flavouring substances are, "generally very poor," because of a lack of data on the concentrations of flavourings in foodstuffs.

Are flavourings safe?

As with all food ingredients, flavourings should be safe for consumption at the quantities in which they are used. However, as flavourings are not identified on food labels, if any associated health problems did occur they would be almost impossible to identify.

Flavourings may have a much wider, indirect effect on our health because of the way in which they are used to improve the appeal of low-nutrient or high fat, sugar, salt (HFSS) foods. Flavourings often replace genuine, nutritious ingredients (a strawberry flavouring is much cheaper than genuine strawberries).

By encouraging the consumption of HFSS foods it is likely that flavourings directly affect our health – and not for the better.

Repeated exposure to flavourings may also negatively affect our reaction to the taste of fresh, unprocessed foods. A sweet, crunchy apple can taste pretty bland and dull when compared to a highly flavoured packet of crisps. Flavourings may thus discourage basic healthy eating, such as the 'five a day' consumption of fruit and vegetables.

Continues over the page

The strawberry swizz

All of the products pictured here appear to contain strawberries, but rather than getting their flavour from real fruit they rely on cheap flavourings. If you want proper strawberries it always pays to check the small print – you may not be getting what you think you are

* **Yazoo strawberry flavour milkshake** loudly claims it is 'low in fat' but neglects to mention it is 'empty of strawberries'. Flavouring and sugar take the place of real fruit.

* **Moo strawberry flavour milk** is made 'as simply as we can, with milk straight from our farmers' lovely cows, packed full of nutrients and natural goodness.' It is also made with flavouring, colour, stabiliser and sweetener – but not actual strawberries.

* **Nesquik strawberry flavour milkshake** mix is basically sugar (almost 98% we reckon) – fortified with a few vitamins and minerals to make it appear healthy. The 'scrummy yumminess' is apparently unaffected by the lack of actual strawberries, and few children will even stop to consider whether this is a good or bad thing. Nestlé actively encourages children to add 2-4 teaspoons to every glass of milk. Would you add four teaspoons of sugar to a cup of tea?

* **Ovaltine Max 4 Milk strawberry milkshake** powder (40% sugar) also contains added vitamins and minerals to make it look healthy, and is described as 'Daily Nutrition' and 'wholesome goodness'. However, the closest thing to a strawberry in this product is the colouring, which comes from beetroot.

* **Alpro Soya Strawberry Flavour Drink** Alpro have added calcium and vitamins but no actual strawberries. Instead, we find sugar and a mix of 'natural flavouring' and 'flavouring'.

* **ASDA Great Stuff Strawberry Milk** has been 'endorsed by ASDA nutritionists' – who apparently think children are better off consuming flavourings instead of real fruit. This bottled product contains just 0.6% strawberry juice – meaning there is less than half a teaspoon of juice in the whole bottle. The carton contains no strawberries at all - and yet ASDA have the nerve to call this 'Great Stuff'.

* **While's strawberry flavour shake** is fruit free, but that has not stopped them plastering the packaging with images of strawberries. The use of strawberry imagery is only allowed if strawberries are a 'characterising ingredient' – so this packaging could well be illegal. However, there is a loophole, as the use of a natural strawberry flavouring would be sufficient to justify the use of such imagery (even though the actual strawberry content would be negligible). This product does not specify the flavouring as either 'strawberry' or even as 'natural', so we have no way of knowing.

* **Friji strawberry milkshake** No artificial flavourings in this product, but no strawberries either. Just another 'natural flavouring' from an unknown source.

Strawberry tea

Cranberry, Strawberry and Raspberry Teabags with 0.2% strawberry from Sainsbury's; Strawberry and Mango teabags with 1.0% strawberry from Twinings; and Tesco Fruit Infusion teabags with just 0.2% actual strawberry.

Strawberries may feature heavily on the packaging, but appearances can be deceptive. All of these teabags contain larger doses of flavourings than real strawberry fruit.

Different types of flavouring

Artificial flavourings

These synthetic flavourings are a cheap alternative to natural flavourings and can also be used to provide flavours which are not found naturally. They are simply labelled as 'flavouring(s)'.

Natural flavourings

A 'natural' flavouring should have been derived from a 'natural' source material of vegetable, animal or microbiological origin, but the process by which it is manufactured may be fairly unnatural, using acids, micro-organisms or enzymes, for example. Natural flavourings can also come from unexpected 'natural' sources, such as carcasses, rose wood, oak wood chips and strawberry leaves.

A natural flavouring in an 'apple' product may well be 'natural', but the flavouring will not necessarily come from an apple. In general, natural flavourings will not be evaluated for safety by the EU, as they are assumed to be safe. It is worth noting that some natural flavourings would have trouble being accepted as new flavourings if they were presented today. For instance, nutmeg is toxic in large doses.

Natural flavourings are the only flavourings allowed into food certified as 'organic', as long as none of the ingredients are derived from genetically modified sources.

Named flavouring

If a flavouring is described as 'apple flavour' or 'natural apple flavour' it should have come wholly or mostly from genuine apples. During the production process most of the nutritional goodness of the apple will be removed from the final flavouring – so we end up with all the taste but none of the goodness.

Named flavourings sound 'healthier' though, and many manufacturers now use such flavourings.

Nature-identical flavourings

Nature-identical flavourings are substances that are obtained by synthesis or isolated through chemical processes. Although they may be 'artificial' in nature, their chemical composition is identical to that of 'natural' flavouring substances, and thus they are known as 'nature-identical'.

Fruit juice or flavouring

This **Hartley's strawberry jelly** claims to have a 'New Fruitier Taste', but it is always worth checking the small print. This product contains no strawberry at all. The new fruitier taste comes completely from unknown flavourings, not strawberries.

Tesco kids strawberry milk contains both flavours and 'strawberry juice from concentrate'. Tesco do not say how much real juice there is, but the label does reveal that this milk drink contains more additives than strawberries.

These **Jubbly strawberry ice lollies** also make a 'real fruit juice' claim. However, it turns out that each lolly contains just 0.6% strawberry juice. Again, the flavour largely comes from unknown flavouring agents, not actual strawberries.

Yoplait's Yop strawberry yogurt apparently comes with 'full on calcium'. We wish we could say the same for the fruit content, which comes in at 'zero'. This has been coloured with E124, ponceau 4R, one of the suspect artificial colourings featured on the **www.actiononadditives.com** website.

Published in The Food Magazine issue 80, 25 February 2008
The Food Magazine is available on subscription for £25 a year. See www.foodcomm.org.uk or email info@foodcomm.org.uk

It's time we cried fowl over cheap chickens

By Helen Martin

NOT since salmonella and bird flu has such a fuss been made over chicken and eggs. Debate is raging – or should that be clucking – over the fear that the welfare lobby may put the price of a nice piece of breast out of reach of the poor. Anyone would think we were talking about a staple such as bread, milk or potatoes.

Indeed, that's how many people have come to regard chicken as a cheap (excuse the pun) product, accessible to all.

Well pardon me for, once again, harking back to my youth, but I remember a time when chicken was for high days and holidays only. At Christmas, birthdays and times of great celebration, a chicken would be acquired.

And if you couldn't afford a roasting bird – as many people couldn't – you could always go for an old boiler, literally an aged egg layer which could, with extensive boiling, become tender enough to eat and produce a pot of soup into the bargain.

In 1957, the blossoming poultry industry had one, iconic goal in mind – to produce a chicken for 10 shillings – (that's 50p for the youngsters). A respectable

poor. Allegedly, you couldn't walk down Auld Reekie's insanitary closes without crunching on a carpet of cast off shells. It was the 1970s before most of us could recognise an avocado or a courgette.

Food and the price of it evolves and changes. Now that we have, as a society, become more concerned about animal welfare we do, as Jamie Oliver and Hugh Fearnley-Whittingstall are advocating with their current campaign, have to make a choice, preferably to buy only free range.

While the Government is, belatedly, laying down rules to outlaw battery farming for egg production, there is as yet virtually nothing on the table to address the welfare of hens bred for meat. For the foreseeable future, the responsibility for that is down to us, the consumers.

Of course it seems unfair that the poor would no longer be able to afford chicken. It's unfair that the poor can't

priced out of their orbit for greedy profiteering, if there was no better alternative, then I'd be first in line to sign the petition.

But it is none of these things. Even free-range chicken is cheaper now than it was in the '50s and we have

Chicken is not cheap, not unless you develop inhumane, cost-cutting ways to produce it

a whole plethora of extra foods from around the world to choose from to fill the gap in the menu.

We have more vegetables, fruit and fish than most of us will ever bother to try in a lifetime. Ask any butcher and he'll tell you he can provide endless cheap cuts of meat that taste delicious when properly cooked – but most people only want to buy the more expensive, recognisable cuts.

There are those who have rejected red meat because they only want to eat chicken and to them I say, well stump up for it. Fussiness comes at a cost.

I'm fussy too. I have no desire to eat monkeys' brains, however much of a

delicacy they may be. I don't want to eat boiled-alive dog either, come to that. I may not yet be prepared to go vegetarian but nor do I want to eat something that has been bred in and confined to a concentration camp for its short life. Chicken's expensive. Get over it.

The Edinburgh Evening News
14 January 2008

And this isn't about money, it's about ethics and humanity

wage at the time was £10 so the very idea that one could buy a chicken for only 5% of your total income had the nation salivating.

Chicken is not cheap, not unless you develop inhumane, cost-cutting ways to produce it.

We shouldn't be surprised by that, nor should we expect common, affordable foods to necessarily stay common and affordable.

Until Victorian times, oysters were the food of the

afford to buy their own home, or a holiday in the Bahamas, or, should they wish to do so, to dine on oysters and caviare every night. It's even more unfair that they can't afford the soaring cost of heat and light. My point is that there are far greater injustices than being deprived of cheap chicken. And this isn't about money, it's about ethics and humanity.

If eating chicken was necessary for survival, if it was unnecessarily being

SOD THIS THEY'RE ONLY £1·99 IN TESCO

ROBERT THOMPSON

The Observer 10th February 2008

Let adult fatties eat themselves to death. The kids we can save

Janet Street-Porter

If the Government really wants to tackle obesity, it should channel all its resources into getting the young fit and healthy.

According to our Prime Minister, obesity is "one of the biggest threats" we face. For some time now politicians have employed the same terminology to talk about health issues as they do about waging wars – which generally entails maiming and killing people. Being fat isn't acceptable – it's talked about as an "epidemic" or a "battle" that must be fought, just like operations in Afghanistan and Iraq.

It does seem a bit rich to be using such emotive language to describe nothing more than a plethora of love handles or beer guts. And I'm not sure that spending millions of pounds on public service advertising telling us all what we all know already – if you eat too much you pile on the pounds – isn't a complete waste of time.

The latest bit of armoury to be deployed against fatties is the extraordinary notion of offering cash or vouchers for leisure centres for successful dieting, copying an idea adopted by some US states, where obese adults are paid $14 (about £7) for every 1% reduction of their weight. The British Heart Foundation is running a competition called The Biggest Loser, which hands out £130 gift vouchers for the entrant who loses the most weight. The Government would like to see this adopted by employers up and down the land – and they may be made tax deductible as an added incentive.

Sadly, when it comes to tacking child obesity, the Government, which set a target three years ago to reduce it by 2010, has revised the target downwards because it is unachievable. Instead, the Department of Health wants the number of overweight children to drop by 2020 to the level it was in 2000 – from the current 30% down to 26%. That hardly smacks of a battle being waged with any commitment, does it?

At the moment around a quarter of all adults are classified as obese, and if the level continues to grow the burden on the NHS will be considerable. New ideas include better food labelling, a £75m advertising campaign to promote healthy diet and exercise, and more cycle lanes. The NHS website will also offer personalised advice about what to eat and how to exercise.

"Don't tell me obesity is a result of poverty. It's a result of wilful self-abuse"

There's some way to go: an episode of Dispatches on Channel 4 the other week looked at why people think they are obese – the reasons offered by the Mr and Mrs Blobbies filmed were patently risible – ranging from thinking it was "genetic" to "glandular". One family claimed to eat a healthy diet but a secret camera filmed mum stuffing food into her mouth with both hands while walking.

I am not quite sure why the Government is spending our money on advertising healthy eating, because the best way to get any kind of message across is through programmes like this, reality shows and popular entertainment. Once you start issuing health warnings it smacks of the nanny state and turns off fatties even more. I've said it before, and still the Government seems reluctant to acknowledge, that by the time a child is 10 the war on a trim waistline is won or lost – and that is where, if we are going to fight a "war" we have to direct all our efforts to teach all kids to cook, understand nutrition and be able to shop sensibly before they leave primary school. Instead of government targets of a paltry two hours' physical exercise a week, kids should have an hour every day, achieved by walking to school or playing sport at lunchtimes.

The number of adults who manage to lose weight and keep it off permanently is very small. Waving vouchers or promising cash as an incentive is doomed to failure. It would be better to abandon the current generation of fatties and pour all resources into ensuring that the next ones grow up fit. Instead of offering stomach-stapling and fat reduction free on the NHS, charge double for it.

Please don't tell me obesity is a result of poverty – it's a result of wilful self-abuse. It's perfectly possible to eat well and substantially on a low income, preparing food that doesn't take hours to cook. We have to stop making excuses and accept that some people are determined to eat their way into an early grave. No government handouts or warning stickers will stop them.

The Independent 27 January 2008

Trust me I'm a...

junior doctor

It's wrong to abuse the obese, says Max Pemberton, but it's right to make them diet

There is a national pastime exercised on a daily basis up and down the country – in people's homes, in Whitehall, in magazine offices, advertising agencies and doctors' surgeries.

It's a strange preoccupation which stands as one of the last bastions of acceptable intolerance. Feeling a bit tired and frumpy? Feel like taking it out on someone? Have a go at a fat person.

It's so easy to do. Walk past McDonald's and scowl disapprovingly as someone orders two Big Macs with double fries. Peer into the shopping basket of a well-proportioned person in the supermarket queue and tut loudly at their ready meals and crisps.

And, of course, the Government loves fat people because they provide it with the perfect scapegoat. All those pesky porkers clogging up waiting lists – blame them for being so damned unhealthy, and then refuse to operate on them. Perfect!

Of course it is shocking that new figures from the NHS Information Centre show that a third of 10-year-olds are overweight or obese. But fat-fascism is everywhere and the BMI (Body Mass Index) has become a new form of social hierarchy: a way of defining and judging yourself and others.

As with any prejudice, it's totally inconsistent. The advertising companies that pump our heads full of images of young, thin women and toned, tanned men are the very ones that then try to flog us king-size Mars bars.

We pour scorn on obesity then shake our heads at the rise in anorexia among the young. I'm always surprised that, in a society that prides itself on its liberal, progressive outlook, we can still be so intolerant of one cohort of people just because of how they look.

Personally, I don't see why someone else's weight is anything to do with me – or indeed anybody else. As a doctor I'll happily provide advice to my obese patients and suggest how they might lose weight, but ultimately we should be free to choose broccoli or burgers as we see fit without interference from the state, or disapproval from our neighbours.

The Government loves fat people because they provide it with the perfect scapegoat

But then, last week, a poll in a medical journal found that some NHS trusts are limiting surgery, such as gastric bypasses or banding, for obesity. There has been an outcry from obesity specialists, calling the decision "outrageous" and "disgraceful".

Now, while I think it is morally reprehensible to withhold surgery for medical problems solely on the basis of a patient's weight, I don't feel the same about this. Those denied obesity surgery will have to rely on lifestyle changes and drugs.

But is that such a bad thing? It was, after all, a lifestyle that got them into this pickle and it seems only right that a change in this lifestyle should get them out of it.

We pour scorn on obesity then shake our heads at the rise in anorexia

In the past five years there has been a 650% rise in referrals for obesity surgery in some areas. It is popular with patients because it absolves individuals of responsibility. They go under the knife; immediately their appetite lessens and they lose weight. No willpower involved.

Even with unlimited resources, I'm not sure this is very healthy. Years ago this type of surgery was reserved for only the most severe

cases, but now it seems anyone who finds WeightWatchers rather arduous feels they can demand an operation.

There are concerns that "people will be dropping down dead" if obesity surgery is limited – as though it were somehow the NHS's fault that people eat too much, and as though there were no other option but surgery.

But with the exception of a few rare diseases, obesity is about choice. I wholeheartedly support the right to make that choice, but with that right comes a responsibility.

It's right that people shouldn't be discriminated against because of their weight, but it's also right that the NHS should be able to evaluate procedures and limit their availability if there are effective and cheaper alternatives.

Diets work. Yes, they can be difficult, but that's not the fault of the NHS. The health service is not abandoning these patients; it's just that they're being asked to put some effort in rather than rely on a quick-fix solution.

Just as people have the right to choose how they live their lives, the NHS has the right to suggest that those who want to lose weight should eat less and exercise more.

Daily Telegraph 25 February 2008
© Telegraph Group Ltd 2008

'I just want to be fit enough to go and see my GP'

Daily Telegraph 2 January 2008
© Telegraph Group Ltd 2008

As if... By Sally Ann Lasson

The Independent 15 October 2007

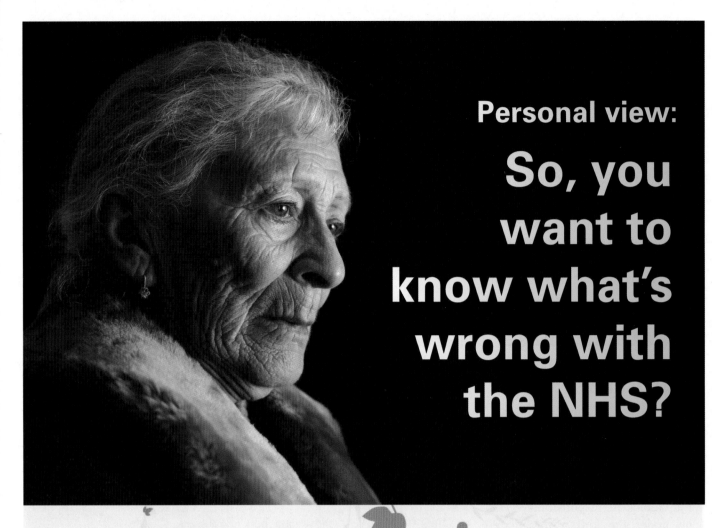

Personal view:

So, you want to know what's wrong with the NHS?

I sat in the waiting room, feeling self conscious. I am usually on the other side of the door, inside the interview room. Now, I was outside, waiting. After five minutes the consultant came out; the big man, the one in charge. We were NHS. He was having trouble interviewing my mother: would I, as a psychiatrist, help him please?

I went into the room. My mum was on the edge of her seat, looking towards me hopefully, giving me that look she had, assuming that everything would be all right now (because "my son" had entered the room). Trusting me. It was then that I learnt what it is like to elicit the first rank symptoms of schizophrenia from your own kith and kin, your own flesh and blood. The great man couldn't manage it. He had the cufflinks but not the questions. He had the style but not the substance. I had the greatest pain I had ever felt in my life. A virtual knife went through my chest as I asked her about the voices, about the thoughts that were not her own, about what the messengers said.

Some tests are done twice, other are not done at all

I have often wondered about the doctor's approach that day, whether he had any feeling at all for what it might have been like, to be us, to be her, to be me – because I really doubt it. I doubt it because it was all in vain. The consultation did not achieve anything. "Follow-up" did not occur; appointments were not kept; action was not taken. And when she went missing so did her notes: there was no "paper trail."

Years went by. Eventually, others would apply the Mental Health Act when the squalor became too great, but only when I had complained to the chief executive of the trust. A note to the wise: complaints in psychiatry are pretty much a waste of time. To be able to proceed you need the "consent of the patient," something of a problem if the patient is missing or does not accept that she is ill. Those who cannot do their jobs, who cannot elicit histories, are curiously diligent when it comes to applying the rules under which complaints can be made against them. They're sticklers for protocol then.

Schizophrenia gave way to Alzheimer's disease. She came to live with me. Times are good and times are bad, and there are times when you need help. You visit the GP, talk to his shoulder, peruse the back of his skull. He sits there with his back turned, looking at his computer screen. He doesn't touch patients; always refers. You wait and see, wait and see.

Recurrent falls take us to the casualty department. We end up on the ward. My mum, now: an elderly woman migrating across five wards over 14 days under at least three different consultants. No one has a plan. Everyone is "waiting to see." You arrive to find out that you are in the wrong place. "Who? No, we haven't got anyone by that name here. Oh... oh yeah, they moved her out this morning." Some tests are done twice (brain scans); others are not done at all (blood tests, which "can be done in the community by the GP").

The "carers" do not care. It does not matter what you say, because they do not listen.

She sits on the fourth ward, frightened, staring across at a woman opposite who is naked except for a nappy, her head stuck between the rails (she's in a cot). The nurses are sitting there, a couple of metres away, chatting, laughing, four of them. My mum wants to get up, to go across. She's been up and down all day. I make her sit. Don't get involved; don't make a fuss; you cannot win: you're an interfering patient, a "busybody." I feel ashamed, ashamed of myself. Ill as she is, my mum has far more guts than me. I want to look away, praying that the naked woman in the cot will soon do something so extreme that someone will come and care, that someone will come and do something, cover her up at least. The nurses are laughing. They appear happy.

The fifth ward, and things are worse. My mother tells me that there are children, running up and down. I cannot see them. There is a man "washing children" in the hall. I go to see the sister, saying, "Actually, my mum is worse." She says, "Well, you know the ward is haunted. Lots of them see children here. I keep an open mind, myself."

Do you laugh or do you cry? And what can you possibly say? Instead, you walk away and make other plans, internally. Walking out to the car park: it's a beautiful, crystalline spring night, yet I feel hollow. It doesn't matter what you do because the "carers" do not care. It does not matter what you say, because they do not listen. We have GPs with computers and consultants with business plans, we have wards that are "haunted," and sisters with "open minds." We have demented women in nappies, their heads wedged between cot rails, smelling of shit. That's what's wrong with the NHS. I took my mum home the next day. We'll take our chances, thanks.

The author wishes to remain anonymous

British Medical Journal (BMJ) Volume 335, 10 November 2007

Those who cannot do their jobs, who cannot elicit histories or examine the sick, are curiously diligent when it comes to applying the rules under which complaints can be made against them

An embuggerance

In December 2007, Terry Pratchett, author of the best selling (and most shoplifted) Discworld series of books, was diagnosed with Alzheimer's disease.

He had started having problems with his hand-eye co-ordination while working on a manuscript. "It was as if I was typing wearing gloves," he said. An MRI scan revealed areas of dead tissue in his brain, suggesting that he had suffered a "mini-stroke" at some time in the past few years and that he was now living with its legacy – early onset Alzheimer's disease.

The first symptoms include lapses of memory and problems finding the right words. As the disease progresses sufferers may experience more confusion, forgetfulness and mood swings – often caused by their frustration with the disease. Terry Pratchett has spoken of his first reaction to the diagnosis as being a sense of loss, abandonment and furious rage.

Pratchett's most famous creation is the Discworld series. Set on a surreal planet carried on the back of four elephants that stand on the shell of a giant space turtle, this is a bizarre yet completely consistent society in which characters and groups inter-react over generations. To someone whose working life has involved creating such a complex yet cohesive world, the disease must seem like a particularly personal insult. The intelligence and imagination behind Discworld and other novels is now

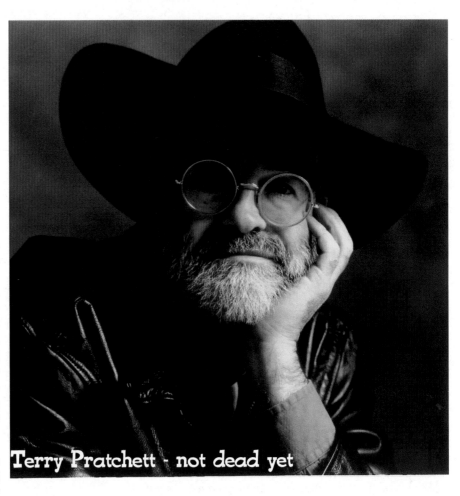

Terry Pratchett - not dead yet

> "As every wizard knows, once you have the true name of something you have power over it."

threatened by an 'old people's' disease for which there is no remedy. Pratchett has decided to confront his situation, using his celebrity and his linguistic skill to break through the almost shameful silence that surrounds the disease.

In an interview with The Guardian he said, "When I found out I thought, 'I have got to tell about eight to ten people who are really close to me.' Then I thought 'Why am I worried about this? Why am I keeping it a secret? I haven't actually done anything wrong!' But I was behaving as if I had, so I decided to stop."

With his typical mixture of humour, fantasy and sharp realism, the author explains why he decided to speak out and to strip away the hesitation and embarrassment over admitting what was wrong: "As every wizard knows, once you have the true name of something you have power over it."

Pratchett made an announcement on the website of his friend and Discworld illustrator Paul Kidby. From the beginning, with his coinage of a new and fantastically expressive term for the dilemma 'an embuggerance', to the humorous PS, the statement is all Pratchett and all defiance.

Since then Pratchett has put much of his energy – and his money – into publicising the need for more research and support. He pledged $1million to the Alzheimer's Research Trust, and told experts at the charity's conference about his frustration with the disease and the lengths he would go to in order to beat it:

"Part of me lives in a world of new age remedies and science, and some of the science is a little like voodoo, but science was never an exact science, and personally I'd eat the arse out of a dead mole if it offered a fighting chance."

"I intend to scream and harangue while there is time."

As in his writing, a light-hearted and humorous view of events is tempered by the recognition that there are "dark places" .

"I am, along with many others, scrabbling to stay ahead long enough to be there when the Cure comes along. Say it will be soon – there's nearly as many of us as there are cancer sufferers, and it looks as if the number of people with dementia will double within a generation. In most cases, alongside the sufferer you will find a spouse suffering as much. It is a shock to find out that funding for Alzheimer's research is just 3% of that to find cancer cures."

In May, Pratchett embarked on a round of interviews – "Another day another sofa" as the website has it.

On the Victoria Derbyshire show on Radio 5 Live he met with other Alzheimer's sufferers. Their discussion was largely optimistic, focussing more on what people could do than what they couldn't.

He voiced his frustration at the rationing of Aricept, a drug which delays the onset of the worst symptoms. At the Alzheimer's Society conference he had put it more forcefully: "The NHS kindly allows me to buy my own Aricept because I'm too young to have Alzheimer's for free, a situation I'm OK with in a 'want to kick politicians in the teeth' kind of way." Those who could not pay for the medicine, sufferers agreed, were being denied the chance of a better life.

Although the participants in the Radio 5 discussion agreed that the best way to cope was through humour – "If we can't laugh at Alzheimer's, who can?" – they inevitably turned to what they called 'the endgame' and the fear of being kept alive long after their original personality had gone. Their fear was less for themselves than for their families "After all **you** won't be there" a doctor had told Pratchett. The author was amongst those wanting the right to decide the manner and timing of their death – and to do so before Alzheimer's took away the ability to make that decision.

Some people expect a cure in the next few years, but not Pratchett, "I expect in five years time we will still be saying there'll be a cure in five years." What he does hope for is a regime to manage the disease. For him at least, Death is an old acquaintance. The Grim Reaper appears frequently as a character in the Discworld books, a skeletal figure, traditionally dressed with a hood and a scythe and riding a white horse – but the horse is called Binky and Death has a very untraditional liking for curry. He has been known to get drunk, go fishing and try dancing. In the Discworld, Death, who is not such a bad fellow when you get to know him, is sometimes thwarted, but that's the difference between fact and fiction.

But it's too soon to mourn. A new book, Nation, has been completed and a bound proof was auctioned on Ebay with the proceeds of £2,427 going to Alzheimer's research. The attitude of the many fans who have expressed their distress on blogs and websites can perhaps be best summed up by something that Terry Pratchett himself wrote in a dedication to one fan at a book signing: "Not dead yet? Good, keep it up!"

An embuggerance

Folks,

I would have liked to keep this one quiet for a little while, but because of upcoming conventions and of course the need to keep my publishers informed, it seems to me unfair to withhold the news. I have been diagnosed with a very rare form of early onset Alzheimer's, which lay behind this year's phantom "stroke".

We are taking it fairly philosophically down here and possibly with a mild optimism. For now work is continuing on the completion of Nation and the basic notes are already being laid down for Unseen Academicals. All other things being equal, I expect to meet most current and, as far as possible, future commitments but will discuss things with the various organisers. Frankly, I would prefer it if people kept things cheerful, because I think there's time for at least a few more books yet.

Terry Pratchett

PS I would just like to draw attention to everyone reading the above that this should be interpreted as 'I am not dead'. I will, of course, be dead at some future point, as will everybody else. For me, this maybe further off than you think – it's too soon to tell.

I know it's a very human thing to say "Is there anything I can do?", but in this case I would only entertain offers from very high-end experts in brain chemistry.

www.paulkidby.com/news/index.html

Sources: Various

Bad teeth – the New British Disease

Alice Thompson

In Britain today, you can stuff yourself on deep-fried Mars Bars, drink 20 pints a night, inject yourself with heroin, smoke 60 cigarettes a day or decide to change your sex – and the NHS has an obligation to treat you. You might go on a waiting list, but it will do its best to cure your lung cancer, patch up your nose after a drunken brawl or give you a hip replacement. It doesn't charge for operations or beds; it may even throw in some half-edible food.

But if you have bad teeth, forget it. You may be rolling on the bathroom floor in agony with an abscess, your gums may be riddled with disease, or people may recoil at the sight of your fangs as you walk down the street, but the NHS doesn't have to help you.

It is now virtually impossible for many people to find an NHS dentist, and if they do manage to squeeze on to a list, they could still be charged 80% of the cost of treatment – unless they are a child, pregnant or on benefits.

The health service under both the Tories and Labour has victimised the dentally challenged – that is, anyone who hasn't inherited strong teeth and a perfect picket fence smile. Few can easily afford to go to any dentist now. My husband went to a private dentist after a 15-year gap, and was left reeling after they extracted £2,000 for 12 fillings. My three-year-old son received a bill for £90 after I stupidly asked my private dentist whether she could have a quick look at his teeth.

A survey by Mori for the Citizens Advice Bureau this week found that seven and a half million Britons have failed to gain access to an NHS dentist in the past two years. In one quarter of the country, no NHS dentists are allowing new patients to join their lists. And despite government targets that every child should have his teeth seen by an expert every year, more than one in three children never see an NHS dentist.

Families such as mine, who have large, unruly teeth, have become part of a new genetic underclass, discriminated against by the state. If my parents had been forced to pay the dentist's bills when we were children, they would have gone broke. My teeth were so bad at the age of 13 that the head of orthodontics at the John Radcliffe Hospital in Oxford heard about me, and took me on as a case history. Three years of tram tracks, elastic bands and the removal of eight teeth later, and I am a shining example of the orthodontist's art; but every time one of my children loses a milk tooth, I know it could cost far more than £1 for the tooth fairy.

The situation for adults is even worse. One friend, Victoria, was told that a crown would cost her £700 privately, the price of her summer holiday. The queue for an NHS dentist was so long that her tooth broke before it was treated and she had to spend £350 having it pulled out. She should have followed the example of the Wiltshire toothache sufferer who told the Citizens Advice Bureau that he now takes out many of his teeth in his shed – with pliers. More than one in 20 have said they resort to DIY surgery.

> ❝ **Those who can't afford the fees have worse teeth than ever before** ❞

There is, of course, the option to go private, but with more and more former NHS patients forced to pay, dentists' charges are now the most expensive in Europe.

Having bad teeth can blight your life. Britain used to be known for its terrible incisors. In Mexico, bad teeth are called "dientes ingles". But gradually we have caught up with America. Now bad teeth are now seen as unacceptably sloppy: no presenter would be allowed on children's television without a polished grin. Even Gordon Brown appeared to have had his teeth fixed before he became Prime Minister. As the public face of the nation's teeth has improved, so has the pressure on everyone else. As a country, we spend £360 million on cosmetic dentistry a year.

But there are increasingly two dental nations in Britain and those who can't afford the fees have worse teeth than ever before. With bad teeth, you are less likely to find a good job or a successful relationship. The elderly, in particular, can find their lives racked by toothache and an inability to eat properly. Gum disease also increases the risk of mouth cancer, and pancreatic cancer in men.

This is a deep-rooted problem that needs a drill taken to it. The Government should start by scrapping the new contract that it introduced for dentists in 2006. Dentists are now paid a fixed fee, in exchange for completing a certain number of units of NHS dental activity a year: the net result is that idle dentists never get round to seeing enough patients – and their funding is subsequently reduced – and energetic dentists are forced to look to the private sector for more work after they fill their quota. In 1990, only 6% of dentists' income came from private patients; now it's 58%. Worse, NHS dentists now receive the same amount of money for six fillings as for one, so there is no incentive to take on complex cases.

Our dentists are trained at a cost of £175,000 by the NHS, so they should be expected to work within the sector for a number of years. And we need more of them. America has twice as many per head as does Poland – half of whom are here. Britain only has 3.7 dentists per 10,000 people. Even if you find an NHS dentist, it's not all smiles: the cost of a filling has gone up from £14 to £43 in the past few years. The NHS budget has doubled in the past decade while dentistry decayed. The Government has finally started filling the financial gap but, as usual it has gone on bureaucracy.

Healthy teeth used to be seen as a sign of a modern society. Now because of our first-world diets and third-world dental care, we have 19th-century teeth. Britain has to take its teeth seriously again or we will soon be back to wooden dentures.

The Daily Telegraph, 18 January 2008
© Telegraph Group Limited 2008

"Make sure he goes private, will you. That impacted tooth is worth a good set of golf clubs at least."

THE ORGAN DONATION DEBATE IS LONG OVERDUE

The writer's husband – who had been diagnosed with cystic fibrosis at the age of three – was rushed to hospital after suddenly suffering from bleeding from his lungs. This is what happened next...

On 23 December 2006, against the odds, he was discharged home for Christmas. We were told he would re-bleed again. The question was when. The hope was to get a lung transplant before that happened.

My husband was given an appointment for a consultation with the transplant team in May 2007. It seemed to us a long, long time to wait, but I understand that the shortage of donor organs means the team has to be very selective in who goes on the list, finding a fine balance between the patient being ill enough to take the risk of transplantation and well enough to survive the procedure. The rehabilitation from having been in intensive care was hard enough. Living with the threat of a re-bleed was terrifying. He continued to have "small" (150ml) bleeds every few weeks. We employed a live-in nurse. I returned to work and, the day before his transplant assessment, got my first consultant post.

Living on the transplant list is a bit like being in suspended animation

After a day of investigations at the transplant centre, we met with the consultant, who described my husband's case as a "no brainer": he needed a lung transplant. He had turned his health around after the period in intensive care, and despite needing 24 hour oxygen, had returned to work, making a joke at the start of his lectures about going scuba diving. But we knew he would re-bleed again and that his chances of surviving another massive episode were slim. His case was fast tracked, and within a week of that consultation he was on the waiting list for a bilateral lung transplant.

Whether to consent is not a decision that can be made easily in those moments of intense shock and grief

Living on the transplant list is a bit like being in suspended animation. There is a need to live every day to the full, but also the sense of the hope of a new, different life hovering somewhere in the future. After a while you stop jumping every time the pager goes off or the phone rings. We followed stories of others who had had successful transplants and sadly of those who died before their call came. There is a guilt that comes from wishing for something that means someone else's demise. There is also a frustration at the statistics: it seems senseless that so many organs go undonated.

I would like to say that this story has a happy ending; that my husband was one of the lives saved every year by someone's gift of life. I would like to say that we have moved into the house we were in the process of buying, that he is taking a well earned sabbatical and will be returning to teaching next term. But I can't. After a series of major bleeds and two further periods in intensive care, he joined the hundreds of people each year who die awaiting organs. Despite the heroic efforts of the intensive care and transplant co-ordination team, there just weren't enough donor organs available to secure his survival.

When a loved one dies, so many things go through your mind. One thought has stayed with me. In the hours after my husband's death, I asked myself whether I would, if it had been possible, said yes to donating his organs. The honest answer is that I do not know if I would have been able to make that decision. I was confused, exhausted, and bereft, and in no state to make a decision about anything. Now, the answer to that question seems like a "no brainer," but at the time I was dazed.

That is why I think that the organ donation debate is long overdue. Whether to consent is not a decision that can be made easily in those moments of intense shock and grief, and my respect and admiration goes out to the families who have done so. No one likes to talk about death or to imagine their own ending or that of a loved one. The opt-out proposal will not mean that those who do not wish to donate their organs will have to do so, or that families will not have a choice. What it will mean is that everyone will be prompted to think about that choice, to make a decision and discuss it with their loved ones, rather than avoiding the issue and thinking, as is all too easy, "there but for the grace of God..."

British Medical Journal (BMJ)
2 February 2008 Vol. 336
The author is an NHS doctor

'Presumed consent' for organ donation is a good idea – no one mad with grief needs to make a decision

Michele Hanson

Gordon Brown is keen to have a system of "presumed consent" for organ donation. Good. He can have mine when I peg out. I want to give them away. But I suspect it's the relatives and friends who tend to balk at these procedures. I did when my father died. Not because someone wanted to transplant anything, but because they wanted to do a postmortem.

What a cheek, I thought. They couldn't be bothered to investigate properly while he was alive. Now they wanted to start poking about when he was dead. So I had a monster scream at the poor woman telling me, and tried to forbid the postmortem. I couldn't, but my little freak-out came as a surprise. I never knew I'd be so furious. But there is something frightful about someone you love being cut open and messed about, especially if they've already gone through hell – even if it will save someone else's life.

My friend Fielding said no to his mother being used for research, because she'd had a horrible time already, with one ulcerated leg and the other amputated. Fielding couldn't bear any more. It wasn't a rational decision, he just felt that she'd had enough. We had both taken what I think chief medical officer Sir Liam Donaldson means by the "default position". It was nothing to do with our true feelings on research or organ donation. More a half-crazed payback for how our relatives were treated in the run-up to death.

So "presumed consent" sounds like a good idea. Then no one needs to make sensible decisions when they're half mad with misery. Much easier to decide in advance. When I fade out, please take any useful bits. If this proposal goes ahead, I won't even need a donor card. I did have one once, but lost it. I think my purse was stolen. Then I never got round to replacing my card. What if I'd died? What a waste.

The Guardian 15 January 2008
© Guardian News & Media Ltd. 2008

... but some patients organisations are opposed

The Patients Association acknowledges the critical shortage of organs for lifesaving transplant operations. This has led to patients travelling abroad or paying for transplants, very often involving donors from third world countries. The idea of presumed consent for everyone has become interesting to clinicians dealing with patients who need transplants to survive.

We do understand that the number of people carrying organ donor cards does not represent the number of people who would be willing to donate an organ. Many of those who would be willing to donate simply haven't bothered or are not sufficiently motivated or aware.

Those with a strong desire not to be an organ donor would still have the right to opt out but we are not satisfied that the opt out always works for everyone. In an emergency situation in a busy Accident and Emergency department, having the right to opt out may still cause distress for families if the harvesting of organs takes place before they are able to pass on to the transplant team their knowledge that a patient did not wish to be a donor.

Director of Communications, Katherine Murphy said, "This could create some difficult problems; therefore we need a public campaign to raise awareness of refusal to be a donor and not a blanket decision taken for everyone. It is dangerous to presume patients' wishes at a time when difficult decisions need to be made immediately. It is not always possible to contact a next of kin in time so we must not take for granted that presumed consent for all is the answer."

The Patients Association
www.patients-association.org.uk

A boy called Alex

Photo: Matthew Whiteman

Alex, who has cystic fibrosis, aims to conduct Bach. This film – and his music – are glorious.

Nancy Banks-Smith

A Boy Called Alex (Cutting Edge, Channel 4) started on an unusually personal note. The director, Stephen Walker, said: "From the moment I met Alex Stobbs, I just knew we were going to get on." As a rule, how you feel about the subject of your film is beside the point, but Alex is quite extraordinarily likable.

There is, it seems to me, something of the Dudley Moores about him. So musical, so small, so ill and so overwhelmingly charming. This is a 16-year-old who plays the organ magnificently while wearing one orange and one purple sock. He is a choral scholar at Eton college, which comes very well out of the whole affair. Eton waives his fees, pays for his nurse, bought him an electric scooter to scoot around the cloisters, coat tails flying, and submits amiably to being bossed about by a boy.

The film is about Alex's determination to conduct the Bach Magnificat, a piece as glorious as it is strenuous, carrying teachers and teenagers along in his slipstream. It is also about the rocketing human

'In his next life, he'll be composing, playing cricket, doing all the things he can't do now'

spirit. Alex has cystic fibrosis, which, sooner or later, will kill him, but he is perpetually upbeat. "To enjoy stuff, you can't be scared. I love it when you read in the newspapers about people with CF doing so much. When I go into hospital you see so many forlorn little faces. You don't want to think like that. Get on with stuff."

His medication for a week covers a table. His pills for a day fill a plate. His body is relentlessly pummelled to shift the mucus that is drowning him. One side-effect of the medication is partial deafness. "It has," he said, "produced some comical moments." Twice during rehearsals he was rushed to hospital. Once when his nurse found him in the morning covered in blood – he hadn't, he said, wanted to bother anyone – and again when one of his surgical implants became infected.

'So musical, so small, so ill and so overwhelmingly charming'

His consultant at the Royal Brompton bowed to his determination to get back to Bach: "I'd as soon try to stop Niagara Falls with a stick of rock as try to stop Alex doing something he wanted to do." He knew feistiness helped to keep his patient alive. Alex's medication was redoubled for the concert. He needed 20 syringes of antibiotic daily, 70 pills and, this time, he needed his mother. "I think he really wants me around," she said, and, as she injected him, he looked at her with an expression I find painful to remember.

He did conduct The Magnificat and it went like a song. His mother said: "I have a profound belief that in his next life he'll be composing, playing cricket, doing the things he can't do now. And he'll be healthy." I found myself smiling to think that, if personality persists after death, the angelic choir, who probably have their own plans for the weekend, will find themselves singing as they have never sung before.

The Guardian 25 January 2008
© Guardian News & Media Ltd. 2008

What is Cystic Fibrosis?

- Cystic Fibrosis (CF) is the UK's most common life-threatening inherited disease.

- CF affects over 8,000 people in the UK.

- Over two million people in the UK carry the faulty gene that causes CF – around one in 25 of the population.

- If two carriers have children each child has a one in four chance of having CF, a one in two chance of being a carrier and a one in four chance of being unaffected.

- CF is caused by a single faulty gene that controls the movement of salt in the body.

- CF is a "multi-system" disease, meaning that it affects many body organs. However, most of the symptoms are to do with the lungs and the digestive system.

- In a healthy person, there is a constant flow of mucus over the surfaces of the air passages in the lungs. This removes debris and bacteria. If you have CF, this mucus is excessively thick and sticky and cannot perform this role properly.

- In a healthy person, digestive juices flow out from the pancreatic duct into the duodenum to digest food. In people with CF, thickened secretions block the normal flow of the digestive juices from the pancreas. This can result in food not being digested or absorbed properly.

- The sticky mucus also provides an ideal environment for bacterial growth. This can put a person with CF at risk of getting bacterial chest infections and pneumonia.

- Other symptoms of CF can include a troublesome cough, repeated chest infections, prolonged diarrhoea and poor weight gain (although these symptoms are not unique to CF).

- A combination of physiotherapy and medication can help control lung infections and prevent lung damage.

- Each week, five babies are born with CF.

- Each week, three young lives are lost to CF.

- Average life expectancy is around 31 years, although improvements in treatments mean a baby born today could expect to live for longer.

- If you have a family history of CF, you can be tested to see if you carry the CF gene before you have a family.

For more info go to:
www.cftrust.org.uk

'IT'S WORSE THAN A CRIMINAL RECORD'

Laura Marcus was hospitalised after a serious nervous breakdown. But that was more than 30 years ago – so why do so many people still make a big deal of it?

There was a time when, if you had seen me on your bus, you would have moved to the other end or got off at the next stop, even if it was miles from your destination. We often joke about the loony on the top deck; well, I was that loony. I spoke to you because I knew you were talking about me – and you wanted me to respond, didn't you?

How terrifying it must have been to find yourself sitting next to me. Or see me loom towards you, eyes wild, my huge presence offering you no

evening classes three nights a week in the hope of a better life. One of the books I studied was George Orwell's 1984, and somehow I got the events at the end of 1974 mixed up with 1984. I started to think everyone was talking in doublespeak. They couldn't speak the truth because there was danger everywhere.

In fact, in December 1974, there really was. This was when the IRA bombing campaign on the mainland was at its greatest, and in my job as a secretary, I had to take all the post to

because I felt compelled to do so. No one ever knew if I would turn up when or where I was expected to. I went missing a lot.

After a few weeks of this very strange behaviour, my friends, my then boyfriend and my parents realised something had gone wrong, so one night, when I was on a trip back to the family home, they called an ambulance. As I was whisked away, I could hear my father killing himself laughing. I always thought people were laughing at me. It was

BEING A FORMER NUTTER DOESN'T MAKE YOU ONE FOR EVER

escape route. I wasn't violent; nor did I ever threaten violence. I didn't need to – I just talked people to death.

Why? Well, without me noticing, my life had become extremely stressful. I was 18 and felt, as teenagers often do, that I had time in my day for anything. So, as well as working full-time with a two-hour daily commute, I was taking A-level

the nearest post office as all the letter boxes were sealed. Then, far more than now, we really were living in times ruled by terrorists.

So my imagined dystopia felt very real. But it was more exciting than scary – I wasn't depressed, I was thrilled. I was starring in my own movie, taking train and bus journeys that went goodness knows where

only later that I found out he hadn't been laughing. He was crying his eyes out.

They took me to Holloway sanatorium in the posh Surrey village of Virginia Water. There were nurses in uniform and, to someone of sound mind, this was clearly a hospital. But I knew they were trying to fool me. It was called Holloway, duh! So I assumed I was in the women's prison of the same name. I had been found out, just as I always knew I would be. But I wouldn't tell them a thing.

And this gothic pile did look like a prison. My youngest brother, on his first visit to see me, christened the place Colditz. In fact, it was nothing of the kind. Holloway sanatorium had always been known locally, and with incredible affection, as "the Sanny". It was in the National Health system and as well as providing sanctuary for the mentally ill, it was an important employer. It had always been a sanatorium but, when built 100 years earlier, provided asylum for the rich only.

illness is never spent. "To complete applications accurately and fairly," the Association of British Insurers later told me, "insurance companies need to know all medical information." The spokesman admitted, however, that "this may seem inconvenient – unnecessary in some cases".

I shouldn't be surprised any more – this happens every time I apply for any kind of health or life cover. It even happened when I applied for a provisional driving licence, nearly 20 years after my breakdown. I disclosed my mental illness on the application form, thinking it couldn't possibly make any difference. It did. They told me I would have to wait before

Mental healthcare can be a positive experience. During the two months I was there, the Sanny was a true sanctuary from a world that had clearly become too much. I was lucky enough to have my psychotic episode when we still had decent healthcare for the mentally ill. Not only was I admitted, as a voluntary patient, to this lovely old building with its occupational therapy unit, cricket pavilion, tennis courts and sumptuous grounds, but I was on a ward full of other young people and we were encouraged to share our experiences, socialise and go for walks in the nearby woods as part of our recovery. So I look back on that time with great

I HAVE DONE NOTHING WRONG – JUST GOT SICK, ONCE

Why am I writing about this now? Last week I decided to get some more life assurance. I have no dependants but I do have a partner, and making sure he's financially OK if something suddenly happened to me seems a sensible, loving thing to do. I went through the formalities over the phone, saying no to every illness I was asked about till, "Have you ever had a mental illness?" Well, yes, I replied, but it was a very long time ago and I've never had a relapse. Sorry, they said, we can't proceed with the application till you've filled in a further questionnaire. I pointed out that a criminal record wouldn't have been an issue. The embarrassed operator agreed, saying that insurance companies regard minor criminal records as "spent" after eight years. But mental

getting my provisional licence while medical check-ups were carried out. So it was another three months before I could even take a driving lesson.

I have done nothing wrong – just got sick, once. I was briefly unable to handle the social cues that most people take for granted; that's why I talked to total strangers on buses. But society seems to be as terrified of mental illness in 2008 as it was in the days of Bedlam. So it must be disclosed whenever you fill in a health form. I'm self-employed, but if I applied for a job and didn't disclose what happened 30 years ago I could be fired if it was later found out – not because of my illness but for lying. Tell the truth, though, and who would employ you? So mental illness tends to stay hidden, as if it was shameful.

fondness, gratitude even, but certainly not shame. The Victorians got a lot of things wrong in their attitude towards mental health but their asylums were intended to be, and often were, just that.

The Sanny, however, is no more. Like many former asylums, it has been converted into luxury flats. As a sop to English Heritage, there are open days when you can see the stunning architecture and gawp at the great hall where I once took my meals.

I mind very much that the shadow of the Sanny still hangs over me because various authorities won't let me forget, but I mind even more that the place is no longer a sanctuary for those who need it. And I wish there was more education about mental illness. Being a former nutter – as many of us are happy to describe ourselves, whatever polite euphemism might be expected – doesn't make you one for ever. And far from being risky prospects when it comes to insurance, or driving, perhaps we are quite the opposite. Our experiences have given us a heightened awareness of the symptoms, so we know what to watch out for – something that surely makes us less of a risk than many stressed-out people who could be on the verge of a breakdown at any minute.

We've shut down all the Victorian asylums; isn't it time we shut down our stupid Victorian attitudes to mental illness as well?

The Guardian 11 February 2008
© Guardian News & Media Ltd. 2008

Depression - the 21st century plague

One in four British adults experience at least one diagnosable mental health problem in any one year. It's time we lifted the lid on the taboo of mental health, allowing those who suffer to come out of the shadows. With so many people suffering, why should they remain in silence?

Depression - THE FACTS:

- 10% of children aged between one and 15 have a mental health disorder.

- Estimates vary, but research suggests that between 8-12% of the population and 20% of children experience a mental health problem in any given year.

- Rates of mental health problems among children increase as they reach adolescence.

- One in four women will require treatment for depression at some time, compared to 1 in 10 men. The reasons for this are thought to be due to both social and biological factors. It has also been suggested that depression in men may have been under diagnosed because they present to their GP with different symptoms.

- British men are three times as likely as British women to die by suicide.

- Suicide remains the most common cause of death in men under the age of 35.

Information from the Mental Health Foundation

Depression - THE FEELINGS:

Case study – Anonymous

I am in my mid twenties and live near the Scottish borders where I work with people who suffer from mental health problems. I work with other sufferers because I hope that I can share the experiences I've had with depression, to help others survive it too.

It's hard for me to pinpoint exactly when it started. Depression seemed to creep over me gradually by the time I was 12-13. Nothing bad had happened to me, I had friends and wasn't getting bullied, my schoolwork was fine and I'd previously always got on with my family. Yet for some reason I seemed to always feel lonely and anxious, constantly on the outside of things, different from everyone else.

These feelings affected the way I was with people. The worse I felt the more I shut out my family and friends and treated them badly. The arguments and fall-outs only worsened things, making me believe that I wasn't a nice person. How could I be if I felt so bad and treated those I loved so awfully?

This behaviour was totally self-destructive. Eventually I felt so low that I started to drink and harm myself. This seemed to offer me some release, but really it just added to my problems. I got involved with people who were no good for me. I truly felt I deserved no better, and the worse people treated me, the more this was confirmed in my head.

My schoolwork started to suffer yet I had no enthusiasm to make any of it better even though I felt so much pain and was hurting those around me. I felt as though my life was being lived in front of my eyes but I had no part in it. I began to frequently think about suicide. I functioned just well enough for those around me to think I was just going through particularly awful teenage mood swings.

When I was nearly twenty, I read an article about people who had suffered from depression. These feeling were so much a part of me, I had never thought that maybe I didn't need to feel them. I went to my doctor who prescribed anti-depressants. Within a couple of months, I felt as though a lead cloud had been lifted from me. Anti-depressants are not magic, and, in most cases, not a long-term solution. However, they allowed me to see things more clearly and start making positive decisions about my life. I decided I should also seek help from a counsellor and at last I began to see a way forward.

I've been free from depression for five years now, although I'm realistic and know that I have a 50-50 chance of dipping into it again. But I do not live in fear of this. I try to look after my mental health as much as possible. If I ever feel low or like I can't manage things alone, I visit my counsellor or open up to my family and friends. I know that depression is treatable, and as soon as I open up and look for help, I step out of its shadows and back into my life.

For further information go to:
www.mentalhealth.org.uk

When the subject is suicide, reporting on it requires the utmost sensitivity

Deborah Orr

In Norway, which has a low suicide rate but has experienced a rise in male suicide that prompts comparison with Britain and the US, the media is forbidden from reporting on suicide at all.

This is an extreme measure, as reporting on suicide, responsibly undertaken, can be positive. All those who champion the freedom of the press need to keep this under consideration.

There has been a great deal of reporting about suicide in the press this week. There has been speculation about the tragic death of the actor Heath Ledger. There have been background reports about the trial of John Hogan, who jumped, with his two children in his arms, from a hotel balcony in Crete, killing his son. Most disturbingly, there has been fanciful elaboration about a cluster of suicides among young people in Bridgend, South Wales, including lurid suggestions that they may have been part of an "internet suicide cult". Yet what seems to have been lost this week is awareness that the reporting of suicide is a very sensitive business in itself.

The MediaWise Trust, which promotes responsible journalism, offers good advice on how suicide can be reported carefully. It is important to do so, because it is well documented that, unless it is assembled with caution, media coverage of suicide can itself promote fatal self-harm. For example, there were 22 suicides on the Vienna underground after a single case was exhaustively and sensationally covered in 1986. The figures fell dramatically after the press voluntarily agreed to limit coverage.

The Trust advises that "sensational headlines, images and language" should be avoided in the coverage of suicide, not only out of respect for grieving relatives, who tend to find the invasion of their privacy deeply unhelpful, but also out of an understanding that imitation is a genuine hazard. The suicides of a shocking number of young people in a brief period of time in one location may be newsworthy. But it is pretty paradoxical that the internet is being openly discussed as a trigger for the spate, when

any form of communication that brings suicide to wide prominence, can usher in the same results. Weird "spikes" in suicide patterns are not rare. A tiny village in Northern Ireland suffered the suicides of three teenage boys in 2007, while a Staffordshire village with a population of 5,000 also recently lost six people to suicide in a year.

Such spikes, more than anything else, stand testament to the insidious suggestibility of hearing about a suicide. The suicide of a friend or of a family member is well understood to be one of the most major triggers for attempted suicide, alongside, mental illness, drug or alcohol dependence and a record of previous attempts.

Widespread reporting of, and speculation about, a cluster of suicides is understandable. The subject is grotesquely fascinating and, of course, we are likely to be drawn towards reports of suicides by people we do not know, and feel sympathy but not real grief for. In the case of Hogan, there has been a lot of talk about his situation and background, some of it extremely dubious and even spiteful.

MediaWise advises that "prominent figures are entitled to privacy, even if they kill themselves", and says that speculation about the cause of a death or the events leading up to it should not be entered into. In Ledger's case, that

guidance has most certainly not been followed, even though a big story about a single suicide can have disturbing consequences. In Australia, a 1995 study found rates of male suicide increased after a suicide was reported, with attempts peaking three days after the first report.

In both the US and Britain, young male suicide has been on the increase for many years, and doubled between 1971 and 1998. Men make up 75% of suicides, and suicides among young men are still increasing. Interestingly, the US and Britain are almost the only countries to have recorded a strong disparity between genders, with the suicide rate almost halving for women over the same period that it almost doubled for men.

It is tempting to attribute such figures to the huge changes in gender roles, especially as the men most vulnerable to suicide tend, statistically, to be working in low-skilled employment or not working at all. Yet even these figures don't respond well to glib analysis. Many more women attempt suicide but tend to opt for "unreliable" methods such as overdoses. Men are more likely to choose a method that is more violent and more decisive. All of this is worth bearing in mind as we absorb speculative coverage of suicide reports of all kinds.

The Independent 26 January 2008

Venturing into the pro-suicide pit

The most startling thing about the vile, venal websites that promote suicide is that their language and outlook appear entirely mainstream.

By Brendan O'Neill

'I continuously want to kill myself. I have tried but have never been successful. I do not know what to do.' 'SOD' is desperate. According to a comment he or she posted on one of the internet's most notorious pro-suicide websites, he or she is seriously sick of life and wants a way out, a 'final exit', a foolproof form of 'self-deliverance'. It isn't long before ghoulish pro-suicide surfers descend on SOD's query, like voyeurs around a car crash that has yet to take place, and offer him or her some bloodcurdling advice.

When death comes to a country village

As anyone whose online surfing has ever gone astray will know, there is a great deal of vile, venal material on the World Wide Web. But the smattering of pro-suicide websites – sinister, garishly-designed advice hubs for the depressed, sick and properly nihilistic – takes things to another level. Here, people who are actually suicidal seek practical and spiritual advice from 'suicide experts', and from surfers who seem to have a perverse interest in discussing suicide methods and their bloody impact on the human body in graphic, salacious detail. These sites are modern meeting places for the depressed and the deranged, where a community of commenters goad each other into taking the final step towards the 'ultimate freedom' – that is, non-existence, blackness, the end of all life, hardship, bad feelings and tough choices.

Yet perhaps the most disturbing thing about these sites is how mainstream they sound. They use the language of mainstream pro-euthanasia outfits and charities, and much of the pro-suicide surfers' disgust for life – both for their own life and also for the idea of human life itself – is heavily influenced by today's misanthropic view of people as a plague and a drain on the planet.

Sanctioning death

Possibly against my better judgement, I decided to venture into this darkest, most morally vacuous corner of the World Wide Web to find out how influential pro-death websites actually are. Visiting these sites, some of which positively celebrate the pleasures of self-destruction and advise the suicidal to 'leave no trace behind' so that 'your stupid family' will spend the rest of their days wondering what happened to you, makes one feel both pity and nausea – pity for the genuine commenters who clearly need to seek serious medical attention rather than submit themselves to the judgement of cheering and jeering pro-suicide death-merchants, and nausea at some of the detailed tips, and accompanying photographs, provided by the pro-suicide lobby.

Yet for all of their self-proclaimed edginess and snuff pretensions, many of these sites are parasitical on mainstream advice and arguments. A pro-suicide site hosted by a Satanist-leaning online outfit gets many of its practical tips from a book by a well-known pro-euthanasia campaigner which offers how-to tips on committing suicide for terminally ill people. Its writer is a mainstream journalist and author who is extremely influential in respectable pro-euthanasia circles on both sides of the Atlantic. Another of the most graphic and ruthless pro-suicide websites lists his work alongside British pro-euthanasia groups in its Bibliography/ Sources. These foul pro-suicide sites arouse handwringing horror in the press – yet frequently they come across like 'mirror sites' for respectable pro-euthanasia organisations, which often win accolades and sympathy in the press for their 'brave campaigning' for the right to die.

Death networking: the latest e-trend

Pro-euthanasia groups will argue that their advice is aimed solely at terminally ill people, and that they have no control over how their material is used and abused by pro-suicide websites. The author of the quoted work wrote: 'In its first 10 years, this book was occasionally used by persons for whom it was not intended – the deeply depressed and the mentally ill. This misuse I regret but can do nothing about. [Some] of us do not have the emotional and intellectual equipment to cope with a lifetime of troubles... and elect to die. Self-destruction of a physically fit person is always a tragic waste of life and hurtful to survivors, but life is a personal responsibility. We must each decide for ourselves.'

This kind of language, which almost normalises suicide as an understandable reaction to hardship, is also widespread on pro-suicide websites. Users argue that they cannot 'emotionally cope' with life or their parents or school, and so they have 'elected to die', or have opted for 'self-deliverance' – the PC phrase for suicide – over perseverance in the face of life's difficulties. Both the public, celebrated campaigns for the right to die and the hidden, derided pro-suicide networks on the web believe that death is a legitimate response to trial and tribulation, whether of the physical or the emotional variety.

Pro-suicide websites also reproduce the language of the euthanasia lobby. Some sites describe themselves as 'pro-choice' rather than 'pro-suicide', and they talk about the 'right to die' or the 'right to commit suicide'. Here, surfers borrow heavily from the euthanasia lobby's transformation of the debate about death into a discussion of 'choice' and 'rights'. Some of the sites also insist that no one should pass judgement against suicidal visitors, but instead should 'accept their decision' and 'encourage the choice they have made' – this normally translates into a free-for-all goading of the suicidal visitor to finish himself off. Yet this is only a more sinister expression of what is a key policy for a mainstream charity like the Samaritans, which also takes a non-judgemental approach, 'Callers remain responsible for their own lives and do not lose the right to make decisions, even if that decision is to take their own life.' Precisely the same rules apply on most pro-suicide websites.

Suicide and environmentalism

Other suicide websites seem to thrive on today's deep-green outlook, which says that the planet is overpopulated and humanity is a diseased mass destroying his natural environment. One US-based, green-leaning, massively misanthropic, population-control group, runs one of the most notorious pro-suicide websites. Its arguments about a 'plague' of human beings overrunning the Earth echo the views of

rather than on putting the case for life, for celebrating the birth of more people, for looking at what is positive in the human experience. In Britain, charity and media guidelines on the reporting of suicide warn media outlets to avoid giving 'excessive detail' about how an individual committed suicide. Unable morally to challenge suicide, or to put the argument against today's widespread green and pro-death misanthropy, the powers-that-be simply seek to remove 'how to' guidelines and hope that this will be enough to put people off suicide. In fact, it only highlights their own inability to assert what is potentially wonderful and meaningful about human life.

'It just seems normal, fashionable almost...'

The end of stigma

The most striking thing that pro-suicide websites and the suicide-concerned mainstream share in common is their belief that suicide should be de-stigmatised. One website slams the 'stigma and ignorance' that surrounds suicide and calls for it to be seen as something rational, as a 'choice'. This echoes the arguments of virtually every mental health charity in Britain and America today, which have uniformly demanded over the past 20 years that the stigma attached to suicide be removed so that we can talk about it more openly. An open and honest debate about suicide would, of course, be welcome. But the main consequence of the campaign to de-stigmatise suicide today, in a time when human life is devalued, has been to normalise it, to present it as an acceptable and even respectable response to personal difficulty.

Webcam showed father's suicide

Stigmatisation in the past no doubt made suicidal people feel isolated, and may have stopped them from seeking help. Yet it also sent a clear message

every mainstream NGO, government organisation and environmentalist campaign group – that if we don't do something drastic to reduce human numbers, then nature will do it for us.

Some European pro-suicide websites celebrate the deep-green thinking of Pekka-Eric Auvinen, the 18-year-old Finn who shot seven people in his school in November last year. They reproduce Auvinen's video testimonies and manifestos in which he argued, among other things, that 'the most central and irrational faith among people is the faith in technology and economical growth', and '[the fact] that there are billions of people over 60kg on this planet is recklessness'. In one Auvinen video, the words 'I wish that death to mankind comes soon' are flashed up. Again, these ideas – that belief in economic growth is seriously misplaced and the planet is overpopulated by overweight people – are entirely mainstream today. The pro-suicide websites take them to their frighteningly logical conclusion by encouraging people to do something about the state of our world: kill yourself.

The focus of those concerned about pro-suicide websites is always narrowly on limiting access to practical information

about the value of life and the ability of humans to overcome terrible obstacles and start afresh. Today, suicide is likely to be discussed as a non-stigmatising personal choice which should be respected; some leading commentators even describe it as brave and courageous. Few think about the impact that suicide has on 'the community', both on the local community and family that is directly affected by an individual's death, and also on the wellbeing and outlook of the broader community if suicide – the final exit, self-deliverance, self-termination – is relativistically accepted as something normal, even honourable.

Pro-suicide websites look to me like the end product of today's normalisation of suicide. In these online arenas, suicide is completely free from stigma, and is openly discussed as a choice, even a 'pleasure', something that will 'free us' from mental and emotional distress or from our selfish destruction of the planet. Banning such sites will achieve precisely nothing – we would do better to challenge the mainstream, above-board culture of fatalism that these sites feverishly feast upon.

Brendan O'Neill is editor of spiked. Visit the website here.
http://www.spiked-online.com
spiked 25 February 2008

NO FUSS, NO FANFARE FOR SPAIN'S OWN MADELEINE

Contrasts with media treatment of McCann case highlighted in disappearance of young Gypsy girl

Paul Hamilos

When Mari Luz Cortés disappeared near her home in Huelva on 13 January, it was perhaps inevitable that comparisons would be made with Madeleine McCann. Five-year-old Mari Luz went missing as she returned from buying a packet of crisps at a local shop. British journalists based in Praia da Luz, the Portuguese holiday resort where Madeleine was last seen, joined the dots between the two stories and drove 200km (120 miles) across the border to the quiet Spanish town. Was she, they wanted to know, the victim of Madeleine's abductor?

The Spanish press has resisted the temptation to label Mari Luz 'Madeleine Two', but there are signs that the eight-month media circus surrounding the missing British girl has changed the way such disappearances are reported. Lola Galán, a writer and former correspondent at El País newspaper, says that in Spain there is no daily tabloid press, so reporting tends to be straighter, but she fears that 'the Spanish press is becoming more like the British – more competitive, with more space for populist stories. This is true of the afternoon television shows as well, which have a similar level of aggression as the tabloid press in the UK.'

Nevertheless, the disappearance of Mari Luz has received nothing like the coverage dedicated to Madeleine. In part, this is because there is less mystery: her parents have not been accused of any involvement and the family wasn't on holiday in a foreign country. This has also removed the element of culture shock that was a key part of the Spanish and Portuguese reaction to the McCanns. Many could

Mari Luz Cortés above, vanished from her home on 13 January. Her parents have poured out their grief to the media

not understand why the family were not showing more emotion in public. To them, the outpouring of grief in Huelva is more comprehensible than the apparent reserve of the McCanns. Indeed, this British reserve may have been one reason that so many people were prepared to believe that the McCanns were involved in their daughter's disappearance.

'It's what the Spanish say whenever there is a strange case: the British are involved. We still think of the British as being eccentric,' says Galán.

Mari Luz comes from a Gypsy family, which has prompted speculation that prejudice may be behind the relative lack of media attention given to the story. The McCanns appeared to be the perfect family and Madeleine's photogenic looks soon became the international image of their personal tragedy. It shouldn't happen, the message seemed to be, to a family like this. The Cortés family, on the other hand, comes from a tough neighbourhood, where crime and drugs are a problem. Some believe that Mari Luz's disappearance might be connected to a feud between two families, or a settling of accounts, and that these are the sorts of things that happen between Gypsies.

But Macarena Orte of Korpa news agency, which produced a TV special on Madeleine McCann, believes the explanation is simpler: 'In the Madeleine case, the family has access to lots of money. In Huelva they are Gypsies and don't have the money to put together a marketing campaign, so they cannot ensure they are on TV and in the papers all the time.'

Even so, Mari Luz's parents have been learning from the McCanns' publicity team, says Manuel Albert, a local reporter covering the story. 'They produced badges featuring the girl's face and the telephone number to call. There are posters everywhere and a website with a bank account where you can contribute to the cost of the search for Mari Luz,' he says.

All of this has been on a far smaller scale, though, with the website thus far having raised *6,000 (£4,467), compared with the £1m raised by the McCanns. Each day the family has organised a press conference outside their house, which has ensured a certain level of interest, although Albert admits that, two weeks on, that has begun to wane.

Like the McCanns, the Cortés family is unwilling to do simply what they are told by the police. They want to take a more active role – hiring their own detectives, organising press coverage and encouraging public support.

Demonstrations in support of the family have been held across Spain, but

Look into my eyes!
Madeleine McCann was abducted from Praia Da Luz, Portugal on 03/05/2007

Should you have any information please contact Crimestoppers UK 0800 555111

A huge media campaign has kept the story of missing Madeleine McCann in the public eye

they have been low-key affairs. Indeed the father, Juan José, a footballer-turned-builder, said he was upset when he learnt that no representative from either the government or the royal family was attending the rally in Madrid. There have certainly been no high-profile visits to the US First Lady, Laura Bush, or TV adverts with footballers David Beckham and Cristiano Ronaldo calling for Mari Luz's safe return. The McCanns flew to Rome for a special audience with the Pope, but the Cortés family is relying on the support of the less well-known Evangelical church.

In any case, the media attention devoted to missing children will inevitably fall away. There are 200 open cases of missing children in Spain alone. According to Rocío Ríos at Antena 3 TV station: 'We made a number of programmes about the McCanns, but Madeleine was the big news story of 2007, whereas we will all have forgotten about Huelva very soon.' After all, she says, a little boy called Yeremi went missing in Gran Canaria just a few weeks before Madeleine, and who talks about him now?

The Observer 27 January 2008
© Guardian News & Media Ltd 2008

STOP PRESS
The body of Mari Luz Cortés was discovered on 7th March 2008. Portuguese detectives have completed their investigation on Madeleine's disappearance but the McCann's private search continues.

FACE UP TO FACTS

HOW THE THINGS THAT SEEM LIKE FUN COULD COMPROMISE YOUR FUTURE

Why not show your employer the photos of you and your mates at that party? Or tell your mum details of your love life? And while you're at it, hand out a few revealing pictures of yourself to a thousand strangers. It sounds unthinkable – but it's just what people do when they allow unlimited access to their social networking sites.

As many as 4.5 million young people have information on the net which they would not want a college, university or potential employer to see – but almost six in 10, have never thought about how what they put online now could come back to haunt them. Even those who are alert to the problem are finding that

"I had a blog a couple of years ago and want to delete it – but I can't, and I had personal details on it!"
(female, 16 Yorks)

embarrassing entries and photos can be very hard to remove. As internet searches are becoming part of recruitment procedures, some young people should be very worried about the electronic footprint they are leaving behind!

"Potential employers could 'google' you and it could give embarrassing information etc"
(male, 16, NW)

The Information Commissioner's Office (ICO) was set up to promote access to official information and to protect personal information. It conducted a survey of 2,000 14-21 year olds and found that most of them were astonishingly relaxed about the amount of information they shared with any virtual passer-by.

Two thirds of young people accept 'friends' on social networking sites that they actually don't know. And, as there is competition to have the most 'friends,' over half leave parts of their profile public specifically to attract new people.

For any fraudster, the personal data on social networking sites can be a goldmine. Date of birth? Yes, there it is in 60% of cases. Job title? Yes a quarter will give you that. Home address? You can get that from nearly one in 10. You can access details that might be used to create passwords eg sibling's name (posted by 23%) pet's

"It sort of scares me to think that what I've written at my age now (17) may come back to haunt me in later years. I did not know this."
(female, 17, NW)

BE SAFE AND SECURE

> "Really annoying, a search on google brings up stuff I put online when I was really young and I can't get rid of it."
> *(male, 16, SE)*

name (posted by a quarter of girls) and even mother's maiden name (posted by 2%). Just the information you need to buy goods or access bank accounts.

Although 95% of those surveyed feel very strongly about their details being passed on to advertisers – Facebook faced a user revolt over just this issue – many young people don't bother reading privacy policies and don't understand how they can manage their personal information.

> "Initial thoughts – who cares? Subsequent thoughts – omg!!!"
> *(female, 14, Scotland)*

Embarrassment and data fraud are not the only risks on the internet. The Child Exploitation and Online Protection Centre (CEOP) is a multi-agency organisation dedicated to preventing offenders using the relative anonymity of the internet to approach, groom and ultimately abuse young people. The CEOP has some particular concerns about internet use.

Their research suggests that one in four of young people are meeting people offline who they originally 'met' online. 83% of them take a friend along – perhaps for safety – but in doing so they are also putting more children at risk. Online chat and instant messenging are still the most reported areas for abuse and grooming is the most frequently reported activity. However social networking, together with online gaming, are new areas where a potential threat exists. As user generated content increases, more children are putting themselves at risk through their postings.

HOW TO AVOID RISK AND EMBARRASSMENT

Be careful what information you give out...

It's important to know who your friends really are. Remember that you don't know who your friend's friends are... or your friend's friends' friends! And you don't know what they'll do with the pictures, phone number or personal details you put on your site.

If there's something you wouldn't be comfortable printing and handing out on the street, then maybe it shouldn't be on your profile – because once it's there, it's out there forever and you won't be able to get it back or control what your 'friends' do with it.

Reputation is everything – what seems funny to you and your friends now might be not be to your teachers, university admissions tutor or prospective employer – or to you in years to come.

Don't blag in your blog

Remember – a blog is for life – if you don't want your thoughts and feelings to be accessible to people in 10 years time, don't post them.

Don't give too much away. Yes, tell the world you're going to a party on Saturday night. But don't post details of where it is.

You could use a nickname or your initials instead of your name if you don't want just anyone knowing who you are. Consider changing your photo to a cool graphic.

Be careful who you agree to accept...

Be careful who you agree to accept into your forums/private chat areas. You're safer to only chat to people you know in the real world.

Know where to go for help...

If you feel anyone is being weird, bullying or abusive contact the administrator of the chat area. If they don't get back to you – you might want to think twice about using the site again.

If it's really serious, report the issue on www.thinkuknow.co.uk using the red reporting button.

Things to think through:

USE your Privacy Settings! Adjust your account settings so only friends that you actually know and accept can instant message you.

CHOOSE sites that give you plenty of control over who can find your profile and how much information they can see. Read privacy policies and understand how sites will use your details.

ONLY upload pictures that you'd be happy for your parents to see – anything too sexy to be passed round the dinner table should NOT make it onto the web, as you don't know who could be looking at it or what they might do with it.

DON'T post your phone number or email address – why would anyone actually need this info when they can message you privately via your social networking site?

DON'T allow people to work out your real life location such as your school, place of work or your usual hours.

DON'T post pictures of you or your mates wearing school uniform – people can work out where you are from it. What you tell people online will affect your personal safety offline.

TICK the "no pic forwarding" option on your MySpace settings page – this will stop people forwarding your pictures to anyone without your consent.

Be password protected

Change your passwords regularly, don't use obvious things like your pet's name, your year of birth or your full name. Don't use the same passwords on social networking sites as you do for things like internet banking.

Sources: Information Commissioner's Office, CEOP

I was dumped on Facebook

Samuel Pinney	
Sex	Male
Relationship Status	Dumped

When a relationship goes sour, it doesn't happen behind closed doors any more. Now it takes place in the middle of the village square of cyberspace. Facebook users can conduct their break-ups online, recording every slanging match for posterity on their 'walls'. If you're dumped on Facebook, everyone in your list of friends is instantly notified of your new status: 'Single'.

Breaking up in cyberspace adds a new dimension to heartache, says Samuel Pinney

I started getting clues that I might be about to become a free man when my girlfriend's friends posted messages to her that read: "Good luck with tonight – it's for the best." When she told me she wanted to talk to me, I knew it wasn't just the usual telling-off about how I ate toast in the wrong way or didn't wash up with enough feeling – both subjects of previous lectures. The break-up talk was, if anything, rather amicable: she said it was over, I asked if I could keep the plants. It would also have been fairly painless, had it not been for the unexpected horrors of social networking that were to follow.

First came the announcement online of my new 'Single' status. Deftly inserted into Facebook's running newsfeed, it informed everyone that both she and I knew that I had been dumped, in much the same way that Reuters proclaims the engagement of a minor Royal. There was no way of deleting it, so it sat there haunting me.

Next were the wall posts. If you are linked to someone on Facebook you are informed of interesting events in their lives. I got a dozen notices telling me that my now ex-girlfriend's friends had posted messages to her that read: "Congratulations!"

I thought things couldn't get worse, and they would soon tire of the news and move on. But then her status updates started to tell a story. Just three days after we broke up, she changed hers to: "2008, new job (check), new flat (check), new man (working on it)."

So I did the honourable thing and erased her from my Friends list; after all we weren't really friends any more and I didn't want to hear about how she was wearing her lucky underwear on a date that night.

It doesn't end there: social networking sites enable people to obsessively check on their ex-partners. I have a female chum who carefully investigates everyone who becomes friends with the ex-love of her life. If they are female and attractive, her cyberstalking goes into hyperdrive. It's not really her fault – she was dumped by this man via Facebook.

It's not just social networking sites: now everything you fought over can be spilled across the internet. Blogs are the new battleground for revenge; they enable you to tell your version of events like an exclusive in Heat magazine. Your ex's blog may only be read by five and half people, but you still don't really want them telling complete strangers how you were unable to put the loo seat down and never really gave the choosing of shelves the attention it deserved, and how these things were symptomatic of your lack of commitment to the relationship.

It makes me think that our grandparents had an easier time. If one of their relationships went bad they could always go to sea – or at least the next village – and never see that person again. They didn't have to fight for custody of the internet. They never had it so good.

Daily Telegraph 11 February 2008
© Telegraph Group 2008

PRAVDA'S BEEF WITH VEGETARIANISM

Seriously... True tales of a mixed up world

The glory days of Pravda – the infamous propaganda rag of the USSR's Communist Party – are long since gone. But even though the newspaper officially came to an end in 1991, in true communist fashion, a number of splinter groups emerged proclaiming to be the one true Pravda. This includes the internet outfit over at http://pravda.ru, which is run by former Pravda employees who still fume over the 'Greek swindlers' who run that other Pravda.

Freed from the shackles of Soviet censorship, the group has fully embraced the Western media model and is now free to give the proletariat the real hard-hitting news that they were, for so long, denied: celebrity gossip, sensationalist appeals to national pride and thoughtful and informative columns such as 'funny strange bizarre and sex news stories'. But the staff at Seriously – being the deeply serious people that we are – prefer to read Pravda's rigorous scientific analysis such as their recent exposé on the dangers of vegetarianism. Here are Pravda's (which means 'The Truth' in Russian) penetrating insights:

'Vegetarians can be referred to as true fanatics. On the other hand, they are seriously misled in their beliefs. Practically nobody argues with them, since it is really difficult to convince a vegetarian of his or her self-deception. Maybe that is the reason why the vegetarian movement develops so actively around the globe and continues to recruit many new members.'

Look out Tom Cruise, here come the Vegetologists!

> **"...a typical vegetarian has dry and fragile hair, dull eyes and an unhealthy complexion... They raise their voice, swing their arms and splutter when arguing"**

'Furthermore, cosmetologists say that a typical vegetarian has dry and fragile hair, dull eyes and an unhealthy complexion. They can hardly stand criticism and have a low boiling point. They raise their voice, swing their arms and splutter when arguing.'

Yes, it's true that vegetarians boil at lower temperatures, but the spluttering only happens when shallow frying on a high heat and that can be easily solved by judicious use of a lid. Deep-frying avoids this problem altogether.

Thanks to our comrades at Pravda for keeping the flame of independent and carnivorous journalism alive. We salute you!

New Internationalist, March 2008

> **"Vegetarians can be referred to as true fanatics. On the other hand, they are seriously misled in their beliefs."**

Petrov, with this article on the evils of steamed vegetables, you have dealt a mighty blow against the forces of degenerate liberalism.

'It's about who's more powerful than who. That's why people kill each other.'

They've dealt drugs, carried guns, knives and axes and seen their friends killed. And they're still only teenagers. Tom de Castella talks to a former gangster about life – and death – on our city streets.

Michael, 17:

I arrived from Ghana when I was about 10. Growing up in Brixton was hard, my mum couldn't help me out cos she was working night and day. At secondary school I was a target to pick on cos I couldn't speak English properly. It got to the point where I flipped and anyone who tried anything I used my strength against.

I'm 17 now, and when I look back our intention wasn't to become a gang, we were just children mucking about. We grew up on the same estate, came back from school and ended up playing together. As we grew up, more friends started joining and we got bigger and bigger. Age 14 and 15 it changed. We started being lunatic; robbing handbags and phones. That's when the name starts coming up – MZ. Murder Zone, my crew. Back in the day everyone from here to Croydon and Peckham knew about MZ.

Being around people that sell drugs, I knew they were making a lot of money so I thought maybe I could do this to help my mum. So I was dealing crack, heroin, weed. I could make a grand a week. I used to use a bike cos I knew the feds [police] target drug dealers in cars.

There was a lot of us, more than 20. It's like a family. What you'd do for a little brother, you'd do for your bredren [brethren].

If one of you is going somewhere and gets stopped by someone, the whole lot of you would jump him cos he's stopped one of your bredren. If you entered their territory alone, it's what we call "slipping" and you can get hit. So when we went out it was as a family – MZ family, we used to call it. If one of my friends gets hit I'm down to do whatever it takes. Let's say he gets beaten up, that means I will go over there and do the same to the youth. I

'If one of my friends gets hit, I'm down to do whatever it takes.'

won't murder them, but I'll beat him till he's unconscious, just like how my friend's unconscious. But if he's murdered my friend, that's a different story. If you've lost a friend, most people my age would think they had to take a life from the other side. Either because of the rep you need – "Yeah, he pulled the trigger he was a bad man" – or cos he was your bredren and you can't let a life go away like that.

At first I was a younger, a "buck". You look up to the big boys, their names are known, they're bad and no one wants to mess with them. You see the jewellery, the fast cars, the fast women, you've heard about their background and you're thinking, "Rah, they've done it, so why can't I?"

MZ made life simple for me. Their reputation made it safer for me to go round certain places. You need to protect yourself if you're

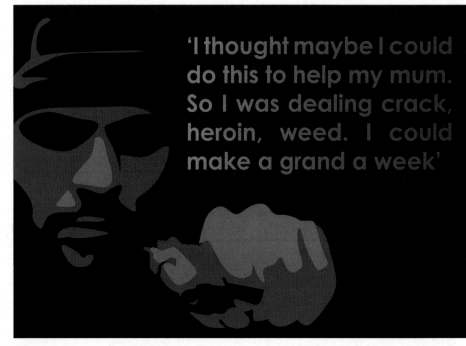

'I thought maybe I could do this to help my mum. So I was dealing crack, heroin, weed. I could make a grand a week'

'I've had a friend dead. He was killed in Kennington, knife to the heart'

leaving your estate. In this generation everyone's trying to rep their own little postcode. It's like with lions. When a lion's got his territory, he don't allow any other male to get through. If the male comes for me, it's a fight, it's a war right there. They just think I need to control my territory, otherwise another male will try and come and take over. If you get caught slipping by another group of boys, then you're going to get it dangerously. It's about who's more powerful than who. That's why people kill each other.

I've had a friend dead. He was killed in Kennington, knife to the heart. There are plenty of knives on the street. I've been sliced on my neck – it was just a little scuff, someone pulled a knife, reached for the back of my neck and just sliced it.

Most of the boys I know have either had a bullet or a knife. I've been shot. I was hit on the arm with a bullet by being in the wrong place at the wrong time. We'd gone to a party and my mate saw an enemy and punched him, we ran off and they started firing after us. I didn't really feel anything until someone told me, "Your hand's bleeding", and then I realised, "Rah, I've been hit." Luckily it wasn't hard enough to go through my bone or I wouldn't be able to use my hand no more.

Disrespecting someone is major these days. When I was growing up, if you disrespect a man you're going to have to rock him one on one with your hands. Now it's about shooting. More young people have got guns and they think it's easier to kill than fight.

Tupac made me change my life around. I don't care about 50 Cent or any other rappers, but he was different. People didn't understand 'Pac, but if you really listen to the guy and his behaviour, there was a meaning to it. I'm not fully out of this yet, but I want to be. It's not like you're going on holiday and you can just pack your bags and go. Imagine you're living this life for eight years. That eight years has made you what you are today. You can't resist that background.

I'm doing A-level art now and I'm hoping to go to art school. I want to write films. I look to [British rapper] Asher D. He's been through similar things. He's been stabbed in the back of the neck like me. He nearly went to prison for firearms. That's why I give him respect. For flipping round. I hope I can do that.

The Guardian 24 November 2007
© Guardian News & Media Ltd. 2007

'I give him respect. For flipping round. I hope I can do that.'

'Ten years ago, in a feat of bravado designed to impress a girl, I vandalised a restaurant where I'd worked.'

William Skidelsky

I have never thought of myself as a violent or aggressive person. So it was a shock to discover, several years ago, that I am capable of behaving like a yob. The occasion of this discovery was a night out in London with university friends, which ended with some of us going back to my parents' (unoccupied) house with a bottle of vodka. Several hours later I suggested, with the ebullience of severe drunkenness, that a girl I quite liked step out with me for an early morning stroll.

Dawn was breaking, and the streets were miraculously empty. We wandered around for a while, and soon came to a restaurant where, the summer before starting university, I'd worked

as a waiter. This combination of circumstances—the bright early morning sunshine, the deserted streets, the presence of a woman to show off to—must have triggered something within me, for I decided that a spot of vandalism was in order. "I hated this place. They were bastards to work for," I declared. "I'm going to smash it up."

When my companion showed no sign of objecting, I set about laying into the restaurant's pair of glass-fronted menu display cases. These were located a few metres in front of its entrance, on a sort of raised patio, and were mounted on gleaming metallic stands. (It was quite a smart restaurant.) Demolishing them was no easy task; several running kicks were required. Nonetheless, within a few

minutes, the metallic stands had been uprooted, and the display cases lay on the ground, their glass smashed. My companion celebrated with a high-spirited giggle. Our morning's work completed, we made our way back home.

What do I make of this episode now, roughly a decade later? As vandalism goes, it was fairly petty stuff: at most I caused a few hundred pounds' worth of damage. But what I did was criminal and, if not totally mindless (I had a motive of sorts), then certainly stupid. If I had been caught, I might well have been prosecuted. My parents and tutors would not have been impressed. In my defence, all I can point to is the fact that I was, at the time, on anti-depressants. These made me feel happy, but also unleashed something manic inside me. When combined with alcohol, the effect was especially pronounced. My assault on the restaurant was only the worst of a string of regrettable incidents during this period. I was getting into a lot of arguments, behaving irresponsibly, and generally was not quite in control of myself.

But the fact that I was on anti-depressants does not, of course, absolve me of all blame. While the pills may have brought certain personality traits to the surface, they were not responsible for those traits existing. The anger that induced me to smash up the restaurant was already inside me, and it is this anger which, looking back, intrigues me most. Where did it come from? What was it about? At the time, I was clear why I hated the restaurant. It was because it had been a miserable place to work. And indeed it was: the hours were long, the pay was low, the bosses were not always particularly pleasant. I had some cause to feel aggrieved.

But if I had been completely honest with myself, I would have admitted that none of this really had anything to do with my desire to smash the place up. The real source of my animus lay elsewhere, in the humiliation I associated with the experience of being a waiter. For the fact is, I wasn't any good at it. Before I started, I had expected to find it easy. I was, after all, interested in food, and considered

But that is also the problem with violence: it invariably hits the wrong target

myself more than qualified for the job. But it wasn't the doddle I expected it to be. I got things muddled up, was too slow taking orders, wasn't confident enough dealing with customers. My hand wasn't sufficiently steady: on one occasion, I deposited a tray full of champagne glasses into the lap of a woman wearing a thin

"I ALWAYS KNOW WHERE MY KIDS ARE — THEY'RE IN A SECURE UNIT FOR YOUNG OFFENDERS."

The Spectator 1 September 2007

cotton dress. And because I wasn't any good, I was unpopular with the other waiters. Most of them tolerated me, but a few were open in their disdain. Once, one of the senior waiters unexpectedly moved to the upper floor, where I was working. "Did you come up here because you wanted to work with me?" I feebly quipped, hoping to ingratiate myself. He looked at me, and shook his head pityingly. "No, that's not why," he said. "You are one of the worst waiters I have ever worked with."

Although I didn't know it at the time, when I carried out my assault on the restaurant that morning, I was getting my own back on this waiter, and on all the other slights and humiliations I'd

endured the previous summer. My act of vandalism was a form of revenge. Somehow, by destroying those menu cases, I was making up for my inadequacy, buoying myself with my ability to cause damage and (so I hoped) to impress a girl. This, I suspect, is the case with most violence: its purpose is compensatory; it allows those who commit it to make up for some humiliation or slight, either real or imagined, in their past. But that is also the problem with violence: it invariably hits the wrong target. Those menu stands weren't responsible for my failure to be a successful waiter, and shouldn't have been made to suffer for it.

Prospect December 2007

Trust and the Teen Tormentor

BY KATHLEEN MARSHALL
Scotland's Commissioner for Children and Young People

A few weeks ago, I participated in the launch of the latest survey by Youthlink Scotland into "Being Young in Scotland." This is their third survey of 11-25 year olds, the others having taken place in 2003 and 2005. Some of the results are, and remain, positive, such as the fact that the 2,500 respondents overwhelmingly identified their parents as the people they most trust and respect. Other findings are more alarming. The relatively short period of four years since the first survey shows a significant decrease in the trust and respect young people have for other groups, including teachers, the law, police, doctors and the Church.

> **Young people constantly tell us they resent the way they are presented by the media as antisocial yobs**

The fact that the question linked "trust" and "respect" may be significant. You are unlikely to trust people that you don't respect, and unlikely to respect people that you don't trust. And you are unlikely to trust and respect people who don't trust and respect you.

Young people constantly tell us that they resent the way they are presented by the media as antisocial yobs. Of course, there is some antisocial behaviour, by people of all ages. Most young people dislike it as much as older people do. "Safer streets" came a very close third in the list of priorities young people wanted me to adopt, polling 24% of the 16,000 votes. So why are some people proposing and adopting "solutions" that assume that all of the trouble is caused by all of the young people?

> **You are unlikely to trust and respect people who don't trust and respect you**

The Mosquito device emits a high pitched sound audible only to people under the age of about 25. The manufacturers say it is merely a slight irritant, causing no harm, but annoying enough to persuade young people to move away from the area in which it is transmitted. Young people describe it differently, some saying it is painful. It is marketed under names like "Teen Tormenter" and "Teen Repellent", locating young people in the same

> **The mosquito device, a slight irritant... young people describe it differently**

kind of category as vermin. It is unregulated. Anyone can buy one. It is being deployed by some supermarket chains, independent business people and private individuals. It is just beginning to make an impact in Scotland, and it should be stopped in its tracks.

It is interesting to compare this with the Dispersal Orders available under antisocial behaviour legislation. The relevant Act of Parliament sets out a procedure to be followed before a dispersal order can be made. The Mosquito device is like a forcible dispersal with no controls whatsoever. It is a sinister development, representing a breach of young people's rights to freedom and dignity.

No-one wants antisocial behaviour, but there are better ways of dealing with it. The Police Violence Reduction Unit publishes a digest of diversionary projects involving the police, in which they attempt to engage with young people in a positive way. Not many have been evaluated, but those which have show the very significant impact that such positive projects can make. Providing young people with accessible and affordable things to do can transform a community, with a huge impact on the kind of low level "hanging around" and boisterous activity that some people find intimidating.

> **Some people sigh and make a mental note to do better when it's their time to rule the world**

We reap what we sow. If we treat our young people with mistrust and disrespect, we will get it thrown back at us – by some at least. Others will tolerate it stoically, sigh and make a mental note to do better when it's their time to rule the world. They may not rebel. They may not turn around and give us the two fingers. But they won't trust us either and, at one level at least, they won't respect us.

We should ban the "Teen Tormentor" and start setting a good example to our young people. We should teach them by example that might is not always right, that trust and respect are the foundations of a decent society, and that our starting point is our trust and respect for them.

Children in Scotland 14 January 2008

I'm sick of hearing people complain about the Mosquito alarm...

Those who claim that the 'teen tormentor' is more of a menace than the kids it's supposed to deter obviously have no idea what life is like in some parts of this country. And to suggest that the problem of menacing kids is only a perceived one is an insult to myself and the people I work with and live near.

I imagine it is easy to believe this problem does not exist, if you live in a vacuum of middle class life, driving your kids to school in your people carrier. However, on my estate, and hundreds like mine, this problem is a living nightmare. The local shops near me were plagued with thugs day and night.

They threw bricks through the windows, stole from them regularly despite being barred for vandalism and would harass people as they passed. When a member of staff in her 60s went out to try and reason with them, she ended up in hospital, beaten to the ground. Not only are these local shops my only means of getting produce for my family (without having to get the bus into town, which is another story altogether) but I have to pass them daily when I take my kids to school and walk to work.

Because of all this the shop has fitted a Mosquito alarm which has driven the thugs away. These alarms are not indiscriminate, they target problem areas where out-of-control youths gather and make life hell for those who are trying to get on with their daily life.

Anonymous, Buxton, Derbyshire

CIVIL LIBERTIES LESS IMPORTANT THAN LIVES

0268101777141277O

Code: 002681017714127770
Woman: 777120014XASC
Status: RST 645
State of health: 222 4 7714
Target group: B

Nr.of Identification accepted / person scanned

In December 2006 the bodies of five murdered women were discovered at different locations near Ipswich in Suffolk. All the victims were sex workers. Following a police investigation, DNA and fibre evidence was found that linked forklift truck driver Steve Wright to the victims. He was found guilty of all five murders on 21 February 2008 and was sentenced the following day to life imprisonment.

BY KENNY FARQUHARSON

THERE'S one detail from the Ipswich murders I cannot shake from my mind. It's the moment Maire Alderton was asked in court about the last time she saw her daughter alive. Twenty-four-year-old Anneli had stopped by her mum's house to drop off some Christmas presents. Asked if she spoke to Anneli as she left, her mother replied: "No, I didn't. She shouted: 'Goodbye mum, I love you.' But I didn't answer."

It's not hard to imagine what scene will be replayed in the mind of Maire Alderton every day for the rest of her life, each time enhanced with different things she wished she'd said as her pregnant daughter breezed out of the door for the final time.

We should keep moments like this uppermost in our minds when we consider the lessons our criminal justice system needs to learn from Ipswich. In particular, we should remember Maire Alderton's grief when we ponder whether we should have a compulsory national database of every British citizen's DNA, as called for by some senior police officers this weekend.

The argument against a compulsory database has some legitimate points to make. Its most compelling argument is that we do not yet know what uses a government might have for our DNA in the future. Could it be used to identify those of us with a genetic disposition towards criminality? Could it determine which of us are worth treating in the NHS, and which of us are so compromised by our genes we're barely worth spending money on? Could insurance companies demand access to the database so they could decide how high to set our premiums for life insurance?

It can be put as simply as this: a compulsory national DNA database would mean fewer serial killers

These are perfectly reasonable concerns. Yet this cannot just be a debate about civil liberties. It must also be a debate about preventing the most odious of crimes. The question the civil liberties campaigners have to ask themselves is this: is your fear about what the government may or may not do with our DNA in the future more important than the prevention of rape and murder? Because let's be clear, if we resist a compulsory DNA database there will be lives destroyed or cut cruelly short that could otherwise have been saved.

Inevitable comparisons have been drawn between Ipswich killer Steve Wright and the Yorkshire Ripper Peter Sutcliffe, and the lesson is a stark one. Wright was caught within 50 days of starting his killing spree, thanks to the fact that his DNA had been taken by police in 2001 after a minor theft. Back in the 1970s, before DNA was used to fight crime, Sutcliffe preyed on women for six long years and 13 lives were lost. Last week's conviction of Mark Dixie for the gruesome killing of model Sally Anne Bowman was made possible by a DNA swab that was taken from Dixie after he was involved in a pub brawl. Within six hours he had been arrested for Bowman's unsolved murder.

But to view genetic science only in terms of its potential dangers is perverse

It can be put as simply as this: a compulsory national DNA database would mean fewer serial killers. Because in many cases the culprit would be identifiable after the first murder. Is this really an advance that can be resisted because of our squeamishness about the state knowing a bit too much about us?

Not only would a truly national database be a revolution in crime detection, it would also be a revolution in crime prevention. What better disincentive is there to committing a violent or sexual crime than the perpetrator's knowledge that he would be extremely unlikely to get away with it? Everyone has seen CSI on the telly. Everyone knows how clever the forensic scientists can be. Everyone appreciates that a flake of skin or a single hair can be enough to link someone incontrovertibly to the scene of a crime.

Here in Scotland the Ipswich case should give us additional pause for thought. South of the border the DNA of every suspect in every crime is kept on file. In Scotland, the DNA is only retained if the crime is sexual or violent. Yet in Ipswich, Wright was caught because his DNA was taken in connection with the theft of £80 from a hotel. Is this distinction between different types of crime really credible? Scotland's chief police officers want the law in Scotland brought into line with that in England. After Ipswich, can this in all conscience now be resisted?

I repeat, this is about the prevention of serial rape and serial murder. Maybe the civil liberties campaigners believe a half-dozen or so lives a year is a price worth paying to safeguard our theoretical notions of personal freedom. Personally, I don't.

I repeat, this is about the prevention of serial rape and serial murder

It's true there are difficulties with DNA evidence that science has still to resolve. When dealing with tiny amounts of human matter it's possible that DNA can become contaminated. When the DNA of two or more people is found together it can produce a misleading genetic profile. But these should be regarded as challenges in a science that is still in its infancy; they are not reasons to reject DNA as a prime crimefighting tool.

The advances in genetic science since James Watson and Francis Crick made their DNA breakthrough in 1953 have changed the world fundamentally. They pose moral, legal, medical and philosophical questions that demand answers from each and every one of us. But to view genetic science only in terms of its potential dangers is perverse.

This scientific advance can and should be a force for good. What's more, it cannot be uninvented, so the dilemmas it raises have to be engaged with honestly and in all their complexity. Simply sticking our heads in the sand and wishing the world was otherwise just won't do.

Scotland on Sunday 24th February 2008

Why do we prosecute primary school children?

**Simon Hickson
argues for a rethink**

The 'age of criminal responsibility' is a technical phrase; legally precise, but concealing much more than it reveals. Let's be clear – we are talking about how old a child has to be before he or she can be arrested, questioned, charged, taken to court and sent for trial. True, children are not always taken to court, but the whole system for dealing with their behaviour revolves around crime and punishment. Even if they are first dealt with outside court, through a reprimand or final warning, they are put on a statutory escalator whose second or third step is the court.

It is the youth offending team (YOT) – and not the children's services – that assesses them and generally supervises them after sentence. YOTs do try to negotiate help from other services but often they receive scant support. Once in the criminal justice system, the child is 'the YOT's problem' – a remark frequently followed by a near-audible sigh of relief.

At what age does this formal system of crime and punishment kick in? In England and Wales, it's 10 years old, and for any offence: the same range as an adult. The punishment could be up to life imprisonment – technically detention at Her Majesty's Pleasure.

THE PROBLEM WITH THE SYSTEM

The Children's Society believes that this system is unsuitable for children under 14.

- Children under 14 are not even 'near-adults'. Individuals vary, of course, but they are still developing in terms of cognitive capacity and emotional maturity, and are often much more impulsive. The more a young person is involved in crime, the greater the gap with adults tends to be. Yet, when barely into their teens, they can be put through and expected to understand a system geared to convicting and punishing adults.

- Children involved in crime, particularly persistently, have often had difficult, deprived backgrounds. These include multiple problems: families who are fractured, traumatised and unable to cope with challenging behaviour; physical and sexual abuse; periods in and out of care; behavioural and learning disorders; educational disengagement; truancy; and exclusion from school.

- We take a markedly more punitive approach to these issues than comparable countries. Our present line is drawn well below most other countries, which typically operate from age 13 or 14 upwards. And yet, our crime levels are higher. Our government should study and learn from their experience rather than persist in the belief that there is only one solution and they have it. Progress is made by learning from, and building on, others' experience.

- Our own system is not even successful on its own terms in dealing with youth crime. Of 10 to 14-year-olds taken to court (the age band used in government statistics), more than half are reconvicted within one year. This percentage rises as the penalties increase – nearly 80% of those who are put in custody are reconvicted.

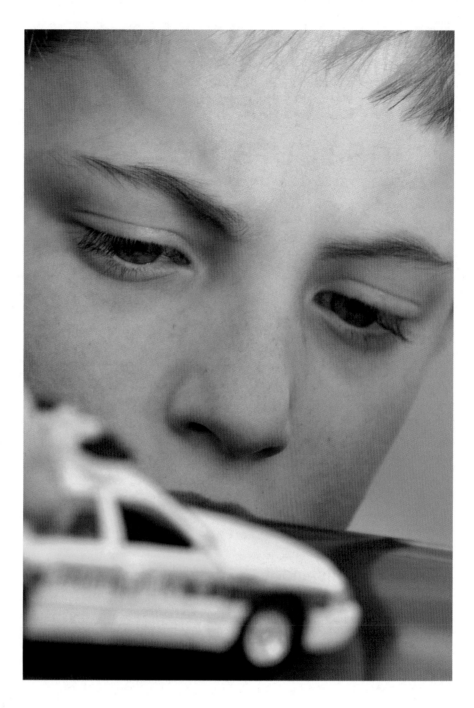

'We should urgently seek to learn from our European neighbours that have higher ages of criminal responsibility and low youth offending.'

Bob Reitemeier, chief executive of The Children's Society, September 2007

POSSIBLE SOLUTIONS

So what should be done for this age group? We do take emerging criminality seriously and believe that, to make a real difference, the new Children's Services Partnerships should be responsible for running specific systematic, area-by-area, multi-agency offending-focused work. This means involving children's social and family services, mental health services, substance misuse agencies, education, the police, youth crime prevention services, and youth activity agencies. Enabling them to handle more serious behaviour that directly harms other people would require a new legal framework based on the civil law and the family courts, or an equivalent.

In the meantime, some progress could be achieved with only minor changes to our present statutory framework. We could take a more preventative approach to early signs of offending behaviour; handle many more children under 14 without formal prosecution or 'two strikes and in court'; and use voluntary engagement with them and their families paying close attention to the behaviour, and what drives it.

Evaluation of The Children's Society's Youth Inclusion and Support Panel in Solihull (run in partnership with local statutory agencies) suggests that such interventions can stop offending and antisocial behaviour amongst children who are at high risk of criminal careers. This was achieved in nearly every case in the Solihull sample, and one of the most important contributors was a clear commitment to preventing young people being drawn into court orders and formal punishments in the first place.

What this and other examples show is that where there's a will, there's a way. What is needed is the will to rethink what we do with younger teenagers, and why we do it.

Simon Hickson is Policy Advisor, Youth Justice, The Children's Society hicksonsb@aol.com

Magistrate Winter 2007

CREATING CRIMINALS: a recipe for an insecure world?

Welcome to England

Vivien Stern describes how UK society is creating an industry out of crime

Crime & punishment

Anyone arriving from abroad at the UK's airports will realise before setting foot on British territory that this is a place where crime and punishment are a major preoccupation. On arrival at passport control notices warn travellers lining up to have their passports scanned, that assaulting immigration officers will not be tolerated and anyone doing so will be prosecuted. Widely-travelled arrivals may be a little surprised. They are more used to seeing signs at airports welcoming them.

If the travellers start reading the English newspapers first impressions will be confirmed. They may read of a new law that penalises parents who have a child who has difficulties at school. If their child is excluded from school such parents are now required to keep that child at home for the first five days of the exclusion and if they fail to do so they are committing a crime and can be fined £50. If they

do not pay the £50 fine within 42 days they face prosecution and a possible £1,000 fine. The visitors may be quite surprised at this too. They might expect any law passed about a child being excluded from a state school would be a law requiring the relevant authorities to ensure that the child receives an alternative education as of right.

Further reading of the newspapers would reveal more surprises. Travellers might read the story of a British 15-year-old disturbed child who lost his liberty for offences of assault and theft, who died whilst being held down by force by three employees in a children's secure centre run by a private security company. Such treatment of children is quite unusual, even in the other jurisdictions of the UK, never mind abroad.

Governing through crime

It will also become clear to the travellers that most British people seem quite used to this way of looking at the world and are only put out when

it seems to go too far, as for example when a young university student is brought to court for the offence of putting her feet on a train seat and risks losing her chance to become a teacher when she qualifies because

> **A student brought to court for putting her feet up on a train risks losing her chance to become a teacher**

she will have a criminal record. Even then it appears that some members of the public are happy that people who put feet on train seats should be prosecuted and acquire a criminal record which could disqualify them from certain professions for life. Much of government policy-making now is, in the phrase of Jonathan Simon from the University of California, 'governing through crime'. It follows therefore that a major part of UK social policy could be described as the creation of criminals.

The creation of criminals has no limit. As the Norwegian criminologist Nils Christie has explained: 'Since crime does not exist as stable entity, the crime concept is well suited to all sorts of control purposes. It is like a sponge. The term can absorb a lot of acts – and people – when external circumstances make that useful'.

Consequences

The consequences do not seem to have a limit either. From people who put their feet on train seats, to those under 18 who carry a firework in a public place, to those who break the conditions of an anti-social behaviour order (ASBO), the criminal creation business flourishes. The consequence is a huge criminal justice business. The leading country in criminal creation is the United States. The US policy of governing through crime has given them a prison population of 750 per 100,000, with 11% of all black men between 25 and 34 incarcerated. According to the Cabinet Office, the UK spends more on public order and safety than any other OECD (Organisation for Economic Co-operation and Development) country.

So how can we account for this change which is a change of a dramatic kind? In England only a decade and a half ago the story was very different. Criminal Justice Bills were rare and new crimes were introduced but sparsely. The number of people in prison in December 1992 was half the figure that it was in September 2007. If children did not go to school a welfare officer visited the family and tried to find out what was wrong. A big government sponsored programme, the Intermediate Treatment Initiative, had substantially reduced the number of juveniles drawn into the criminal justice system.

Increasing inequality

What happened that propelled crime into the prime policy seat? How did we come to the point where an 82-year-old Second World War veteran was sent to prison for breaching an ASBO he received over a boundary dispute, and a 60-year-old partially sighted woman with long-standing psychiatric problems was jailed for swearing at people living near her sick mother? Why is it that parents cannot get their children into the special schools or

mental health units they need, but will find there is no shortage of places when their children do harm to something or someone and are charged, tried and locked up? These are not questions to be answered in a few words. Clearly, the world of 2007 is very different. The criminal justice system we have now fits the ideology of the Washington economic consensus and the world shaped by that consensus. It fits with a world of widening and gross inequalities, the removal of security of employment and pension rights, and the shrinking of the welfare safety net for the less fortunate and those with fewer talents to sell in the market society. Those who have provided answers to these questions suggest a process rather like this: growing inequality and social exclusion lead to more violence (and indeed research from many different parts of the world shows a connection between levels of inequality and levels of violence) (Stern 2006). Governments adhering

> **A major part of UK social policy could be described as the creation of criminals**

to the current economic ideology are not going to reduce inequality nor spend huge sums on reducing social exclusion. So there is only one way of dealing with it. More draconian systems of control and punishment will have to be introduced. Governments might also conclude that an electorate upset about the insecurity which surrounds their daily lives might find some relief in scapegoating others. The government therefore moves into a mode of satisfying the public with a daily drama of retribution against people who are traditionally not liked: criminals, badly behaved teenagers, parents who do not bring up their children properly.

A different approach

This policy might also make sense to certain types of government because in the globalised economy there are many unwanted human beings. There is no room for so many people who are not high-skilled now that manufacturing work can be done in China and even skilled work like answering calls on

how to sort out a computer that is malfunctioning can be done from India. Also, it cannot have failed to occur to some of those involved in developing such ideas that creating a big penal system for large numbers of unwanted

> **Growing inequality and social exclusion lead to more violence**

people might have an upside. It could be turned into a business. It will need some changes of course to make it easy to sell and to buy. But once it has been broken down into specific services that can be provided by contractors and then reconfigured to give economies of scale, there are good business possibilities.

However, we do not seem to make society safer or more secure with these policies. Security and low levels of crime come with a very different approach, with more social inclusion, more equality. If we want to be secure, feel secure and live in peaceful neighbourhoods we need to be more like Norway. According to the paper on the Cabinet Office website dated January 2007 (Cabinet Office 2007) Norway has persistently low crime rates relative to other European countries. It convicts relatively few people. Its imprisonment levels have not changed much since 1950 and are low. It abolished life sentences in 1981. It spends much less on policing than the UK. The number of police per head in Norway is less than half the EU average. It focuses on prevention rather than enforcement. It has a strong welfare state. There is an active Crime Prevention Council. Very high levels of social trust are correlated with low levels of fear of crime.

Let us hope Gordon Brown's advisers get to read this information about Norway before it is deleted from the Cabinet Office website because it was put there by the staff of the former incumbent.

Baroness Vivien Stern CBE is a Senior Research Fellow at the International Centre for Prison Studies

*Centre for Crime and Justice Studies
Winter 2007*

OUR CRIMINAL SYSTEM IS A PERSISTENT RE-OFFENDER

Jenny McCartney

The curious uniformity of the mugshots of the three teenagers convicted last week of Garry Newlove's murder said it all: the pallid, hollow faces, the vacant, defiant eyes and the little spikes of hair teased low over the forehead in approved thug fashion.

I am sure that each individual cut rather a pathetic figure at the trial, shorn of all drunken bravado and the bogus security of their baying gang. Jordan Cunliffe, 16, and Stephen Sorton, 17, both hung their heads and cried when they were convicted of murder, as though they finally realised the gravity of what they had done to Mr Newlove, and to themselves.

Adam Swellings, 19, also known as "Swellhead", didn't cry: when the police first arrived to arrest him on suspicion of Mr Newlove's murder, his reported response was, "Fair enough." Swellings had been released on bail on August 10 last year, just hours before he and his friends beat to death Mr Newlove, a 47-year-old father of three, who had had the temerity to object to them vandalising parked cars. It should, well before then, have been amply clear to any court that bail restrictions meant precisely nothing to Swellings.

In court on August 1 he had admitted repeatedly breaching a harassment order and committing an assault against a young woman. Once bailed, he went on to assault a young man that same day. On August 10, he admitted this fresh assault and to obstructing a police officer while on bail. He was once again granted bail, despite the opposition of the police and the Crown Prosecution Service, on condition that he did not go into Warrington. Can the fact that Swellings went into Warrington that night really have surprised anyone?

Mr Newlove's widow Helen has rightly demanded to know why Swellings was bailed yet again. Jack Straw, the Justice Secretary, has simply observed that such cases highlight the difficult decisions that have to be taken by the judiciary.

Such a response is surely more worthy of an Injustice Secretary. We all appreciate that granting bail is a delicate judgment, and that occasionally the wickedness of an offender will surpass a judge's reasonable expectations. That is not the question here. In this instance, the judge did not need a crystal ball to predict Swellings's insouciant attitude to bail conditions: it was clearly evident in the violent history of his behaviour. The real question, surely, is why the magistrates did not give Swellings a custodial sentence, which would have permitted them to deny bail.

I suspect, however, that Mr Straw is well aware that our prisons and remand centres are overstuffed, and violent offenders such as Swellings are granted bail or released on probation every day and appallingly monitored thereafter. The judges know it, the police know it, and any former home secretary, such as Mr Straw, will know it too.

Every so often the public discovers the gruesome inefficiency of the present system – usually by means of a particularly horrifying murder or rape – and there will be an outcry. Nothing thereby changes. You might remember Richard Whelan, stabbed to death on a north London bus in 2005. His murderer, Anthony Joseph, had been released from prison only 11 hours earlier – by mistake, it turned out, because there was an outstanding warrant for his arrest on another matter. Apparently, the error occurred because Joseph's details had not been uploaded on to a national police computer.

He was released on bail just hours before he beat Mr Newlove to death

Or perhaps you recall the brutal murder of the financier John Monckton during a robbery in 2004: his killer, Damien Hanson, had been released halfway through a 12-year sentence for attempted murder and was supposed to be under the supervision of the probation service. Among other glaring errors, his probation staff had failed to include any assessment of Hanson's risk of re-offending in their report for the Parole Board, despite an earlier assessment that there was a 91% likelihood he would re-offend. Four probation staff were suspended for their mistakes in this case: within two weeks they were all back at work.

There is no doubt that neglect and family dysfunction have shaped the characters of Mr Newlove's killers. But a sense of defeatism among our police and judiciary has then allowed them free rein to destroy another family forever.

Time and again, an incredulous public asks why persistently violent offenders are so frequently released, unsupervised, back into society. Time and again, we hear that there has been some regrettable error in the system, but that it appears to be no one's fault. Yet it is the fault of individuals – further compounded by a shoddy, creaking system – and we deserve to know exactly who will be held accountable and what will be done to change matters. Otherwise, you can bet that in years to come decent people will still be dying to find out.

The Sunday Telegraph 20 January 2008
© Telegraph Group Ltd 2008

'My daughter needed prison'

My eldest daughter is now 23 but between the ages of 14 and 18 she was a nightmare to cope with. The problems were exacerbated by drugs and alcohol use and a fruitful shoplifting career.

My husband and I (both of us are responsible professionals and caring parents) tried early on to approach the youth service to support us in dealing with her behaviour and to halt the decline. We were told clearly that many services would not become involved until she became a "habitual offender."

We received no help for at least a year. Each time we went to court with her for yet another offence, reports would be produced with a softly softy approach to my daughter while we, her parents, were begging authority figures to ensure she experienced some sort of consequences for her actions. (Oh, she did have to write a letter of apology to someone she mugged!)

We, her parents, were begging authority figures to ensure she experienced some sort of consequences for her actions

Her offending became increasingly serious, as did her drug and alcohol use. Supervision orders were extended and extended.

When I now ask my beautiful daughter "What could we have done to change your behaviour?" she insists there was nothing

Youth services and social services only became involved when they no longer had a choice, by which time my daughter was well and truly an "habitual offender" with a serious drug and alcohol problem. As her parents, we were on first name terms with many of the local constabulary who acknowledged our frustration with the lack of consequences for our daughter and our almost powerless position of responsibility.

This cycle of despair came to a head when her latest offence ended up in crown court and she was sent to Holloway Prison at the age of 15 and a half.

My husband and I were horrified at the thought of her in Holloway and felt she, and us, had been let down by a system that had refused to respond until she was a prolific criminal and drug user. But we also experienced a sense of relief that at last someone else cared enough to call a stop. This milestone was the start of her recovery.

When I now ask my beautiful daughter "What could we have done to change your behaviour?" she insists there was nothing.

When I asked her "What was it that made you start to turn things around?" her reply was very simple and straightforward... "To be made to face real consequences" – in her case, that meant prison.

Name and address supplied

Community Care 13 September 2007

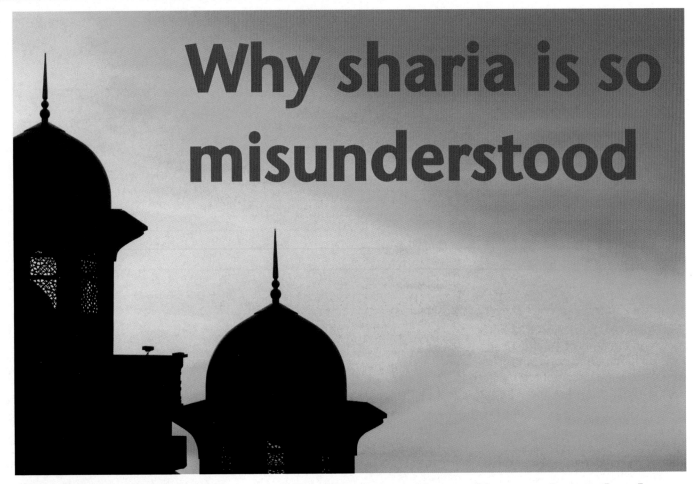

Why sharia is so misunderstood

Sharia is complex, and needs to be aligned with the process of civil law, says Mona Siddiqui

Religious voices are either ignored or sensationalised; they are rarely heard with careful consideration. The Archbishop of Canterbury's lecture at the Royal Courts of Justice, in which he mentioned both sharia and Britain in the same breath, has evoked blistering attacks from an array of political and religious voices.

To hear the leader of the Anglican Church call for any sort of "constructive accommodation" of Muslim practice is more than many can bear, especially in our current climate. When the head of the Anglican Communion directs his attention to Islam in the UK rather than pronouncing on a moral vision for Christianity, many hear nothing other than alarm bells.

One could legitimately ask: did the Archbishop really not expect that any serious consideration of sharia and its possible place in Britain would be construed by many as a threat to both British society and its Christian heritage?

Despite the tolerance we all value in Britain, public debates on Islam

public has developed an intolerance of any Islam-related issues.

Not only does Islam appear increasingly like an idiosyncrasy in the West, but most of the stories related to the faith conjure up medieval and barbaric images, completely at odds with Western notions of individual freedoms. This is

you begin. Misleadingly, but commonly translated as "Islamic law", the term has become synonymous with penal law, and stripped of its broader ethical dimensions and the fluidity of juristic reasoning.

As contemporary Muslim scholars attempt to contextualise the debates on Islamic law and ethics,

The Danish cartoon crisis, the veil issue, and then the teacher and teddy bear fiasco — it is hardly surprising that much of the public has developed an intolerance of any Islam-related issues.

often associate Islam as a faith with Islamism as an ideology. When you compound this with the big stories of the past few years, such as the Danish cartoon crisis, the veil issue, and then the teacher and teddy bear fiasco, it is hardly surprising that much of the

why, despite his attempts to qualify and explain the complexities of sharia, many in the media could see little beyond chopping off of hands and stoning of adulterers.

The problem with starting any conversation on sharia is finding exactly where

they are constantly battling against the bloody-mindedness of some Muslim states, which refer to sharia as God's law, but only as a tool for self-interest and political expediency.

God's law must be simple to be implemented. Unfortunately, this

sentiment is also rife among many Muslims in the UK, who feel that all aspects of sharia can and must be applied without due consideration of time, place, and individual moral agency.

Yet the argument is even more complex than that. The Archbishop is right to say that aspects of sharia are already in place here, and, while some are accepted, even encouraged, others are condemned for disregarding individual human dignity. For example, sharia-compliant financial packages, while regarded by many Muslims as little more than wordplay on the term interest, are nevertheless on the increase. Our own Prime Minister sees the lucrative fallout from such religious convictions, as London veers to becoming the financial epicentre for such ventures.

In the area of personal law, most Muslims marry according to their religious law, and register their marriage under the civil law of the land. For decades, the two systems have existed side by side, and there is nothing here that contradicts the law of the land or the faith; no principle is being violated here.

But, if arranged marriages are premised on adult consent, forced marriages ignore this premise, and should be seen as nothing less than a crime against the state and the individual.

The problem is not in the existence of religious law, but in the nebulous status of certain aspects of religious culture. Many in the legal profession are aware that Islamic divorce proceedings must be done in the framework of both religious and civil law. However, they are also aware of the dangerous position this leaves women who become victims caught between two legal systems.

Two different conversations must be held here. The first is about how an Islamic process can be aligned with a civil process – which would be both possible and desirable on all sides. A second, more important conversation, is about those who administer the religious sharia institutions.

These are mostly men for whom women still bear the burden of honour in society. While they may appear to be independent arbitrators, narrow and conservative thinking or religious morality often underpins their pronouncements – the complexities of modern life rarely feature in their decisions.

Muslims have once again been put on the defensive: some distancing themselves from the Archbishop's words, and some doubting his very intentions in raising such issues. But, having worked closely with Dr Williams on several occasions, my feeling is that he had the courage as a senior public figure and theologian to start a debate that many are too scared or simply too arrogant even to contemplate.

Church Times 15 February 2008
www.churchtimes.co.uk

What is sharia law?

Sharia is the body of Islamic religious law based on the Koran, Muhammad's teaching, the actions of his followers, and centuries of precedent.

It is the legal framework for the public and some aspects of private life for all people in countries with an Islamic legal system (and for all Muslims).

Hardline followers of sharia believe the laws are eternal and should be followed to the letter whereas liberal Muslims say sharia law is not a definitive code but is open to interpretation.

Sharia deals with many aspects of day-to-day life, including family, sexuality, hygiene, social issues, politics, economics, banking, business, contracts.

Cutting off the hands of thieves and the flogging of drunkards and adulterers are perhaps the best-known practices of sharia law to non-Muslims. However, most of the laws are concerned with prosaic issues such as financial arbitration, divorce or personal hygiene.

Although sharia is not legally binding in Britain, there are a dozen sharia courts which operate out of mosques. They deliver judgments on personal law, including financial issues and divorce.

Britain's oldest sharia court is in Leyton. In operation for 25 years, it has Charity Commission status, issues around 10 fatwas (judgments) a day and hears around 50 divorces a month.

What he wishes on us is an abomination

Yasmin Alibhai-Brown

What Rowan Williams
Archbishop of Canterbury
wishes upon us is an
abomination and I write
here as a modern
Muslim woman

He lectures the nation on the benefits of sharia law — made by bearded men, for men — and wants the alternative legal system to be accommodated within our democracy in the spirit of inclusion and cohesion.

Pray tell me sir, how do separate and impenetrable courts and schools and extreme female segregation promote commonalities and deep bonds between citizens of these small isles?

What he did on Thursday was to convince other Britons, white, black and brown, that Muslims want not equality but exceptionalism and their own domains. Enlightened British Muslims quail. Friends like this churchman do us more harm than our many enemies. He passes round what he believes to be the benign libation of tolerance. It is laced with arsenic.

He would not want his own girls and women, I am sure, to "choose" to be governed by these laws he breezily endorses. And he is naive to the point of folly if he imagines it is possible to pick and choose the bits that are relatively nice to the girls or ones that seem to dictate honourable financial transactions.

Sharia is nothing but a human concoction of medieval religious opinion

Look around the Islamic world where sharia rules and, in every single country, these ordinances reduce our human value to less than half that is accorded a male; homosexuals are imprisoned or killed, children have no free voice or autonomy, authoritarianism rules and infantilises populations.

Many women, gay men and dissidents came to Britain to escape Islamic tyrants and their laws

What's more, different Muslim nations claim to have their own allegedly god-given sharia. In Saudi Arabia, women cannot drive (What in Allah's name could the Koran have warned about cars?). In Bangladesh and Pakistan, they have no such bar to driving, although increasingly Saudi Wahabi Islam is taking over and we see Saudi sharia taking hold.

It is growing in influence here, too. Ten years ago, the only fully shrouded Muslim women around were from the Arab fiefdoms, the many wives of sheikhs often drawn by cartoonists to convey the absurdity and inhumanity of such cloaks. Now all of Europe has these girls and women rendering themselves invisible in public spaces. It is their elected sharia, so they claim without credibility. There is no agreed body of sharia, it is all drafted by males and the most cruel is now claiming absolute authority.

In Pakistan, on the statutes are strictures on adultery introduced by the military dictator Zia ul-Haq. Women activists in that country have given their lives protesting against the injustice of those laws where women suspected of adultery, or rape victims, are punished in hideous ways and the man goes free.

The Iranian theocracy changes its regulations from year to year, capriciously playing with the lives of females. The morality police hound women and girls, beat them up, imprison them for showing an ankle, walking too provocatively or singing in the streets. They fight back but are ground down eventually.

Most sharia contradicts the letter and spirit of the Koran, distorts the transcendental text

Two Iranian friends chose to die rather than live under the demeaning religious orders. Go to Afghanistan if you fancy a 12-year-old bride — a practice approved by the mullahs. That's sharia for you. Many women, gay men and dissidents came to Britain to escape Islamic tyrants and their laws. Dr Williams supports those laws and, by default, makes the refugees victims again.

Four years ago, a Saudi woman in her fifties came to my home. She was divorced from a Saudi prince who had sent her away and kept her children. What she said about sharia cannot be repeated. She had money, this princess, but no parental rights and she howled like a child in excruciating pain in my living room.

Yet, family disputes, says Dr Williams, would be easier, within sharia. For whom exactly? The polygamous men who live in this country, yes, certainly. Not for their wives who will be told that God intends them to lower their eyes and accept unjust verdicts.

Many will be sent back to bastard husbands or flinty-eyed mullahs will take their children away. In Bradford and Halifax, they may be forbidden to drive or work where men are employed. Adultery will be punished. I don't think we will have public stonings but violence of some sort will be meted out (it already is) with lawmakers' backing.

Sensing the drift in their direction, British sharia "experts" today shamelessly direct female medical students not to wash their forearms, essential to prevent the spread of infections, because that exposes their flesh.

Does the Archbishop even know that sharia comes in many guises and that several schools of jurisprudence have their own versions? The list is long — Hanafi, Maliki, Shafi, Hanbali, Jafari, Salafi and on and on. Ayatollah Khomeini preferred his DIY set of crimes and punishments when he came to power.

No women are allowed to be imams or serious jurists, so cannot help make their own fair and free set of female-friendly sharia. All the systems insist on ultimate truths, hard certainties. Sharia cannot provide solutions to the complex challenges of modern life and many violate fundamental human rights as established by the United Nations.

Taj Hargey, a historian and Islamic theologian, runs the Muslim Education Centre in Oxford. He, with me, is a trustee of British Muslims For Secular Democracy which is attempting to educate Muslims out of authorised obscurantism and non-Muslims into a better understanding of the progressive and evolutionary nature of the practice of Islam.

What did Rowan Williams – The Archbishop of Canterbury – actually say?:

"… as a matter of fact certain provisions of Sharia are already recognised in our society and under our law; so it's not as if we're bringing in an alien and rival system; we already have in this country a number of situations in which the law the internal law of religious communities is recognised by the law of the land."

"Nobody in their right mind I think would want to see in this country a kind of inhumanity that sometimes appears to be associated with the practice of the law in some Islamic states the extreme punishments, the attitudes to women as well."

"I don't know enough about the detail of the law in the Islamic law in this context; I'm simply saying that there are ways of looking at marital dispute for example within discussions that go on among some contemporary scholars which provide an alternative to the divorce courts as we understand them. In some cultural and religious settings they would seem more appropriate."

"We have orthodox Jewish courts operating in this country legally and in a regulated way."

"There is a place for finding what would be a constructive accommodation with some aspects of Muslim law as we already do with some kinds of aspects of other religious law."

"We have got a fragmented society at the moment, internally fragmented, socially fragmented in our cities and fragmented between communities of different allegiance. Now I think that there would be a way of talking about the law being more positive about supporting religious communities that might be seen as deepening or worsening that fragmentation."

"So how does the law engage critically and intelligently – the law of the land – with the custom, the imperatives, the principles of distinctive religious communities? It's a large question, much larger than the question about Islam and I think it's a question which the Church can quite reasonably be thinking about."

He is incandescent that Dr Williams backs a perilous Islamic conservatism, already too powerful in Britain: "Sharia is nothing but a human concoction of medieval religious opinion, largely archaic and outmoded and irrelevant to life today. Most sharia contradicts the letter and spirit of the Koran, distorts the transcendental text."

During his sermons Dr Hargey explains to congregations that, for example there is no blasphemy in the Koran, that the Prophet himself allowed a man to mock the divine revelations. Apostasy, says the holy text, will be dealt with by Allah in the afterlife. Sharia policemen insist apostates should be tortured and killed.

Dr Williams says Muslims want the choice to opt for sharia. What he believes to be choice is, in truth, inner compulsion, the result of brainwashing which begins in the madrassas when girls and boys are young enough to mould.

I have often admired the Archbishop's lofty thoughts, his intellectualism, the passion for human rights, his guts when the Government needs to be chastised. But this time his kind indulgences betray his own invaluable principles and deliver Muslim women, girls and dissidents into the hands of religious persecutors – an unforgivable intervention, which I hope he now sincerely regrets.

The Independent 9 February 2008

Facebook knows I'm an atheist

Social networkers are broadcasting their unbelief all over the web, says Bill Thompson. And in doing so they might just help raise the profile of atheism

Facebook knows I'm an atheist, and if Facebook knows it then the CIA probably knows it too, which could be a problem if I tried to stand for election in South Carolina, Mississippi or any of the other seven US States which require candidates to believe in a supreme being.

Fortunately I'm not a US citizen so the problem doesn't arise, rather as Liberal Democrat leader Nick Clegg's admission of his own atheism is unlikely ever to trouble the press office at 10 Downing Street.

But any believers among the 500 or so "friends" I have accumulated on this rapidly-growing social network site are now aware of my lack of belief in their god, and I can only assume that a variety of government agencies, marketing departments of large companies and other organisations have added this key fact to their databases, under "Thompson, Bill".

They know I'm a self-declared heterosexual too, that my politics are "very liberal" (since there's no way to tag oneself as a socialist) and that I'm currently "in a relationship", although I haven't made an explicit connection to my partner and don't reveal whether she is herself a Facebook user. Not believing in God is one thing, revealing who you're sleeping with is far too intimate to be exposed on anyone's website as far as I'm concerned.

I'm a pretty understated atheist, of course, so I can't count myself among the ranks of the "New Atheists", standing beside Dennett and Grayling in the battle for reason. It's just there on my profile if you want to look. I haven't signed up to any of the atheist groups, not even the delightfully named "Jesus College Atheist Society" and I've resisted the temptation to install the "OUT" application, which puts a big red "A" on my page, even though I'm assured it stands for "atheist" and not "adulterer".

I added my lack of religious beliefs to my profile on Facebook, MySpace, Orkut and the other social network sites that I've joined in the same way that I tell other people where I live and what I do, and I am not alone.

A quick look at the profiles of my various friends reveals that, somewhere between "fish with legs rules" and "mild", there are a refreshingly large number who plainly state that they prefer a universe without a creator whose approval they need to seek. While the Data Protection Act would insist that religious views count as "sensitive" data along with medical details, sexual orientation or political opinions, it seems that millions of people are rejecting the protections offered by the law and revealing themselves online.

The point of stating my religious beliefs is not so much a campaign as a decision not to treat them as worthy of protection, and this may be the important thing about it. Users of social network sites are encouraged to share information with their "friends" without any clear definition of what a friend might be, and as a result many people are finding that boundaries between lovers, acquaintances, old schoolmates, employers, work colleagues and (in my case) random listeners to their radio programme are blurring and dissolving.

This is often portrayed as a bad thing, and certainly anyone who decides to tell their mates what they really think of their employer without realising that they've added their line manager to their list of friends is asking for trouble. We will need to find new social norms for this new space for interaction, just as the '80s ravers developed social practices around the use of ecstasy that differed significantly from earlier alcohol-based subcultures, but they will emerge in time.

> **Facebook encourages us to treat religious views as of no more significance than preferred pizza toppings**

Of course it's easy for me to come clean. I live in a country and a culture that does not discriminate against me for my lack of religious belief. I won't have to testify to a belief in a Supreme Being in order to stand for election, as is the case in North Carolina, and I won't be pursued as an apostate by the vicar who baptised me into the Church of England as a child.

A recent Pew Research Centre survey of US voters found that 53% of those polled had an unfavourable view of atheists while 61% would be less likely to vote for a candidate for president who didn't believe in God. While these attitudes remain common it is hard for people to be honest about their lack of religious belief, but of course that makes it less likely that the prejudices will be confronted or challenged.

Perhaps Facebook will help, simply because it encourages us to treat religious views and sexual orientation as of no more significance than favourite movies or preferred pizza toppings. In the end this could matter more than any number of "Brights" t-shirts or big red A's, because it will simply relegate religious belief to the level of other superstitions, habits and personal preferences. Where, of course, it belongs.

New Humanist January 2008

Suddenly I'm totally incensed. But only in a good way

Miranda Sawyer

Recently, somewhat to my surprise, I've been going to Mass. I'm not a Catholic, but my husband is and he'd like our son to be brought up in the faith. As a wishy-washy, non-practising Anglican, let me strum meaningfully 'pon my acoustic guitar and assure you that I have no problem with that. I'm a religious liberal. Believe what you like, mate. I spent years convinced that maths was the holiest of holies and then joined the mass cult worship of Our Saviour Jarvis Cocker. These days, I'm open to anything that doesn't involve wearing a red string round my wrist or a suspiciously heavy belt.

The whole experience is simultaneously reassuring and new

At the moment, our church-going is having little noticeable effect upon our son. He has but one true God: Gordon the Big Express Engine from the Thomas the Tank series. Oddly, however, Mass is having an effect on me. I enjoy it. I like the chapel: big, dark, crumbly,

impressive. I like the congregation: all ages, wages, nationalities. The atmosphere - formal, friendly, tolerant towards children and what you wear – is very different from the snooty, suburban churchiness I remember from my youth. Not much competitive hat-wearing. No rush for the best pews.

He has but one true God: Gordon the Big Express Engine from the Thomas the Tank series

Sometimes, our son and I go to the Sunday school next door, for a few Bible stories and some restful colouring in. When we do go into the service, I'm not too out of step: the Anglican Eucharist is very like the Catholic one. Admittedly, it can be hard work keeping up with the

order of play while ensuring your child isn't using other people as a trampoline; when I've managed, I've found I know the words, apart from the Hail Marys.

I am a religious liberal. Believe what you like, mate

The whole experience is simultaneously reassuring and new, which is the type of experience I like.

I don't want to leave everyday life entirely – I like everyday life – but the niggly specifics of it can mean you spend your time fussing over the detail rather than considering the bigger picture. It's nice to stop microscoping and, instead, spend some time pondering other people, charity, the world, old stories. To silence the mind's circular chatter about deadlines and who's taking the kid to the childminder and have we got any milk and whither mortgage rates, and open it to the possibility that living might be about something more.

The Observer 20 April 2008
© Guardian News & Media Ltd. 2008

LEGAL RESEARCH UNDER THE ICRW

WWW.icrwhale.org

More Sushi than Science

There has long been a history of whaling, and there has also long been a history of dispute between whaling and non-whaling countries. Countries who choose to kill whales argue that it is possible to take whales while preventing them from becoming extinct. Anti-whaling countries assert that there's no possibility of taking whales without extinction, and that all whales are endangered. This dispute has continued for more than two decades

Photo courtesy of Australian Customs

How can Japan continue to defy the law under the guise of science?

In 2007, at the International Whaling Commission meeting, the Scientific Committee strongly criticised Japan's self-proclaimed 'scientific whaling' for having killed nearly 7,000 minke whales and failing to deliver conclusions of any scientific value. Darren Kindleysides, the Campaign Manager for International Fund for Animal Welfare (IFAW) explains "Japan's 20 years of 'scientific whaling' has delivered thousands of dead whales and next to no useful knowledge of the whales they 'study'. The meat is packaged and sold in the fish markets in Japan. This has more to do with sushi than science."

Despite the negative press Japan has shown no signs of stopping hunting whales. This season it is seeking to kill up to 935 minke whales and 50 larger fin whales, all in the name of science. So far condemnation of such killing has been the job of animal welfare and environmental groups such as IFAW, Greenpeace or Sea Shepherd but the release of new photos has marked a significant shift in whaling politics.

Taken in February 2008, these pictures show the horrific reality of Japan's self-proclaimed 'scientific' whale hunt in the Southern Ocean, with a slaughtered adult minke

whale and calf being hauled on board a Japanese factory ship. And these pictures were not taken by the various environmental activists who spent much of January harassing the whalers on their Antarctic hunt, but by officials working for the Australian government. Other images include gory footage of a harpoon being shot into a whale, which is then hauled on to the ship.

For a government to become so actively involved in such an issue has raised the stakes in a dispute, which has most of the international community disagreeing with Japan. Officials in Tokyo reacted with anger and a warning to Australia that this was "dangerous emotional propaganda that could cause serious damage to the relationship between our two countries". But there was a much deeper anger felt by officials in Australia. Peter Garret, former member of the rock group Midnight Oil and current Australian Environment Minister said: "It is explicitly clear from these images that this is the indiscriminate killing of whales, where you have a whale and its calf killed in this way." He went on to say that he felt "sick and sad" looking at them and added: "To claim that this is in any way scientific is to continue the charade that has surrounded this issue from day one."

While Japan claims that such brutal killing is necessary in the name of scientific research, to date they have revealed little that is useful, apart from a lot of dead

Japan's 20 years of 'scientific whaling' has delivered thousands of dead whales and next to no useful knowledge of the whales they 'study'

whale meat. As Darren Kindleysides explains "In contrast, research in countries such as Australia, Argentina and Brazil has delivered information on their life history, including population trends, to a precision that lethal researchers could not even dream of. How many times must Japan be told – you don't need to kill whales to study them."

And while the Australian government have been gathering visual evidence, part of Greenpeace's work in the Southern Ocean has involved an undercover investigation to reveal that much much more than US$60 million worth of 'by-products' are being sold each year. Undercover investigators have revealed dramatic evidence of an embezzlement ring involving crew members on board the giant Nisshin

Photo courtesy of Australian Customs

Maru, the Japanese whaling boat. The activists were told by informers on board the ship that officials and senior crew members from Kyodo Senpaku, the commercial arm of Japan's ICR, simply turned a blind eye to the whale meat theft and have been allowing it to continue for decades. One informer associated with Kyodo Senpaku said that officials from the ICR are most likely aware of the thefts as well.

Junichi Sato, Greenpeace Japan whales campaign co-ordinator, said on their website that "the information we have gathered indicates that the scale of the scandal is so great, it would be impossible for the ship's operating company, Kyodo Senpaku, not to

know." He continued to say "Kyodo Senpaku is turning their back on large scale corruption and theft of taxpayers' money. What we need to know now, through a full public enquiry, is who else is profiting from the whaling programme? Who else has allowed this fraud to continue?"

Such widespread embezzlement of whale meat indicates that the US$60 million worth of declared 'by-products' is merely the tip of the iceberg. This either means that 'researchers' are killing more whales than they claim they are, or the number they are killing is simply not justified in the name of science, as most of the whales caught are simply being sold commercially via Kyodo Senpaku,

Prospect, March 2008

"So in summary, if you harpoon a whale enough it dies"

Photo courtesy of Australian Customs

The History:

In 1982 after 10 years of internal debate, the International Whaling Commission (IWC) agreed to a trial five-year ban on commercial whaling, to last from 1986 to 1990. In 1994 it was declared that there was to be an indefinite 'pause' in commercial whaling. Norway objected to the ban in 1986 and was thereby exempt under IWC rules; Japan and Iceland, in contrast, quickly developed an intense scientific interest in the whale species they had previously hunted commercially. Japan set up the Institute of Cetacean Research (ICR) to continue the research. The institute receives its funding from government subsidies and from Kyodo Senpaku, a profit making company. It was established in 1986 following the ban, and conducts the collection, processing and wholesale selling of the by-products from the whale research on behalf of the IWC. It sells roughly US$60 million worth of whale products each year.

or being embezzled for high profits by its employees – possibly with the company's consent.

According to three separate panels of independent, international legal experts (commissioned by IFAW) Japan's whaling programme

What Australia calls 'indiscriminate killing' and Japan regards as 'random sampling'

breaches the United Nations Convention on the Law of the Sea, the Antarctic Treaty System and the Convention on International Trade in Endangered Species (CITES) and the International Convention on the Regulation of Whaling.

Following the pictures taken by the Australian government the Humane Society International

has urged them to launch a case against Japanese whalers in the International Tribunal of the Law of the Sea.

For IFAW, Darren Kindleysides said "The world's best legal minds have made the case. Japan's whaling is not just cruel, it's criminal." He concludes that "if there is to be a permanent end to whaling in the Antarctic then the burden for action rests with the Australian Government and other conservation minded governments worldwide to challenge the Government of Japan through international courts."

The key question is: will Australia risk a confrontation with a near neighbour to prevent what they call 'indiscriminate killing' and Japan regards as 'random sampling'.

Sources: Various

'Climate change' is preferable to 'global warming,' but the public doesn't like change, so let's call it 'a different weather opportunity'

Prospect, March 2008

The miracle of sight – because of the miracle of science

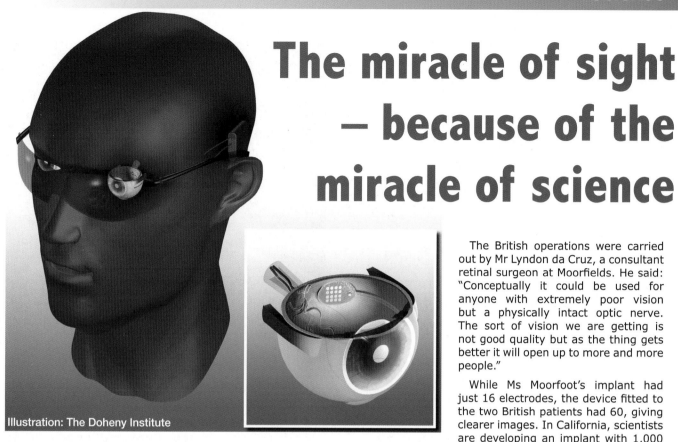

Illustration: The Doheny Institute

It must be one of the most powerful examples of the miraculous potential of modern science and technology – restoring sight to the blind. For the first time in Britain, patients have had their sight restored by the use of a 'bionic' eye – a tiny device implanted into the retina. Surgeons say the procedure 'is straight out of science fiction', but it will give hope to thousands of people.

The operations on two patients at Moorfields Eye Hospital, London, were conducted as part of an international clinical trial of the technology, known as the Argus II retinal implant. This is an electronic device which is implanted into the back of the eye. A tiny camera mounted in a pair of glasses transmits a wireless signal to a small processor which the patient wears on a belt. The processed signals are sent back to an ultra thin electronic receiver and from there to the panel of electrodes in the device.

The electrodes stimulate the remaining retinal nerves so a signal can be passed along the optic nerve to the brain. The spots of light are then processed into a picture – and the blind can see!

Although the vision the patients gain is not perfect, it does allow them to get around without a stick or a guide dog and to pick out different objects on a table. It is generally not possible for patients to see faces or to read but even this limited vision holds the promise of them being able to lead an independent life.

Linda Moorfoot was one of a few American patients to be fitted with the earlier version of the implant. She had been totally blind for more than ten years due to retinitis pigmentosa. She can now see a rough image of the world made up of light and dark blocks. She told Sky News: "When I go to the grandkids' hockey game or soccer game I can see which direction the game is moving in. I can shoot baskets with my grandson, and I can see my granddaughter dancing across the stage. It's wonderful."

The first patients in Britain to be given the operation were also completely blind due to the same condition as Ms Moorfoot. This inherited eye disease causes the loss of cells in the retina so that vision gradually disappears. Eventually this technological miracle could be offered to thousands of patients as the devices are developed and perfected.

The British operations were carried out by Mr Lyndon da Cruz, a consultant retinal surgeon at Moorfields. He said: "Conceptually it could be used for anyone with extremely poor vision but a physically intact optic nerve. The sort of vision we are getting is not good quality but as the thing gets better it will open up to more and more people."

While Ms Moorfoot's implant had just 16 electrodes, the device fitted to the two British patients had 60, giving clearer images. In California, scientists are developing an implant with 1,000 electrodes, which should allow facial recognition.

American researchers are also hoping eventually to develop a camera the size of a pea that could be implanted within the eyeball, replacing natural tissue with artificial technology. Mark Humayun, Professor of Ophthalmology and Biomedical Engineering at the Doheny Eye Institute in Los Angeles, California, which developed the technology, said: "The camera is very, very small, and very low power, so it can go inside your eye and couple your eye movement to where the camera is. With the kind of missing information the brain can fill in, this field is really blossoming. In the next four to five years I hope, and we all hope, that we see technology that's much more advanced."

Sources: Various

HOW THE IMPLANT WORKS

Camera
Receiver
1
Processor 2

Lens
Retinal implant
3
4
Retina
5

Implant electrodes stimulate retina and send signal to the brain

Space Debris May be Catastrophic to Future Missions

Ian O'Neill

Kessler Syndrome could be a frightening situation for space travel. No, it's not a health risk to the human body in zero-G and it's not a psychological disorder for astronauts spending too much time from home. Kessler Syndrome is the point at which space travel becomes impossible without hitting into a piece of space junk, jeopardising missions and risking lives. In extreme predictions, collisions between bits of rubbish may become more and more frequent, causing a catastrophic cascade of debris multiplying exponentially, falling through the atmosphere and making space impassable.

In the meanwhile, space mission controllers must be acutely aware that there could be an odd bolt or piece of old satellite flying toward their spaceship at velocities faster than the fastest rifle shot. Spare a thought for the space debris trackers as they try to keep a record of the 9,000+ pieces of junk currently orbiting our planet.

Strict international civil aviation-style laws may need to be imposed on the world's space agencies if future generations of the human race are going to make it in space. This stark warning comes from Tommaso Sgobba, Director of the International Association for the Advancement of Space Safety. Sgobba's main argument comes from the danger associated with the escalating accumulation of space debris in Earth orbit; should these high speed bits of junk hit a spaceship, satellite or an astronaut, death and disaster may ensue. It may get worse than this, possibly paralysing the Earth from having access to space at all.

Other scientists agree with Sgobba, recommending that future missions into space abide by some strict codes of practice (possibly more strict than those imposed on international civil aviation) to drastically cut the rate of orbital littering by the 20 countries currently able to send stuff into space.

Even the most tightly controlled missions, such as the International Space Station, are expected to shed bits and pieces over the course of their lifetimes. Space junk comes in all shapes and sizes and can be anything from a small screw to entire dead satellites. Recorded examples of space junk include an old glove lost by

> ## Kessler Syndrome is the point at which space travel becomes impossible without hitting into a piece of space junk

Ed White during the first ever US space walk in 1965 (during the Gemini-4 mission), a camera that Michael Collins let slip in space in 1966 (during the Gemini-8 mission) and a pair of pliers that International Space Station astronaut Scott Parazynski dropped during an EVA (Extra Vehicular Activity) last year.

It is hoped that tighter controls on the rockets, satellites and spacecraft will slow the rate of junk increase, but the problem is already pretty worrying for long-term missions in orbit around the Earth. The two critical regions filling with debris are in low Earth and geosynchronous orbits, a few hundred and 22,300 miles high respectively. Low Earth orbit will cause problems for spacecraft to actually leave the atmosphere and geosynchronous orbit may hinder future communication satellite insertions.

To safeguard our access into space, and avoid an increase in debris-related incidents, action will need to be taken.

http://www.universetoday.com
24 February 2008

Afghan girl defies death threats over Olympics

By Tom Coghlan in Kabul

A teenage athlete has overcome a campaign of intimidation including death threats to become the only female member of the team to represent Afghanistan at the Beijing Olympics.

Mehboba Ahdyar, a shy 19-year-old from Kabul, will face the worlds best 1,500 metre runners in August wearing a veil and a baggy tracksuit.

While she is unlikely to mount the winner's podium, few of her opponents will have endured such a perilous training regime to get them to the Games. Training for Mehboba begins after nightfall. At 8.30pm, when Kabul residents are transfixed by the daily episode of the country's most popular soap opera, a racy Indian drama named *Because a Mother-in-Law was Once a Daughter-in-Law Too*, Mehboba slips out of her house in a poor suburb and starts running.

"In spite of the taunts and death threats, she insists she will run for national pride"

She runs up and down the streets for the duration of the programme. It is the only time when, as a woman, she can supplement her official training sessions without threats or harassment.

She recently had to destroy the Sim card on her mobile phone because the number had become known to fundamentalists who bombarded her with death threats.

"They say that they will not leave me alive," she said, with a shrug.

Mehboba, whose father scrapes a living as a carpenter, is a devout Muslim and insists that if she is forced to wear the sort of figure-hugging kit favoured by other international athletes she will not take part.

But such dedication to her faith has not prevented further intimidation. After a Western journalist visited her house

"Three times a week she trains for three hours at the national stadium, a concrete track around the field where the Taliban used to perform public executions."

this week a rumour spread that she was entertaining foreign men as a prostitute.

Mehboba received a visit from the police, while her family were warned that they might have to leave their house.

In spite of the taunts and death threats, she insists she will run for national pride.

"I will compete against heroes," she said, although she could not name any of the world's leading middle-distance runners. "We have trained for three years. I hope for a medal or at least to break Afghanistan's record."

Her personal best is a full minute outside the 1,500-metre world record, but she has beaten all comers in national competitions.

Three times a week she and her fellow Olympian, Masood Azizi, a 20-year-old sprinter, train for three hours at the national stadium, a concrete track around the field where the Taliban used to perform public executions.

Mehboba and Azizi, along with a wrestler and a Taekwondo competitor will today fly to Malaysia for five months of intensive training to give the four-athlete team their best shot at Olympic glory.

Mehboba was excited and nervous. "I have never left the country," she said, "except for a refugee camp in Pakistan."

Daily Telegraph 29 March 2008
© Telegraph Group Ltd 2008

'Sometimes I light up as I jog along; and if there's a good pub along the way I might drop in for a pint'

Essential Articles 11 • www.carelpress.com

Photo: Matthew Lloyd/PA Wire/PA Photos

KEEP ON RUNNING

It's hardly the ideal training regime for long-distance runners, but booze and fags have not held Buster Martin back. At 101 he's limbering up for the London Marathon. Julian Champkin reports

All sorts of people run the London Marathon. There are proper, serious runners, there are runners dressed in rhino suits and as deep-sea divers. And there is even one who is made up to look like a 101-year-old man.

Well, actually, no. That *is* a 101-year-old man running the London Marathon. Buster Martin will be out there at the start line on April 13 with the best of them; and if all goes to plan he will be there at the finish line 26 miles and, at a guess, some five hours later.

"I don't run as fast as I used to but it's a bit faster than a jog," he says. "I don't promise to finish, because I never make promises I cannot keep, so when I have actually finished is when I will promise."

Buster is a phenomenon. You may remember him from The Zimmers, a rock group of 80-year-olds and above who recorded their version of My Generation for a TV programme last year. Buster was their oldest singer. He is also Britain's oldest working man. For three days a week a firm of plumbers in Pimlico employs him to clean and valet its vans – and he still belongs to a boxing club.

Buster is obviously fit. He attributes this to the past 96 years of his lifestyle. "You stay fit by working, and I have been working since the age of five."

He was born in France, but his mother abandoned him in a Cornish orphanage when he was three months old. "They got five years' work out of me at the orphanage, then they slung me out when I was 10 because I was eating too much. They paid my train fare to London. I got there at 10.30am and by 12 I had a job setting up stalls in Billingsgate market." He joined the Army at 14 – nipping out of the barracks before dawn each morning, he says, to earn extra money on the market.

He was a PE trainer, and ended up as Regimental Sergeant Major. "You have to be a bastard to be an RSM. I always say I was born one."

He married in 1920 – he was 14 at the time. His wife, Iriana, was 12. They married in France, where it was legal. "I don't say how I got to France. That might not have been quite so legal." They had, believe it or not, 17 children: "Twins, triplets, singletons – all sorts. Our first-born is 86 now." Iriana died in 1955. "I still talk to her each morning, and ask 'How is my guardian angel?'"

He made headlines again last year when three muggers attacked him. If you talk to Buster for long you won't be surprised to hear that it happened when he was leaving the Fox and Grapes pub. You also won't be surprised to hear that they ran off after he fought them back. "A hard kick where it hurts," he says.

The first time he visited a doctor, he says, was in 1982. "Well you didn't, before the National Health, not when you had to pay for it. They gave me a flu jab. I've had a cold ever since." The only time he was ever off work was for an ingrowing toenail.

And now he is running the Marathon. Why? "Cos they asked me to." He has a trainer, Harmander Singh, who also trained 96-year-old Fauja Singh to run marathons. They train together three times a week in Brixton, once a week round Buster's patch in Lambeth. He prefers Lambeth. The route, he says, takes him past more of his favourite pubs. "Not always without stopping."

His training methods are as unusual as he is. Other runners carry rehydration fluids in plastic bottles. Buster shows me what he claims is his training aid: a pint mug with a chunky handle. Other support systems he carries include a packet of fags stuffed into a pocket.

"I like to light up as I jog along; and if there's a good pub along the way I might drop in for a pint."

He says he has been smoking and drinking since he was seven, and after 94 years it would be dangerous to stop now. There is no disputing his endurance. "I was round the park four or five times yesterday – that must be eight or nine miles. And last Wednesday, when it was pouring with rain, I was out from 11.15 till three. Came home soaking wet." His trainer reckons he does 20 odd miles a week.

He goes for runs at 2.30 in the morning on occasion.

"Well, you don't get the nutters out then. Leastways, the only nutter out then is me."

"Why run? Well, I enjoy it. If you're alive you ought to be happy. They tell old people that we are good for nothing, they give us a Zimmer frame and sit us in a chair doing nothing all day – no wonder people seize up and give up and are as miserable as sin.

"I want to show other people that we are not past it. Old people can do things if they want to. How will I feel afterwards? Bloody knackered. And if I'm not, I will be bloody amazed!"

The rest of us are bloody amazed already.

Saga April 2008
www.saga.co.uk

London Marathon 13 April 2008
Buster ran to raise money for the Rhys Daniels Trust, which provides families with somewhere to stay when visiting children in hospital.
www.rhysdanielstrust.org

STOP PRESS

Guiness World Records has refused to verify Buster Martin's claim to be the oldest Marathon runner suggesting that he is 'only' 94 since he was born on 1 September 1913 not 1906.
Mr Martin said: "I know how long I have lived. There are always rumours from a lot of people who are jealous"
He finished the race in just over 10 hours.

Get your kids fit... the easy way

Schoolkids could soon be spending their lunchbreaks playing computer games... but don't worry, it's to help them get fit.

A scheme getting kids to mimic sports such as tennis and bowling by playing the Nintendo Wii has been trialled in six schools in Worcestershire.

And after winning an award from the Youth Sport Trust, it may be extended across the country.

A pilot scheme involving Wii clubs at lunch and break-times is reported to be in the pipeline. While some parents may be horrified that their children will be indoors playing virtual sport rather than outdoors doing the real thing, action needs to be taken to get our kids fit.

Child obesity levels have trebled in the past 20 years, causing life-threatening health problems, so parents and teachers are trying to find more inventive ways to help children to stay healthy.

"It's a move in the right direction if it gets results," says Chris Mundle, director of Destination Health & Fitness (www.destinationw1.com), who is a personal trainer and sports coach specialising in working with young people.

"Children must find something they enjoy that keeps them active – inside and out.

"All children should be getting 20 to 30 minutes of aerobic activity – swimming, running, etc – three times a week.

"But playing a game like the Wii or Swingball is beneficial, as long as children are doing it as well as regular exercise."

We got Ivan Copeland, aged nine, Dylan Ajani, eight, Owen MacDonald, eight, and Freddie Ajani, five, to put five popular action games to the test and asked Chris to give his verdict.

GIANT RETRO SPACE HOPPER

Chris says: "This is a great anaerobic exercise that involves both balance and co-ordination. It's good for inner-thigh muscles which you use to hold on to the ball, and it also works the abdominals. What's more, it builds strength in shoulder muscles and forearms."

CALORIES BURNT IN 30 MINS: 180

THE VERDICT:

Ivan: "Good but it's hard work to get your balance and a bit dangerous once you get going – it bounces really high."

Dylan: "This is my favourite. It's good for your legs and you're getting fit while you're sitting down!"

Owen: "Brilliant! Can I take one home?"

Freddie: "A bit difficult for me to get on, but really boingy. Also good for fighting with. I would play with it lots."

SWINGBALL CENTRE
(includes volleyball, tailball and shuttleball)

Chris says: "This involves constant movement, like tennis, so it's a more aerobic form of exercise. It's excellent for working out the lower body - legs, lower back and abdominals."

CALORIES BURNT IN 30 MINS: 200

THE VERDICT:

Ivan: "Great practice for learning to play tennis. You could take this to the park."

Dylan: "There are loads of great games on this, so it would be perfect for a sunny day."

Owen: "I think this one would be better in the garden – you need space."

Freddie: "I didn't like this. The pole kept falling off."

Wii MARIO & SONIC AT THE OLYMPIC GAMES

Chris says: "The races that involve pumping your arms are good for arms and shoulder muscles. Some of the games are more explosive – where you have to whack something – which is anaerobic (helping to build up muscles). Although this is an active game, kids would need to play it for more than 30 minutes consistently for their overall health to really benefit."

CALORIES BURNT IN 30 MINS: 120

THE VERDICT:

Ivan: "I like this, I could play it for hours. It really makes your arms tired."

Dylan: "I love this – it's a really cool video game that you play standing up, so it forces you to move, which is good for you."

Owen: "I like it but it's quite hard – I'd like more practice!"

Freddie: "My favourite. I won the swimming one!"

TWISTER

Chris says: "This is like ashtanga yoga! You're holding the positions for a long time, so it's all about strength, balance and co-ordination. It targets specific muscles and is a good all-rounder for fitness."

CALORIES BURNT IN 30 MINS: 140

THE VERDICT:

Ivan: "This one really makes you stretch your body. I like it but it's a bit slow."

Dylan: "This makes your legs ache, but it's worth it – it's fun."

Owen: "I love this – I play this a lot with my mum and dad, but they always get tired before I do!"

Freddie: "Really good but it made my legs ache."

DANCE MAKER DANCE MAT

Chris says: "This involves stopping and starting, so it's anaerobic exercise – you're using energy bursts rather than constantly burning energy. A good all-over workout."

CALORIES BURNT IN 30 MINS: 160

THE VERDICT:

Ivan: "This is better than I expected, I'd definitely play it again."

Dylan: "I thought this would be girlie but it's quite good actually – you have to move fast."

Owen: "It's good fun, but not my favourite."

Freddie: "I loved it – it makes you move about. The music is annoying though.

Daily Mirror 7 February 2008

TEEN READING – A CONTRADICTION IN TERMS?

"Today's young people are exposed to a wider variety of reading material than any previous generation," according to Honor Wilson-Fletcher, director of the National Year of Reading, because of the explosion of digital media.

A report "Read up, Fed Up: Exploring Teen Reading Habits in the UK Today" does seem to establish that young people are reading different things from previous generations, and responding in a different way. In the list of things they love to read, magazines and blogs feature higher than books and the loathed list is dominated by material teenagers are forced to read.

Song lyrics and computer game cheats may not rank alongside War and Peace in terms of sustained reading but they do add to a picture of a varied reading diet

Given the way the survey was conducted, it is not surprising that online material features strongly. The research started with a series of online focus groups which produced a list of 20 loved and loathed reads. Teenagers were encouraged to have their say via the social networking and web building site Pizco and a further 1,340 users of the site were surveyed.

Song lyrics and computer game cheats may not rank alongside War and Peace in terms of sustained reading but they do add to a picture of a varied reading diet which includes some old favourites and some surprises. A typical teenage perversity is evident in the lists. Although Bliss and Heat rank at the top of the 'loved' material, the fourth most loathed item is "reading about skinny celebrities in magazines". The Harry Potter series features in both the most loved list (at 5) and in the most loathed (at 8). Old favourites like The Lion the Witch and The Wardrobe are in the loved list while Facebook is loathed.

For homework to be at the top of the loathed list is not surprising but the inclusion of The Beano and the Financial Times is puzzling. Perhaps this represents scorn for things that are on the one hand too childish and on the other too serious.

Although it may be worrying that Shakespeare and 'Books over 100 pages' appear among the most hated material,

it is also surely unhelpful that 45% of teenagers said they had been told off by adults for reading something that was not 'proper reading'.

One very positive item appears in the loved list in fourth place – 'my own blog or fan fiction' – which suggests a strong link between reading and writing. Fan fiction – in which people use characters and storylines originally created by others to create their own stories – is a good example of the way digital media allows the combination of reading, writing and social networking. Fans invent new scenes or situations for characters from a book (or film or TV series). These may continue the story or even fill in events before and during it. They often submit their work to a small group to critique and edit in a beta version and then put the product 'out there' for a wider audience to read and review. The results can range from the worthless to subtle and moving pieces, but this whole process can only exist because of digital media. A massive 80% of those surveyed said they had written their own story, film, play or song.

What can we conclude about what young people read? It seems likely that the survey has been biased by the method chosen to collect the data. The sample appears to have been restricted to teens who were online and it was self-selecting, so that only those with strong views in either direction were likely to respond. Perhaps there is a an undiscovered group of teenagers who are sitting in their rooms, with their computers turned off, reading War and Peace – or, if the survey is correct, re-writing it.

Sources: Various

READ UP: THINGS TEENS LOVE TO READ

1   Heat magazine
2= Bliss Magazine
2= Song lyrics online
3   Computer game cheats online
4   My own online blog or fan fiction
5   The Harry Potter series
6   Anne Frank's Diary
7   Film scripts
8   Books by Anthony Horowitz
9   The Lion, the Witch and the Wardrobe
10= BBC Online
10= Books by Louise Rennison

FED UP: THINGS TEENS LOATHE TO READ

1   Homework
2   Shakespeare
3   Books over 100 pages
4   Reading about skinny celebrities in magazines
5   The books I am made to read by school/ my teachers
6   Encyclopaedias and dictionaries
7   The Beano
8= Music (scores)
8= The Harry Potter series
8= Maps/directions
9   Facebook
10= Financial Times
10= Anything in another language

Is our children reading?

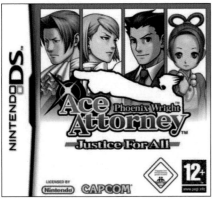

Steven Poole

As George Bush nearly asked: "Is our children reading?" The answer appears to be no, according to the 2006 report of the International Literacy Study. As the Guardian summarises its findings: "England has plummeted from third to 19th in an international league table of children's literacy levels as pupils replace books with computer games."

Imagine the headline 100 years ago: "Children spending too much time playing outdoors with hoops and sticks, says minister; should be forcibly enclosed to study improving literature." There's always some apparently pointless youth activity to scapegoat.

As has always been the case, though, the adult paranoia expressed here about the supposedly harmful influence of videogames depends on a sublime ignorance of the form. In fact, you're not going to get far in most modern videogames if you can't read. And some of them make you read an awful lot.

News headlines don't tell you, for example, about the wonderfully batty series of games for the Nintendo DS starring Phoenix Wright. These games, in which you play the part of a defence lawyer in a series of increasingly surreal criminal trials, take place almost entirely through conversations that you have to remember and then sift for contradictions, before triumphantly shouting "objection!" in a crowded courtroom. At a rough estimate, one Phoenix Wright game contains at least as much text as your average children's novel.

Meanwhile, another game for the DS, The Legend of Zelda: Phantom Hourglass, not only has innumerable scripted conversations and written signs to read, but makes you write as well – scribbling notes on your maps (via a touchscreen and stylus) so you can solve the puzzles and navigate through increasingly tortuous temples. A child playing this game is probably more passionate about reading its prose for clues and taking detailed notes, than he is about doing his homework. But that's not the game's fault.

> Youth literacy isn't actually decreasing; it's just moving into arenas that the fogeys don't know about or understand or have any idea how to quantify

Ah, but is the writing in these games any good? Well, it's variable, like the writing in books. Some of it's rubbish and some of it is very good. (In my opinion, Phoenix Wright is funnier and cleverer than most TV made for adults.) But quality doesn't really matter. My memory of reading as a child is basically that of voraciously hoovering up any old crap. (This turned out to be excellent training for becoming a book reviewer.)

Not all of the games that children are playing are so dependent on reading, of course. Doubtless children are also playing a lot of games where you race shiny cars or shoot zombies into bloody chunks with massive guns. Well, everybody has to relax now and then. To insist that a young person spend every minute of his or her waking day in adult-mandated forms of self-improvement would be a kind of child abuse.

There is a larger paranoia about decreasing literacy among the young caused by maleficent new technologies. It seems at least as plausible that youth literacy isn't actually decreasing; it's just moving into arenas that the fogeys don't know about or understand or have any idea how to quantify – like videogames or instant-messaging or writing in internet forums, or the wonderfully playful transformations of English in Lolcat captions.

At any rate, it's clear that young people aren't put off games like Zelda or Phoenix Wright because they demand reading skills. On the contrary, the games reward reading. As the experts and politicians commenting on the report wonder aloud how to put the "buzz" back into reading, Phoenix Wright and Zelda are already doing it.

So if English children are not so much interested in picking up a paperback, maybe that says more about the quality of books currently being foisted upon them than it does about the evils of digital entertainment. Children are, after all, quite discriminating. If someone writes a new Harry Potter, they'll curl up with it for days. If not, there's always the games console.

The Guardian 1 December 2007
© Guardian News & Media Ltd. 2007

The soldier's tale: return from Iraq

It's now five years since the Iraq war began. And ever since the first casualties started to arrive back in Britain, former paratrooper Stuart Griffiths has been documenting their struggles. Here he presents his moving portfolio.

This has been a slow process – not every wounded soldier wants to talk or have their picture taken – but even as the war broke out, on 20 March 2003, I knew their stories would need to be told. These portraits are about honouring their sacrifice, but they are also a protest against the difficulties and injustices they face as they return to civilian life. I know from my own experience as a soldier how hard that readjustment can be.

In 1988 at the age of 16 I joined the Parachute Regiment, went straight to Northern Ireland and became unit photographer, taking everything from passport photos to PR shots. I was attached to the intelligence section and there I began to learn things about the way the Army worked that made me feel uncomfortable. After a few years I left the forces and moved to Brighton to do a degree in photography.

In 2000 I went to London to try to work full-time as a photographer but my accommodation fell through and I ended up on the streets. Someone gave me the number of the Ex-Forces Fellowship Centre in East London and they gave me a room that night. That's where this project really began. There were 100 ex-servicemen living there at the time and most of them were dealing with physical and psychological injuries, as well as alcohol and drug addictions.

I lived there for about a year until I moved in with my girlfriend, but I went back when the war broke out in 2003, as I thought the story of the hostel needed to be told. My original plan was to do something on the residents there, to coincide with the first anniversary of the war. This would be a kind of warning of problems up ahead, because these guys are the people that the soldiers fighting in Iraq could eventually become. Then I began photographing the Iraq veterans themselves.

I think my own soldiering background has helped them open up to me. They know I have respect and empathy for them and that is how I wanted to convey their injuries. I don't want to be brutal or sensational, but I do want to challenge the viewer with the reality of what serving your country means. We used to be saturated with television images of fighting in Iraq, but as more and more of these guys come home it all goes quiet.

Death and injury are inevitable parts of soldiering but what is different with this conflict is that it has been controversial since the start, and that hasn't been good for these veterans psychologically. It isn't about directly defending our country, so they aren't treated as war heroes in the usual sense. And they have to rely on the NHS, which can barely cope with the needs of the ordinary public, and on mental-health charities such as Combat Stress. It's a struggle for some of them even to get a war pension. There is a lot of bitterness and anger at the fact that they have given so much and are getting so little in return.

I hope with this project to be able to reach out to as many people as possible with this alternative viewpoint of the British armed forces. I support the Army, but there is no glory in war and certainly not in the way these casualties have been treated. I'm still taking these photos and will continue to do so until I know in my heart that it is time to stop. At the moment, things are still relatively recent for these guys coming back from Iraq. I just wonder where they'll be in ten years' time.

> " There is a lot of bitterness and anger at the fact that they have given so much and are getting so little in return. "

Jamie Cooper, Age 19
Served as: Private
Time in Iraq: September 2007-November 2007

Following a mortar attack on his Basra base, Jamie Cooper became the youngest soldier to be wounded in Iraq, two months into his tour. Shrapnel from the rockets sliced through his stomach, leg and hands causing massive internal injuries. After being airlifted to Selly Oak Hospital, he spent the next nine months recuperating.

It was a difficult recovery and the conditions in the NHS ward, according to Cooper, were appalling. "I was disgusted at the hospital," he says. "My colostomy bag kept bursting and at times I was left in my own faeces all night." He also caught MRSA twice, which hampered his recovery. Complaints from his parents prompted a media outcry.

Cooper has spent the past eight months at Headley Court, where his progress has amazed the doctors. "It was a shock when I started walking again, as I wasn't meant to," he says. He now hopes to be able to rejoin his unit in Germany, albeit not in a frontline capacity. "When I first got injured I wanted to quit," he says, "but what changed my mind was when I was taken back to visit all the lads. I still felt like I wanted to be part of it all."

"They don't understand what you're suffering"

Chris Thompson, Age 23
Served as: Private
Time in Iraq: January 2004-March 2004

Chris Thompson was 18 years old when his vehicle was caught in a roadside bomb explosion in Al Amarah in 2004. The device, packed with ball bearings, damaged Thompson's right foot and lower leg so severely that, by the time he was flown back to Birmingham's Selly Oak Hospital, doctors were forced to amputate to avoid infection.

Thompson returned home to live with his mother in Bishop Auckland to await discharge and some kind of compensation. He has been overwhelmed by the support of his local community but is less impressed by the treatment he has received from the MoD. He feels that he and many other injured soldiers have simply been abandoned.

Thompson was happy to be photographed and talk about his experiences despite the fact that he says he has been warned off talking to the press by the MoD. "I wasn't having it," he explains. "You fight for your country and then they just forget about you."

Chris Thompson
Photo: © Stuart Griffiths

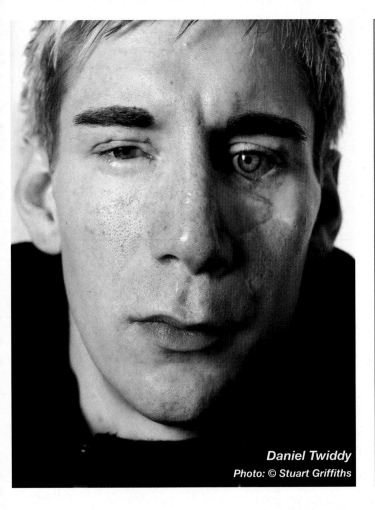

Daniel Twiddy
Photo: © Stuart Griffiths

Andy Anthony Julien, Age 23
Served as: Cavalryman
Time in Iraq: February 2003-March 2003

Five days into the war, the tank in which Andy Julien was travelling was hit by 'friendly fire' from another British tank. Two of his comrades were killed instantly and a third, Daniel Twiddy suffered 80% burns. Julien's legs were badly damaged, but it is the psychological effects that have been harder to bear. "The physical recovery was very difficult but at the moment it's more about dealing with the mental issues. I'm still trying to get my head around it now, especially when I go back over what actually happened out there."

Julien feels that, while his colleagues were a great source of help, the MoD was less forthcoming. "The people in my regiment kept their promise and looked after me, putting me in touch with Combat Stress so I could get counselling – at one stage I was going rapidly downhill – but I wasn't prioritised because I wasn't a serving soldier. I think the MoD should have given me more support at that point, when I really needed it."

Although Julien was keen to get back into Army life as soon as possible, he was physically and mentally "downgraded" by doctors working on behalf of the MoD and medically discharged in January 2005. He is now back home in Manchester working in customer services.

"All I am is a number that they need to replace"

Daniel Twiddy, Age 27
Served as: Lance-corporal
Time in Iraq: February 2003-March 2003

Daniel Twiddy was involved in the same friendly-fire incident as Andy Julien. He spent a month in hospital in the UK recovering from 80% burns and severe shrapnel wounds to his face. "My mum says she could look straight through my nose into my mouth at first," he says. He lost all hearing in one ear and is partially deaf in the other.

Twiddy has made a good recovery – although he is still undergoing treatment for his injuries – and is working again in his own business as a plasterer.

"I'm a determined person so I've just got on with it really. The Army has been good to me – my old regiment and the British Legion have helped a lot – but the MoD don't give a shit. All I am to them is a number that they need to replace. I asked for £60 a week for a private physiotherapist and they refused. They say they've done their best by me, but it's not true."

Twiddy has no regrets about his decision to go to Iraq. "I'd be out there now with my mates if I could."

Hayley Murdoch, Age 26
Served as: RAF cartographer
Time in Iraq: February 2004-June 2004

Hayley Murdoch severely damaged her back and hip while providing cover for a Land Rover patrol in 2004. As an RAF cartographer, she had not trained for the duty she had been performing, something she says is symptomatic of the poor way the MoD has handled both operations in Iraq and her subsequent aftercare.

"The accident was the easy bit, it was waiting for treatment back home that was a nightmare. You think things will soon get back to normal and then you get left on a shelf. No one likes to watch their life ebb away."

When Murdoch did finally manage to get treatment at the MoD's Headley Court rehabilitation centre, she was more than satisfied with the help she received. She has taken an administrative job in the family business and still uses a walking stick occasionally, but it is the non-visible signs of damage that she regrets the most.

"I joined the military as an outgoing, confident person," she says, "and that really took a beating on my way out."

"Did we make that much of a difference that we can pull out now? I honestly don't think we did"

Interviews by Rhiannon Harries

The Independent 16 March 2008

Craig Lundberg
Photo: © Stuart Griffiths

Craig Lundberg, Age 22
Served as: Lance-corporal
Time in Iraq: 2003 and 2007

Craig "Freddie" Lundberg joined the Army after finishing his GCSEs. In 2003, shortly after his eighteenth birthday, he was sent on his first tour of duty in Iraq. Four years later he was back in Basra on his second. "It was different this time," he says. "It was a lot more dangerous."

On the night Lundberg got hit, his section was involved in an operation to arrest a group of local insurgents when they came under fire. He was hit by two rocket-propelled grenades, which caused the loss of his left eye, serious damage to his left arm and severe burns and shrapnel wounds to his face. Lundberg's right eye was also damaged, leaving him blind.

Lundberg, who has fought to remain in the Army in any capacity available to him, is devastated by the idea that British troops could soon be withdrawn. "I just think all I've done was a waste. Why has it taken me to be in this state and two of my best mates to get killed for them to say, 'Oh yeah, we're getting out now'? What difference did we make in that tour? Did we make that much of a difference that we can pull out now? I honestly don't think we did."

Lundberg and his family have since set up a charity, The Freddie Fund, which raises money for the soldiers wounded in Iraq and Afghanistan and their families.

It's not only the public who don't respect a uniform

Andreas Whittam Smith

The Royal Air Force has had a base at Wittering, near Peterborough, for more than 90 years. You would think that by now it would have become an accepted part of the local scene. Yet the station commander, Group Captain Rowena Atherton, recently gave the order that RAF personnel should not wear their uniforms in the city because of the verbal abuse they might receive.

When this came to light last week, people were shocked. Even the Prime Minister came forward to say: "All our armed forces should be able to – and be encouraged to – wear their uniforms in public and have the respect and gratitude of the British people for the huge commitment to public service they show."

What seems to have led to the ban is the experience of an RAF nurse in Peterborough. The windows of her home and of her car had been smashed. She told senior officers she was being targeted because she wore her uniform in public. A spokesman said a number of personnel who lived in the city and its outskirts had suffered abuse when openly wearing their uniforms. The verbal attacks had come from a "cross-section" of the community, he added.

Hearing this story, I first asked myself whether senior officers at RAF Wittering had drawn the right conclusion from the reports they received. Could the violent hostility experienced by the RAF nurse have been a further example of the proliferation of mindless violence in certain areas, rather than of hostility to the armed services?

Checking the archives of the local newspaper, I noticed that, quite close to where the RAF nurse lived, another family with no connection to the services had a horrific experience earlier this year. Two of the young daughters of the household have disabilities. They were verbally abused, the parking space for their disabled car was barricaded, bad language was etched into the side of their motability van and on to the walls of their house. The windscreen of their parents' car was smashed.

I wondered, too, whether military personnel did have a strong desire to wear their uniforms in public when they were off-duty. My experience as a soldier doing National Service was that we never wanted to wear our uniforms outside the barracks except when hitch-hiking home. We enjoyed our fun in civvies. The RAF nurse was a member of a Ministry of Defence hospital unit which operates within the NHS hospitals in Peterborough. She was wearing her uniform to go to and from work.

These reservations made, however, I believe there is a genuine problem. For instance, when the RAF staged a parade in Peterborough to mark the freedom of the city, young teenagers found it funny to run between the ranks. I call that instinctive disrespect. General Sir Richard Dannatt, the head of the army, warned last year of a growing gulf between soldiers and the nation. And an independent study by the Labour MP Quentin Davies, is believed to show that there have been various incidents where military personnel have been turned away from shops, airports and pubs, even when in civilian clothes.

Doubtless, some of this is a form of protest at Britain's involvement in the Iraq and Afghanistan wars. This is unfair to our troops, 175 of whom have been killed in Iraq and a further 89 in Afghanistan. But if the Government of the day systematically reduces the scope for protest against these misbegotten policies, as Labour has done, disapproval will be shown in less pleasant forms than, say, demonstrating outside Parliament or heckling ministers at public meetings, both now liable to be treated as illegal activities.

Nor, despite Gordon Brown's hasty statement, does the Government show much meaningful respect for the armed services. Coroners' inquests have repeatedly shown that troops have died because of avoidable deficiencies in their equipment. Returning casualties have sometimes lacked the medical treatment they deserve. Veterans who suffer trauma have been badly served. And when the dead arrive home in coffins, do ministers show their gratitude by turning up at the airfield. Did Mr Blair ever do that? Does Mr Brown? Does anybody?

The decision taken by the RAF station commander in Peterborough was prudent but lacking robustness. On the same day that her bureaucratic decision became known, Flight Lieutenant Michelle Goodman was awarded the Distinguished Flying Cross, the first woman ever to be so honoured. In Iraq, Fl-Lt Goodman had been exceptionally brave. She flew her helicopter at night into the middle of Basra under heavy gun and mortar fire to rescue a soldier who lay critically wounded and got him out. Thank God for such heroes.

The Independent 10 March 2008

> **"And when the dead arrive home in coffins, do ministers show their gratitude by turning up at the airfield. Did Mr Blair ever do that? Does Mr Brown? Does anybody?"**

The most dangerous job in the world

Photo: © Johnny Ring

Bomb disposal experts rarely get to tell their story. **Cassandra Jardine** talks to a 'Felix' who defeated the best efforts of Iraqi bombers

Chris Hunter says he sleeps well. For four months in Iraq he did what he calls "the most dangerous job in the world in the most dangerous place in the world" but, meeting him now, you would scarcely believe that he hadn't taken up his alternative career choice and become a restaurateur.

Bomb disposal experts are known in the army as "Felix" because they are like cats with nine lives and Hunter is certainly a cool cat.

He has written his memoirs, *Eight Lives Down*, under an assumed name and he lives under tight security for fear of reprisals from jihadists who have

> "Do you want to be James Bond?" Of course, he replied "Absolutely"

much to pay him back for, yet he claims that his only worry is how to pay his mortgage on the house near Hay-on-Wye.

In a world full of macho heroes, Hunter, 34, appears to be an oddity. He's a man with a Queen's Award for Gallantry who considers what he did to be almost a routine technical job.

His citation is neatly filed away with his young daughters' school reports, but to read it is to be transported to a world far from the green, rolling hills of Herefordshire, to his four months in southern Iraq in 2004, an experience so "outrageous" that he laughs with incredulity when he thinks back over it.

"We were neutralising expensive rockets at such an astonishing rate that it was costing them money and making them look foolish"

Duty

The citation mentions his selfless devotion to duty, to the way he gave no thought to personal danger as he took those long, lonely walks across open ground to defuse bombs – despite the constant risk of being picked off by a sniper.

He didn't bother to wear body armour, it says, because it hampered him, made him less effective. His efforts saved thousands of lives.

Later, when he moved into intelligence gathering, he was instrumental in disabling a whole bomb factory. He treats it as all in a day's work.

"I wouldn't say I was blasé about danger," he says, "but it becomes second nature. I never felt scared as I walked up to a bomb. I would break out in a sweat and my mind would be racing but that's just the adrenaline, I couldn't control it. The really hard bit was operating in the heat."

He's been reliving those days in writing the book, which is probably unique. Bomb disposal experts have never told their stories before, because it puts them in too much danger. "It used to be because of the IRA; now it's the Islamists," he says. "The Arabs are incredibly dignified people, but they take revenge very seriously." I hope they read his book because it may make them think again.

Deeply moved

Hunter is no gung-ho Rambo type, he's a man who believes it is his duty – as it was his father's before him – to save innocent lives. The moments that touched him most were his encounters with Iraqis. He's scarred by the memory of the man who beat his pregnant wife in front of him because she had inadvertently shown her face to British soldiers. And he remains haunted by the girl whose throat was cut by her father for the dishonour of talking to squaddies.

But he was also deeply moved by the men, women and children who thanked him for saving their lives. "When you've been to somewhere a bomb has exploded and seen the carnage it causes, and then the next day been able to prevent that happening again, you do think you are doing humanitarian work.

"People say that one man's terrorist is another man's freedom fighter and I've some sympathy with that view. But when someone plants a bomb with the intention of injuring civilians, I don't think that is ever justified. Maybe we could stop them by giving in to what they want, but the current government guys wouldn't subscribe to that, so you have to mitigate the threat."

Atonement & the buzz

People go into bomb disposal for three reasons, he believes: atonement, duty and "the buzz". He pleads guilty to all three. He says he was atoning for the minor-sounding sin of "having too many girlfriends" – before he met his wife Lucy.

The duty he felt was to continue the work that his father had done (but rarely spoke of) during the Second World War. And the buzz? "For me it was about standing on the edge, wondering: 'Do I go in or don't I?' and 'What course of action do I take?' When you start the long walk towards a bomb, suddenly you are on your own, totally focused. I miss that. The only reason I got out was for my family."

Iraq was the pinnacle of his 17 years in the Army. He joined, aged 16, picking a career in intelligence initially because he was asked at his interview: "Do you want to be James Bond?" Of course, he replied "Absolutely" and then spent the next two years in a language laboratory learning Russian.

After that he sat, feeling bored, at a desk. It was only when he was commissioned and sent to Sandhurst that he found his calling. Watching a bomb disposal expert at work he thought: "I could do that."

"I knew something strange was going to happen... Other soldiers had gone up to the car and (the bomb) hadn't gone off, so I knew it was meant for me"

Two hundred exams, and many psychological tests later – designed to weed out the risk-taking hero types – he was allowed to make the first of many lonely "long walks" while others stood back in case, this time, the bomb exploded before he could cut through the wires or shave the explosive away from the detonator.

He served in Northern Ireland, Colombia, and Afghanistan, but his four months in Basra were more dangerous than the previous 10 years put together.

Experience and luck

The work was non-stop and the conditions horrendous. Every day there was another bomb at a roadside or under a bridge to defuse or disable. Each time a mixture of his level head, experience and luck allowed him to save the day. Soon, he was such a well-known enemy of the

Shia militia that he became the target himself.

"We were neutralising expensive rockets at such an astonishing rate that it was costing them money and making them look foolish," he says, "and getting lots of forensic evidence that helped us identify who was planting the bombs and where they were getting their equipment from. That's why they wanted to get me.

Death trap to desk job

"I knew something strange was going on because every time we rocked up to defuse something there would be a television crew and a crowd of spectators. They were waiting to see me blown up. I knew for certain that this was the plan when they planted a car bomb outside a Sunni hospital. Other soldiers had gone up to the car and it hadn't gone off, so I knew it was meant for me. They had booby trapped it – which bomb-makers don't often do because it is more dangerous for them."

Ideally, he would send in a robot or disable it himself. Failing that, he would fire a water-filled missile to explode the shell but without detonating the bomb. In this case, all he could do was clear the hospital and then let the robot set it off. No lives were lost but Hunter had become a liability.

He was promoted to major and given a desk job hunting down the bombers. He was spectacularly successful, but it wasn't the work he loved most. And by then he knew the time had come to put his marriage first.

He knows he was lucky to escape with a deaf ear, a bullet hole in his leg and scarring from broken glass on his hands. Two colleagues had their legs blown off and have begun a long, slow recovery.

He also doesn't mind having only been paid £32,000 a year for a job that meant risking his life daily, but he wishes there was more recognition in Britain for the sacrifices soldiers make.

"The year after I left Iraq I went to Washington. I walked into a bar wearing my medals and everyone stood up and cheered. I thought the President must be behind me, but it was me they were cheering. Being British I was both touched and embarrassed."

In January he left the army. Now he's slowly returning to civilian life, making a living out of counter-intelligence consultancy and writing more books, fiction and non-fiction, about his work.

"Psychologically, I would say I have no issues. My wife told me I screamed in the night last week, but I didn't register any dreams."

Perhaps it's not just toughness, but the sense he did a job that was unequivocally worth doing that allows him to remain such a calm and happy man.

Eight Lives Down by Chris Hunter (Bantam)

The Daily Telegraph 24 October 2007
© Daily Telegraph Group Limited 2007

A portrait of life and death in Gaza

Photo: Mohammed Abed/AFP/Getty Images

This desperate scene, captured moments after an Israeli attack, moved *Tim Butcher* to investigate the fate of the young casualties

It was a stunning picture. Friction between Israelis and Palestinians generates countless images, but the photograph of a prostrate teenager in agony next to an inert, almost restful figure on a road by an abandoned bicycle somehow stood out.

So vivid was the light and so dramatic the shell-damaged Jeep backdrop that you could almost hear the boy's scream. Look closely at the second figure's white shirt and its bloom of crimson red might even be growing in front of your eyes.

But while pictures might be worth a thousand words, this one – taken by an agency photographer who arrived at the scene minutes after the blast – told you nothing of who the boys were, how they came to be there and what subsequently happened to them.

'Mahmoud and Khalil came from starkly different backgrounds, but the Israeli war machine is no respecter of class'

To piece that together took days trawling ill-equipped hospital wards, false leads, interviews with traumatised mortuary assistants, and luck.

The incident took place in Gaza last Wednesday as the sun sank in the spring sky. The clearing of winter clouds is normally a harbinger of good, but not in Gaza, where clear skies mean one thing - an increase in Israeli military activity. Bombers, attack helicopters and surveillance drones all perform better without cloud.

The issue of "who shot first" has long become academic in this troubled corner of the Holy Land. Around 1.5 million Palestinians, about a third of whom were driven from their homes in what is now Israel, when the Jewish state was founded 60 years ago, are crammed into a scruffy sliver of Mediterranean littoral known as the Gaza Strip.

Without a meaningful economy, meekly dependent on aid and with a creaking infrastructure providing piecemeal power, sewage and water, it is a festering Petri dish for Palestinian resentment. And it is no surprise where that resentment is aimed. The strip has a short land border with Egypt, but the rest of its frontier, airspace and marine approaches are under Israeli control.

Violence between the two sides has been going on for decades. Put crudely, Palestinian militants launch attacks against targets inside Israel - often using primitive rockets aimed at civilians - and Israel responds hard and heavy.

The Jewish state insists it fires only at confirmed military targets, but the death toll among Gazan civilians dwarfs the number of civilian Israelis killed.

Mahmoud abu Khobayze, 16, heard the sounds of pre-dawn clashes when he woke up in the tatty breezeblock home he shares with his navvy father, Ibrahim, 40, mother, five brothers and two sisters in the village of Mughraqe.

The village is home to some of Gaza's oldest population, the once nomadic desert Bedouin. It is dirt poor, with domestic animals fenced in not by wire but by hurdles of desert scrub.

Mahmoud had to get up early as he faced a long walk to the Ain el Hilwa secondary school on the outskirts of Gaza City. Days of border skirmishes had led Israel to shut off fuel supplies and there was no school bus.

"It was just a routine day. I could hear some firing, but it was a long, long way off, so I just went to school," he said. "I cannot even remember what we studied – English and Arabic, I think."

'I heard the first explosion, dropped the bicycle and fell to the ground'

In a much smarter part of Gaza City, the Sabra suburb near the centre, 19-year-old Khalil Dogmoush was preparing for work.

The oldest of eight children, he had followed his father, Ismail, into the stonemasonry trade and ran a granite-cutting workshop to the south of the city. "He was a clever boy and could have done anything," said Ismail. "But he showed great skill as a businessman.

No one could believe he was only 19, he was so like a more experienced man. And he employed seven people at his own factory, at a time when work is very rare here in Gaza."

The Dogmoush family is one of Gaza's largest. Some of its more extreme elements were responsible for last year's kidnapping of Alan Johnston, the BBC journalist, but Khalil clearly belonged to the mainstream part of the family.

He was so successful that not only did he own a small car pimped out with tinted windows and go-faster stripes, he also had enough money to afford fuel (cooking gas for an engine that had converted because of petrol shortages) at inflated prices. Listening to music as he tooled down Salahadin Street, Gaza's main north-south axis, he might not even have heard the sound of fighting.

Mahmoud and Khalil came from starkly different backgrounds, but the Israeli war machine is no respecter of class. It was the sight of a press Jeep near Mughraqe that first caught Mahmoud's attention.

He had walked home from school and eaten a late salad lunch before

'You can clearly see the muzzle flash from the tank about 1,500 yards away. And two seconds later, just before the film dies, you can see something dark exploding above Fadel. He died instantly'

strolling over to the eastern edge of the village where it is bordered by Salahadin Street. He was with a friend, Mohammed abu Shalouf, 18, who had an old mountain bike that he used to ride to school. Mohammed was hanging back a bit, perhaps sensing something was wrong, happy for Mahmoud to wheel the bike.

The Jeep, owned by Reuters, had two of the news agency's award-winning Gaza team inside. Clearly marked as a press car, they were seeking a vantage point from which to film Israeli forces.

"I saw the Jeep stop where there is a view over the fields and the guys got out and set up their tripod and their camera," said Mahmoud. "A couple of boys from the village walked right up to the cameraman, but I was still about 50 metres away."

Parents across Gaza tire of telling their children not to go outside during fighting, but they also tire of their children ignoring them. What else could be as interesting as watching fighting from a safe

distance, say the kids. The problem is that with the tactics used by Israel in the cramped conditions of Gaza, there is rarely a truly safe distance.

The Reuters cameraman, Fadel Shana, 24, filmed the tank that killed him.

On his film you can clearly see the muzzle flash from the tank about 1,500 yards away. And two seconds later, just before the film dies, you can see something dark exploding above Fadel. He died instantly, almost decapitated by shrapnel. The two boys who Mahmoud saw next to the tripod were also killed in the blast.

"I heard the first explosion, dropped the bicycle and fell to the ground," said Mahmoud. "I had cuts on my neck and chest, but I could move, so I started crawling away."

The detonation of the first tank round was heard by Khalil as he drove home from a day's work. It was so close he heard it above the stereo. He had two friends in the car, but pulled over on Salahadin and ran up the spur road towards the damaged Jeep, to see if he could do anything to help.

It was just as he passed Mahmoud crawling back along the asphalt that the second tank shell exploded. This one contained hundreds of inch-long steel darts, known as flechettes (French for little arrows). They make

It was just as he passed Mahmoud crawling back along the asphalt that the second tank shell exploded

disarmingly small entry wounds but do terrible damage once inside the human body. Khalil was hit by several, but the one that killed him punctured his heart.

Blood can be seen on the front of his white shirt in the photograph that was taken in the seconds after the second tank shell detonated. Mahmoud was also hit by a flechette, puncturing the top of his left thigh. It meant he could no longer crawl and by the time the photograph was taken it was all he could do to drag himself up on his arms and scream.

Doctors managed to remove two pieces of shrapnel from Mahmoud's neck and chest that night before he was moved to Shifa Hospital, the biggest in Gaza, while experts work out what to do with the flechette then lodged deep within his pelvis. An orthopaedic specialist, Dr Ahmed Akram, said the flechette had already caused extensive nerve damage and if Mahmoud walks again he would do so with a limp.

They buried Khalil on Thursday after midday prayers. Hundreds of Dogmoush family members gathered outside the five-storey apartment building where his family have lived for decades.

His 90-year-old grandfather, for whom the boy was named, has lived through three foreign occupations of Gaza, two wars and decades of violent insurgency and he used to boast that he had never cried in public. At the sight of his grandson's corpse, he fell to the ground and wailed.

Last Wednesday's incident might just be a footnote in the bloody history of Gaza, but for those affected it was the day their lives changed for ever.

The Daily Telegraph 23 April 2008
© Telegraph Group Limited 2008

When suffering gets personal

On his return from Afghanistan, BBC world affairs editor John Simpson reveals how his attitude to covering stories about violence and suffering has changed.

The explosion was just close by. The windows of my hotel billowed inwards like sails in a storm, and the walls shuddered. A pause, then the alarms and sirens started up all round. My camera team and I got there quickly. The stench of high explosive still hung over everything. The screaming had mostly stopped, and the rescue workers were dealing with the still-living and collecting up bits of bodies. The police were starting to take out their frustration and anger on the photographers. This was in Kabul just the other day but I have seen these things dozens and dozens of times during my career.

Shock of new life

I have never been a great one for the kind of reporting that tells you how the journalist feels when something terrible happens. It seems to me that we need reporters to be crisp and accurate and unexcitable, like ambulance crews. You certainly do not want an ambulance-man leaning over you and telling you how he feels about your injuries. You just want him to say they will get you sorted

out in no time flat. But in Kabul the other day, and in Baghdad a couple of weeks earlier, I could not help noticing a change within myself. I tried to find out dispassionately what had happened, of course, but when I looked at the bodies on their stretchers and the injured moaning in pain I felt a new kind of anger. I knew immediately what it was all about.

Last year, after four miscarriages over a period of some years and virtually giving up all hope of having a baby, my wife and I had a son: a healthy, active, jolly little boy we have named Rafe (short for Ranulph). With six billion people on earth, having a child is scarcely a rarity. But in our case it was so unexpected, so gratifying, that Rafe seems to us like a miracle.

Gut anger

I already had two daughters by my first marriage and have always, fortunately, been close to them: even more so, now that we all – weirdly – have children of the same sort of age. But I confess that when my daughters were young I was not so aware of

> **"To see the miracle of other people's lives snuffed out wantonly on the streets of Baghdad or Kabul, or London for that matter, for some scarcely understood political or religious motive, seems to me nothing short of blasphemy"**

their uniqueness: everyone of my age seemed to have children then. I understand things better now. And to see the miracle of other people's lives snuffed out wantonly on the streets of Baghdad or Kabul, or London for that matter, for some scarcely understood political or religious motive, seems to me nothing short of blasphemy.

I do not just loathe the stench of high explosive, I have come to loathe the attitudes of people who use high explosive for their own purposes: insurgents, terrorists, the intelligence services of a dozen countries, governments which target towns

"I have finally understood something, through the blessing of having another child late on. It is that life itself is immensely valuable...

...All lives."

and cities and always have a ready apology when they kill the wrong people.

High explosive means hospitals with blood on the walls and corridors, and ordinary people like you and me, lying on the floor or on a wheeled stretcher, ears ringing with the noise of the explosion, nostrils filled with the stench of it still. The screams of others who are worse hurt than us. The fear and despair of the small number of doctors who have to deal with so many life-or-death cases, and know that they are condemning many of them to a slow, painful death. "The armed struggle," said an African resistance song from the 1980s, "is an act of love." Try explaining that to the people lying in the hospital corridors.

Everybody hurts

The idea that some civilians are decent and righteous, while others deserve everything they get, or else should not have been in the way, seems to me to be intolerable. I

hope I never did think that attacks on civilians – any civilians – were justified but now I know for certain they are not. Having been through the first and second Gulf Wars, and watched the wars in the former Yugoslavia and the Nato bombing of Belgrade in 1999, I do not really care any longer what the cause is. It is the civilians on the receiving end who matter.

I am sorry if this sounds pious or sentimental. I do not mean it to be. But I have finally understood something, through the blessing of having another child late on. It is that life itself is immensely valuable. Not just the lives of people who think and look and maybe worship like you and me, people who are attractive or well-educated or rich, people who are the right type of Christian or the right type of Muslim. All lives.

I realise this is terribly sententious: the moral equivalent of a motto from a Christmas cracker. Still, just because something is obvious does

"I do not really care what the cause is. It is the civilians on the receiving end who matter"

not automatically mean it is totally lacking in value. I am certainly not going to stop going to the kind of places where these things happen. But, at the grand old age of 62, my reaction to them has changed.

The fact is, my time reporting on violence and bombings in places like Baghdad and Kabul has shown me one essential thing: that the lives of the poor, the stupid, the old, the ugly, are no less precious to them and to the people around them, than the life of my little son Rafe is precious to me.

From Our Own Correspondent
BBC Radio 4 28 July 2007

MASAI MARATHON –

Photo: SANG TAN/AP/PA Photos

RUNNING FOR LIFE

Most people would recognise the iconic image of the Masai warrior – a lean solitary figure decked out in red robes and elaborate beaded jewellery. The scene, synonymous with East Africa, is an unexpected one in Central London

BUT six young Masai men left their village in Tanzania to run in the London marathon and to raise both money and awareness concerning the desperate plight of their people.

The Masai people are one of the last distinct tribes in Africa to retain their cultural identity. Traditionally their diet consists of blood and milk. No household is without cattle which are seen as the 'money'

and 'bank accounts' of the Masai people. For this reason cattle are rarely killed and eaten, except on special occasions such as traditional ceremonies.

However, Tanzania has suffered years of drought and for the Masai the search for water had become increasingly desperate. Initially it was the cattle that died, the very thing that the Masai depend on to live. Then the village Elders, the sick and of course the most vulnerable of all, the children. All for the want of something we all take for granted every day: clean drinking water.

Their young men are proud warriors who are renowned for their physical strength, agility and ferocity in battle. The traditional warrior role – stealing cattle from other villages or killing a lion – was no help in the face of this predicament but the young warriors were not prepared to wait passively for outside aid and took a different view of their role as protectors. They decided to undertake the journey and task of a lifetime: to find a way to provide their village with clean water.

The solution came about as part of an English lesson by volunteers from the charity Greenforce. Work on verbs led to a discussion of running and an explanation of the word 'marathon'. For the Masai – for whom running is almost as natural as breathing – the idea of raising money by running was immediately almost irresistible. They decided that they would form a team to run the marathon.

> **For the Masai – for whom running is almost as natural as breathing – the idea of raising money by running was immediately almost irresistible**

While running may come easily to the Masai, organising the journey to England to allow them to take part was a difficult undertaking. Greenforce worker Paul Martin, known to the Masai as 'Soldier Bob', who was their guide and co-runner, records that "Greenforce struggled to even find the funds to cover the costs of bringing the Masai over to the UK and even on the day of arrival as I drank hot sweet Masai tea with Isaya I was concerned that maybe I would not be able to fulfil my promise to him." Greenforce also felt it necessary to prepare the Masai for the cultural differences they would meet, just as they would have prepared European volunteers for life in a Tanzanian village.

Their training consisted mainly of their normal life. The spokesman for the group was Isaya. As the first born in his family and the leader of his age group in the village, Isaya grew up with many responsibilities which restricted his education to three years at primary school. Nevertheless, he found the time to learn English with the assistance of Greenforce. His confidence and charisma as well as his keen interest in other cultures was evident in the interviews given to the media. He explained that a young Masai might run every day to steal cattle

from other villages or to chase lions away from the herd of his own. He also had a keen ear for a soundbite: "The marathon is easy" he is quoted as saying, "There are no lions."

In a concession to their culture, they were allowed to run carrying their shields and sticks and without wearing race numbers on their traditional robes. In a concession to our culture, they were supplied with underpants by Marks & Spencer. Far from the high tech footwear of the elite runners, the Masai wore sandals made from old tyres.

Despite their natural advantages, the Warriors' intention was not to break any records; their purpose in running was not personal achievement but to benefit their village. On their many TV news appearances the dignified demeanour of the young men and the boldness of their endeavour caught the imagination of the viewers. The donations began to come in. As 'Soldier Bob'

> **In a concession to their culture, they were allowed to run carrying their shields and sticks, in a concession to ours, they were supplied with underpants by Marks & Spencer**

records: "Shortly after our first TV appearance on the BBC, I had a call from my office that donations had started to appear in my inbox. Not huge amounts, not the big sponsors I had hoped for, many were just £5 - £10 with the occasional £50 but donations nevertheless. Isaya and I, along with the Warriors, continued our whirlwind tour of TV studios and press conferences and the donations increased in frequency and continued to increase throughout the week. It was obvious that it was not the big companies, the rich benefactors of most sporting events that would support us but ordinary people. Ordinary people with a desire to help, not because they wanted product placements or their logos emblazoned on a Masai shield, but purely because they wanted to help ordinary people elsewhere in the world who were struggling for survival with dignity and pride."

"I don't think I'll ever live to see another day like it"

On the day of the marathon itself, the Warriors sang and chanted as they ran, attracting a great deal of support and encouragement from the watching crowds. Unfortunately one of their team fell ill and had to go to hospital, accompanied by another Warrior. The remaining four crossed the finish line in just under five and a half hours. As Isaya said, however, "..the finish line of the Flora London Marathon is not the finish. The finish is when we can turn on a tap in our village and get clean drinking water!"

Far from their minimum aim of £20,000 to cover their expenses, the Warriors have so far raised more than £114,00 and a major supplier has donated a water pump. In addition their presence at the marathon has vastly raised the profile of the problems facing their people - and continues to do so via Youtube and other sites.

Race director David Bedford was in no doubt who stood out in the 2008 marathon. "The Masai Warriors have to be the defining image of this race. The reception they got and the colour they gave the event will probably end up as one of the greatest memories I've got in the history of the event."

And he was not the only one who found the Masai presence, and the connection they made with the crowd, an emotional event.

'Soldier Bob', experienced volunteer and ex-Army and French Foreign Legion veteran wrote: "Personally as a cynical Londoner and a well travelled soul I don't know which is more amazing. The participation of the Masai in the Flora London Marathon, or the reaction and support of the thousands of ordinary people that lined the streets and donated to the Masai cause. I'd never believed it could happen. It makes me proud to be British, proud to be a Londoner and has renewed my faith in human kind.

I don't think I'll ever live to see another day like it."

Sources: Various

Masai Guide to England

The Masai men had never left their home so Greenforce prepared a guide for them on how to behave and what to expect – just as they would prepare European volunteers to visit the Masai.

"You may be surprised by the number of people that there are and they all seem to be rushing around everywhere. Even though some may look like they have a frown on their face, they are very friendly people "

"You cannot rely on the sun to tell the time accurately and will have to rely on clocks and watches. The sun will rise and set at different times."

"You will see many people who are wearing only small clothes and you will wonder why they are cold and may think they are being disrespectful. This is normal for England, especially when it is sunny or in the evening."

"When nature calls it is advised to seek out a public convenience as opposed to using a tree or a bush."

"Whereas at home it is acceptable to spit, in England it is not. If you have to, you must do so in a sink or in some trees when no one is looking."

"If you see something that someone else has, like a bracelet, and you like it, the person will find it very unusual if you were to take it and wear it."

"You may see animals in a field seemingly left alone. It is important to remember that these animals are owned by someone and are being looked after."

"Many people drink alcohol in England. They do so at bars, at home or at clubs – the English equivalent to a Masai party. When people drink they seem sillier or different."

The 21st century slaves here in the UK

Children trafficked into the UK from Africa, and Nigeria in particular, are living a life of exploitation by better off relatives and others

Photo posed by model

Debbie Ariyo

The two brothers walked through our office doors at Afruca – Africans Unite Against Child Abuse. Sobbing, they recounted details of their terrible experiences spanning many years at the hands of various relatives to whom they were sent as children for a "better life" by their mother following the death of their father in Nigeria. They ended up as domestic slaves.

Now in their mid-twenties, the two young men have spent the bulk of their lives in the UK in abject penury. Denied the opportunity of a decent education, they are now homeless, jobless and unable to produce any documentation as proof of their identities. Effectively, they are in limbo, living from hand to mouth, not sure of their next meal or their next bed for the night. These two young men are part of a growing underclass of young people trafficked into the UK as child slaves.

Over the past six months, as a result of a media campaign ran by Afruca on African satellite TV stations, we have continued to receive young people who have tales of woe similar to the two brothers. We have supported at least 15 young people in various ways since January 2007 to enable them to deal with the impact of trafficking and

exploitation so they can move on with their lives. While all their stories are different, their experiences of abuse and exploitation as domestic slaves are very similar. More and more young people are coming to us for help, evidence of the growing phenomenon of child domestic slavery in this country.

Our experience is supported by recent research into child trafficking. A recent report produced by the Child Exploitation and Online Protection Centre (CEOP) identified 330 victims of trafficking, a third of them coming from different African countries with most of them destined for domestic slavery. This is corroborated by the results of another study on child trafficking in the north of England by ECPAT UK.

Nigerian problem?

Without wishing to stigmatise any community, it is pertinent to add that all the 15 victims mentioned above, including the two brothers, are of Nigerian origin. In the same vein, all the victims of domestic slavery identified in the two research reports referred to above are also all from Nigeria. As a Nigerian myself, this fact is quite disconcerting. Why are Nigerian children being trafficked into the UK for domestic slavery?

The practice of using children for domestic servitude is undoubtedly a very common phenomenon in Nigeria itself.

According to local non-governmental organisations campaigning against this practice, almost every middle class household employs domestic servants many of whom are children. Due to the growing poverty level, the widening gap between rich and poor Nigerians, many parents are wont to give their children to better off relatives in the belief that they will be well looked after and given an opportunity of either going to school or learning a vocation. However, most of these children end up being used as slaves and servants.

Yet the idea of giving children away to relatives is nothing new or strange in many African countries. The practice of fostering, where children are given to relatives to look after is not an act borne out of cruelty or ignorance. In the past, this system has afforded many children from poor backgrounds the opportunity of a good education leading to a prosperous future. The notion that it takes a village to raise a child meant that the extended family were responsible for ensuring children had access to a decent life which their poor parents were unable to give them. Unfortunately, this system of community support has been abused by unscrupulous individuals with ulterior motives. The sad case of Victoria Climbié, the Ivorien girl trafficked into the UK and tortured to death by her relative comes to mind here.

The estimated two million Nigerians here are probably the most rooted nationals from any African country in the UK, bearing in mind that many have been living or visiting the country since the 1960s and 1970s. With a growing middle class population, it is not surprising that the practice of fostering is equally taking hold here as well. Unfortunately, however, many children and their parents have been deceived into coming to the UK for a so-called better life and a good education. Instead, these children end up being used as slaves, to look after the families of their exploiters and cater for their every need. Many have been subjected to a life of suffering, multiple abuse, excessive child labour and harm. Instead of the better life and the good education promised, only a childhood of exploitation awaits.

The physical abuse experienced in many cases results in long-term poor health. Some of the victims we worked with at Afruca were also sexually abused by their exploiters. Most terrible of all is the rupture with their own families. A young girl we supported was brought into the UK at the age of nine years. Now at the age of 19 she has never been in touch with any member of her immediate family as she was prevented from doing so by her exploiters. It is doubtful whether she will ever be able to locate them.

Denial of right to family life

This broken family link, the denial of rights to a decent family life, is a serious form of emotional abuse. Added to the lack of parental care given by the exploiters, many child victims exist in an emotional vacuum, with no love, no affection, and no attention ever paid to them. The deceit, abuse and exploitation experienced at the hands of those they expected to care for them and help them achieve a better life result in a deep emotional and psychological scarring. In fact, many of the victims who come to us have revealed that at one time or another, they either attempted suicide or had many suicidal thoughts.

Yet the implications of their experiences do not end with their slavery. Every single young person we have been in contact with has a serious problem proving their true identity. In many instances, traffickers employ false identities in order to be able to procure travel documents to bring their child victims into the country. Now as adults, many of them have no way of ascertaining their true names, age and date of birth because authentic documentation is unobtainable.

One consequence is that young people are disbelieved by the authorities when they attempt to regularise their status in the UK and they cannot get jobs.

Why are Nigerian children being trafficked into the UK for domestic slavery?

Photo posed by model

Many victims of trafficking do come to the attention of different agencies – be it social services, schools, doctors and others. But practitioners are often unable to identify the indicators of abuse and exploitation and to safeguard the young people. At least one victim we worked with had run away to seek help and support from her local social services department. Unfortunately, not only was she denied any form of help, she was reprimanded for running away from home and was returned to her exploiters.

No prosecutions

No one has ever been prosecuted here for child domestic slavery. Many of the victims we have worked with have taken the steps to report their cases although to date no action has been taken. Yet the UK government is a signatory to the European Convention on Human Rights, articles 3 and 4 of which clearly highlight the rights of people not to be subjected to torture or to inhuman or degrading treatment or to be held in slavery or servitude. Since the government is obliged to protect these rights, it is a mystery that no one has ever been prosecuted.

Until someone is prosecuted, this practice will continue unabated. The government has got a policy in the form of its National Action Plan on Human Trafficking, but it is not enough. Not only should their exploiters be made to face the music, but victims need to be given the support and assistance they require to enable them to prosecute their exploiters and seek compensation for their lost childhood.

It is also imperative that action is taken to raise awareness in source countries such as Nigeria about the implications of handing children over to a "better life". Unless everyone is aware of the facts, the endless stream of children looking for a better life will continue unabated.

Debbie Ariyo is Founder and Executive Director of AFRUCA – Africans Unite Against Child Abuse, an organisation promoting the rights and welfare of African children in the UK.

Community Care 13 December 2008
www.afruca.org

Zimbabwe: an eyewitness account

No soap in a hospital? Can you believe it? But this is Zimbabwe, a country whose public health system was once the envy of neighbouring countries and that now has the lowest life expectancy in the world: 34 for women and 37 for men. This statistic continues to shock and disturb me; Zimbabwe is, after all, not a country at war

O f course, HIV has had a great impact. But it is mainly the policies pursued by Robert Mugabe's Zanu PF party that has moved Zimbabwe, once the bread basket of this part of Africa, to a basket case.

In late October 2007 I spent 10 days in Zimbabwe. I am a trustee of a charity, Zimbabwe Health Training Support, whose aim is to support the training of health professionals and medical students in Zimbabwe. During my stay I ran workshops on medical ethics for junior doctors and consultants. I gave a talk to GPs in Bulawayo on how quality is assessed in general practice in the United Kingdom. While in Bulawayo I stayed with a physician and spent part of my week shadowing him. I also shadowed a GP.

HIV seemed to pervade all healthcare encounters. As many as 70% of inpatients in the public hospital in Bulawayo had an HIV related disease. Many people present with advanced disease – a death sentence. The HIV clinic

in Bulawayo is supported by the Clinton Foundation, but a shortage of drugs and resources has meant that it has been closed to new entrants since August except for children, pregnant women and healthcare workers. I spoke to a pharmacist concerned about the future supply and reliable delivery of antiretrovirals.

A lack of catheter bags and pads meant that incontinent and immobile patients had to lie in urine

Some Zimbabweans who work in South Africa get their antiretrovirals there. One young man had fraudulently been given painkillers as part of his triple regimen therapy. He presented with an immune reconstitution syndrome. He needed chemotherapy, but this wasn't easily available and anyway he didn't have the money to pay for it.

The HIV clinic has 2,500 children on its register. A morning spent with the paediatric nurses revealed the human tragedy. I met numerous orphaned children with HIV being cared for by aunts and grandparents. Because

Healthcare professionals are leaving their work daily. No one begrudges them for leaving, but work schedules become more intense for those remaining

of the food shortages in Zimbabwe a charity was donating food to people with HIV to help feed their families.

I wondered why there seemed to be so many small children and babies with HIV, given the availability of treatment for pregnant women. A paediatrician said one reason is that there is no easily accessible milk in Zimbabwe, so mothers continue to breast feed beyond six months, putting their babies at further risk of acquiring HIV.

Shortages of medical equipment and drugs are severe. Thermometers were being shared between wards, no glucose sticks were available for monitoring diabetes, and certain antibiotics could not be obtained. A lack of catheter bags and pads meant that incontinent and immobile patients had to lie in urine. One patient had metastatic pancreatic cancer. There was no morphine to control his pain or dexamethasome to reduce his brain swelling. Patients in outpatient clinics told us they had difficulty getting basic drugs for ordinary medical conditions such as heart disease, diabetes, and asthma. One patient couldn't afford to buy a steroid inhaler. A girl was walking around for a week with a fractured arm not in a cast as neither of the public hospitals had plaster of Paris. The tragedy is that it never used to be like this.

Healthcare professionals are leaving their work daily. A paediatrician and a physician had left the week before I arrived. No one begrudges them for leaving, but work schedules inevitably become more intense for those remaining. Non-governmental organisations try not to poach health service staff, but they pay in hard currency. Inflation continues to soar – during my short stay prices increased by a third. Nurses I met couldn't afford to eat on their pay. A typical nurse's monthly salary of 17 million Zimbabwean dollars (£290) doesn't go far when transport to and from work costs $Z400,000 each day. One nurse I met relied on financial support from a relative (a nurse) working in Britain.

Simply surviving in Zimbabwe is exhausting. People spend a lot of time searching and queuing for food. Basic foodstuffs such as bread, sugar, and flour are hard to find. Many people survive on one meal a day. There is a desperate shortage of fuel, and people have to go to Botswana to get it. Every day there are cuts in power and water supplies – one part of Harare had not had any running water for six weeks.

I have great admiration for the healthcare staff I met. They had to be so resourceful and were constantly having to solve problems. I was impressed by the clinicians' skills. As is

The HIV clinic has 2,500 children on its register. A morning spent with the paediatric nurses revealed the human tragedy

the case in many developing countries, doctors' clinical and interpretive skills are often very sharp as so few tests and investigations are available.

I was left with a lasting impression of people who, in spite of incredibly difficult circumstances, had not lost their humanity, sharing food and water and helping each other out in whatever way they could.

Kate Adams is a general practitioner in Hackney, London, and a trustee of Zimbabwe Health Training Support

Simply surviving in Zimbabwe is exhausting. People spend a lot of time searching and queuing for food

British Medical Journal (BMJ), Volume 336
12 January 2008

Chinese celebrities scorn one child policy

Fines are a small price to pay for the rich to expand their family

Wealth and fame may buy celebrities in China endless privileges, but it does not make them exempt from China's one child policy, warn family planning officials

China has historically had a high population. Almost one in five human beings alive is a resident of China (1.3 billion out of a global total of 6.7 billion). The one-child policy was introduced in 1979 to ensure that China, which has always been prone to floods and famine, could feed all its people. The 'one child' policy stipulates each couple living in the cities should only have one child, unless one or both of the couple are from an ethnic minority or they are both themselves from one child families. In most rural areas, a couple may have a second child after a break of several years. Officials have pointed out the introduction of the policy has made the population an estimated 400 million lower than it would have been. Yet despite the fact that it has reduced environmental pressures, there have still been many concerns.

At present, couples face fines of up to 10 times the local per capita income if they break the law. Penalties are believed to average around 100,000 yuan (£7,000) in Beijing. But because the gap between the rich and the poor has widened so considerably, these fines are almost small change to the rich, and a small cost to pay to be able to have a second or even third child. However, the rich sports people, pop stars and business men who violate the one-child policy will soon be facing harsher fines and tarnished credit records.

The warnings from the senior official come amid growing bitterness about the ease with which the well-off flout the rules while others are crippled financially for having a second child, rubbing salt into the wound of the increasing class divide.

Footballer Hao Haidong was reportedly fined 50,000 yuan (£3,500) for having a second child, although this would little affect him as he has an annual salary of 5m yuan (£350,000).

Pop star Sun Nan, who has won the heart of millions of fans with his love songs, is likely to become less popular with the authorities as he and his wife, who already have a daughter, are expecting another child.

> **These fines are like pocket money to the rich, and a small cost to pay to be able to have a second or even third child**

> **The number of men is now thought to exceed women in China by more than 60 million**

Zhao Benshan, an actor and director, has four children – although those with his second wife are twins. The exemption of multiple births from the one-child policy is thought to have encouraged some couples to turn to fertility drugs so they can enjoy a larger family without penalty.

According to an online survey of 7,900 Chinese netizens jointly conducted by China Youth Daily and www.qq.co, more than 60% of respondents said it was unfair that stars and the affluent could breach the rule with 68% seeing the issue to be a major social problem.

Because of the policy in China, single children are even more precious

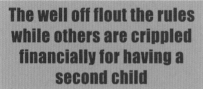

The well off flout the rules while others are crippled financially for having a second child

Some well-off people can afford to submit forged documents saying their first child suffers from a congenital disease, some "buy" the birth permit for a second child while others simply pay the fine without noticing much change in the bank balance.

"How can they violate the national policy just because they have money?" asked one netizen on the survey. Some feel so strongly they are even suggested amending the law, making it a crime to have more children than permitted.

The one child policy has already promoted atrocities such as forced abortion and the killing of female infants because of the traditional preference for boys. The number of men is now thought to exceed women in China by more than 60 million. Increasing the penalty might only increase the lengths people would go to avoid the consequences.

But tension is rising. The director of the state family planning commission has described famous offenders as a "negative social influence" and officials have promised to tackle the issue by naming and shaming rich and influential offenders, or banning them from receiving awards and honours.

According to Xinhua, the state news agency, a threefold system of punishment – tougher fines, the inclusion of family planning violations in personal files in the national credit system and the censure of party members – is being planned. It is hoped that the measures on credit

It's rubbing salt in the wound of the increasing class divide in China

records – affecting the ability to borrow – will make celebrities and businessmen think again.

The government argues it must continue with its restrictions because of demographic pressures. China's population is expected to continue growing over the next two decades, peaking at 1.5 billion. If the government cannot find a successful way to prevent celebrities from flouting the law, not only the population, but the tension within the population, between the 'haves' and the 'have nots' will increase still further.

Sources: Various

Boycott Burma: to go or not to go?

By Andrew Buncombe, Asia Correspondent

Tourists have long been discouraged from travelling to Burma. But the argument – which has been reignited in the wake of Cyclone Nargis – is far from simple. Here three people who know the country make the cases for and against.

There's nothing like having your preconceived ideas shaken up a bit by meeting people who are personally involved in an issue you thought you knew about.

I had always thought the arguments of those who supported a travel boycott of Burma made sense: why should foreigners provide money to the military regime that runs the country in such a brutal way? Why should tourism provide a gloss of acceptability to the generals and hadn't Aung San Suu Kyi – the imprisoned head of the National League for Democracy opposition party – asked tourists to stay away?

Why should foreigners provide money to the military regime that runs the country in such a brutal way?

But when I was in Burma most recently covering the aftermath of Cyclone Nargis, I spoke with people involved in tourism who made me begin to rethink the whole issue. They told me that in a country wrought with poverty, tourism was one of the few ways people could make a living. Admittedly only a small number of the Burmese population work in this sector, but at least those people were being helped. Other people have argued that while it was once all but impossible to travel to Burma without putting money into the coffers of the regime, one can now stay in privately-run guesthouses or hotels and fly non-Burmese airlines.

The more I thought about it the more I thought I needed to consult on the issue. What follows are the opinions of a former British diplomat who runs his own web-based newsletter about Burma, a staff member of the indefatigable Burma Campaign UK and a statement from Lonely Planet, who have been widely criticised for publishing a guidebook to the country.

I admit I'm still somewhat undecided on the issue. I'd like to know what you think.

Lonely Planet, publishers of Lonely Planet Myanmar Travel Guide

"Our aim in publishing this guide is to provide objective information to help travellers make informed decisions about whether or not to visit Burma. No one reading our guide could be in any doubt about our opinion of the current regime, which we describe as 'abominable'.

"We do not accept the view that publication of a guide to Burma encourages people to visit the country for tourism purposes. People make the decision to go for themselves and would go irrespective of whether we produced a guide or not. Lonely Planet's Burma guide outlines the arguments both for and against visiting the country: without such information travellers could make the decision to visit Burma without being aware of the situation in the country.

"The first chapter of the guide presents objectively the issues and starts with the question 'Should You Go?' It includes the views of Aung San Suu Kyi and the Burma Campaign UK, details of activist websites, shows how the regime profits from travellers, and, for those who do decide to go, information that enables travellers to maximise their support for the local population, and minimise the prospect of any money which they might spend going to the military regime. When such travellers return, we encourage them to speak out about what they have seen, to write to the local Burmese embassy and to share their experience with others, perhaps by participating in Lonely Planet's own discussion forum, the Thorn Tree.

"In conclusion our decision to publish is not a show of support for the current regime and we fully support the aims of the restoration of democracy in Burma. We do not, however, believe that you create new freedoms by stifling information or banning books."

Derek Tonkin, Chairman, Network Myanmar

"The hostility shown by the military regime in Burma to immediate and generous Western offers of assistance to the people of the Irrawaddy Delta devastated by Cyclone Nargis has shocked many people, and has lead to allegations ranging from xenophobia to inhumanity. In point of fact, the Burmese response to similar offers from China, India and Asean (Association of South East Asian Nations) countries has been much more forthcoming. Many now realise that attempts to isolate and ostracise Burma over the past 20 years have been a disastrous failure, for it has been the Burmese people who have suffered, and not the generals.

The notion that all the money from tourism goes into the pockets of the generals can be dismissed out of hand

"Western sanctions include the discouragement of travel and tourism to Burma by most EU countries, notably the UK whose political leaders have urged travel operators not to offer Burma as a travel destination on the grounds that the leader of the Opposition National League for Democracy, Aung San Suu Kyi, was opposed to any action which might bring financial support and respectability to the military regime. In point of fact, her call for a boycott of travel to Burma only related to the 'Visit Myanmar Year 1996' and both in statements at the time and subsequently she has acknowledged that some might have good reason to visit her country as "responsible tourists".

"The notion that all the money from tourism goes into the pockets of the generals can be dismissed out of hand. A mere US$198m gross were earned from tourism in the Financial Year ended 31 March 2007, and the results for the year ended 31 March 2008 are expected to be considerably down after the "Saffron Revolution" in September. When operating costs have been deducted, notably the provision of goods and services, very little remains by way of operating profit in an industry which has so long been depressed. Indeed, Thailand earns in only four days what Burma earns in a whole year from tourism. International class hotels, most of which are 100% foreign owned, find it difficult to pay their taxes and land rentals as well as to service their debts. Indeed, far from propping up the regime as critics allege, a respectable case could be made to show that the regime actually subsidises tourism to Burma. By way of comparison, some US$2.16bn were earned from natural gas sales to Thailand in the same period.

"The tourism industry was largely privatised after 1988 and at least 300,000 Burmese people are directly employed, not counting the many tens of thousands of postcard sellers, taxi drivers, handicraft workers and stall holders who depend on tourism for their livelihoods. Together, they support families of well over 1.5 million people. Visitors to Burma say that they meet no one who even hints that they ought not to have come. The Burmese people crave contact with the outside world.

"Those who support a travel boycott cannot possibly have the interests of the Burmese people at heart."

Hlaing Sein, Campaigns Officer, Burma Campaign UK

"It is impossible to visit Burma without funding the military dictatorship.

"Some people in the travel industry argue that tourists bring information from the outside world to the isolated local people, but what do we learn from the copies of Hello! magazine that they leave behind? If we talk about political things to tourists we risk being arrested. Only regime trained tourist guides are allowed to speak with tourists, and those tourist guides are told by the regime what to say to foreigners. As a Burmese citizen I personally didn't experience the benefit of the tourism. The regime declared 1996 as 'Visit Myanmar Year' but in the same year there were some student protests in the Rangoon University and the universities were closed for several years. Even as the regime opened the doors to tourism they were still committing human rights abuses.

"Tourism helps fund the regime that oppresses us. A very small number of people make their living from tourism, and so of course they defend it, but all of us suffer from the regime that keeps us living in poverty and in fear. Three quarters of the population are farmers and these people are not benefiting from the tourism industry. Luxury hotels import foreign goods for tourists instead of using local products. Tourists sit by swimming pools in hotels like those owned by Orient Express and pay $5 for an imported can of coke. How do we benefit from that?

"The regime identified and promoted tourism as a source of foreign exchange, not as a way of providing jobs for the people. Front page articles in state owned newspapers talk about the importance of tourism to Burma, but they only mention foreign exchange, not employment for ordinary people. They need foreign dollars to buy the guns they use to rule over us. Not only does tourism fund the regime, tourist facilities have been built by forced labour. Ordinary Burmese people have been forcibly removed from their homes to clean-up areas for tourism.

The regime spends around half its income on the military, that shoots at monks who are peacefully protesting, and uses rape as a weapon in its war of ethnic cleansing

"Some have tried to argue that the presence of tourists could help prevent human rights abuses, as the regime would not do certain things in front of tourists. But during the uprising last September, even before the crackdown, tourists were hiding in their hotels until they could get on the first flight out. Our people are struggling for freedom and democracy in our country.

"Tourists should think twice before they consider Burma as a tourist destination. How will their money be spent by the regime? Bear in mind that the regime spends around half its income on the military. This is the military that shoots at monks who are peacefully protesting. A military that uses rape as a weapon of war in its war of ethnic cleansing in the east of Burma, even raping girls as young as six. They torture, they assassinate, they mutilate and behead people. This is what your tourist dollars help pay for. By visiting Burma, tourists are not providing financial or moral support to us, instead they fund our oppressors. Stay away."

The Independent 2 June 2008

Tale of two disasters

Separated by nine days and less than 2,000 miles, two huge natural disasters occurred in May 2008. One in Burma and one in China. Yet the way each country has dealt with the aftermath has more to do with political and social division than anything geographical. Where does the natural disaster stop and the man-made disaster begin?

Burma, also known as Myanmar, has a population of 48.8 million and is ruled by a military junta which suppresses almost all opposition to its rule and wields absolute power, despite international condemnation. Cyclone Nargis struck it on the 3 May 2008.

China is the world's most populated country, with a population of 1.33 billion. After stagnation under communism, it is now the world's fastest growing economy and is described as going through its second industrial revolution. The Sichuan province was struck by an earthquake on 12 May, 2008.

Both Asian countries were reeling from the horror of tens of thousands of people probably dead and hundreds of thousands more made destitute and homeless. Both were also historically reluctant to involve outsiders in

The different ways they responded were evident in the sights and smells of the two stricken areas

national affairs – yet the immensity of the disasters put them far beyond the means of any single country. And the different ways they responded were evident in the sights and smells of the two stricken areas.

In Burma the dead were left to lie where they fell, filling the rivers and the lakes with bloated unidentified bodies while surviving family members searched not only for them, but also for aid to keep themselves alive. In the Sichuan province of neighbouring China both the dead and the living were

dealt with. Corpses were collected and buried, allowing families, where possible, to feel the sour comfort of a body to grieve over, and a point to rebuild the remains of their lives. They were kept going with aid from uncountable trucks of relief supplies coming into the villages.

People all over the world donated their own money to both causes and international aid was on offer right from the very start. Burma initially responded to this aid by declaring that it was "not ready to accept foreign aid workers" and by hounding reporters covering the effects of the storm out of the country. Eventually they allowed international aid relief – limited to food, medicines and other supplies – as well as financial aid. But either due to the lack of manpower and organisation or, as some even suggest, by an act of wilful neglect tantamount to genocide, the aid did not reach storm victims, allowing hundreds of thousands to be threatened with starvation, exposure and disease.

While Burma finally accepted the presence of foreign aid workers within the country it remained staunchly against any foreign military aid – which might have helped overcome logistical difficulties. A report from Amnesty International indicates that the Burmese military were trading aid for physical labour – exploiting their people using the global aid that was meant to save them.

China was once like this. In 1976, under Chairman Mao, the Tangshan earthquake, struck close to the capital Beijing. At least 250,000 people died. The Chinese government then refused to accept international aid

from the United Nations, and insisted on self-reliance. Its efforts were beyond inadequate. The political repercussions of the disaster and its aftermath contributed to the end of the Cultural Revolution in China, which had gripped and halted educational and economic development.

This time however, China couldn't have acted more effectively. Whether because of the magnitude of the quake and the media attention on the forthcoming Olympics or just as a reflection of development, China proved to be the model of disaster relief. Accusations about why so many buildings, particularly schools, collapsed so easily during the quake (there were instances of schools crumbling to dust, while the teachers' dormitories next to them remained standing) may point to local corruption. However, a distinction must be made in modern China between the local administrations and the central government – the national government today is certainly doing its best to make up for the mistakes.

International recrimination is being directed at the Burmese generals for their "inhuman" response to the disaster, bordering on a "crime against humanity". In contrast, China is being showered with international praise, for not only its reaction to the disaster but also the openness with which it has allowed the details to be reported. In 2008 for the Olympics, the Chinese government has lifted travel restrictions on foreign journalists for the first time. Though the eyes of the world are on Burma, it appears that the junta feels no shame while its people suffer.

Sources: Various

The languages of extinction: the world's endangered tongues

**Every fortnight, another language dies; some 40% of the world's languages are thought to be at risk. Now a new study has identified those that are most endangered.
Claire Soares reports**

For the Nivkh people of eastern Siberia, it's not as easy as one, two, three. Depending on whether they are talking about skis or boats or batches of dried fish, there are different ways of counting. Twenty-six different ways in fact. Small wonder, then, that 90% of Nivkhs choose to communicate in Russian but that choice has put Nivkh on the list of endangered languages.

And it is not alone. Linguists believe half the languages in the world will be extinct by the end of the century. The 80 major languages such as English, Russian and Mandarin are spoken by about 80% of the global population, while the 3,500 linguistic minnows have just 0.2% of the world keeping them alive.

"The pace of language extinction we're seeing, it's really unprecedented in human history," said Dr David Harrison, author of the book When Languages Die. "And it's happening faster than the extinction of flora and fauna. More than 40% of the world's languages could be considered endangered compared to 8% of plants and 18% of mammals."

The pace of language extinction we're seeing is unprecedented in human history

When dolphins or eagles become extinct, people can get sentimental and mourn their passing but the death of a language is an unnoticed event, despite the fact it's happening more frequently, with one language being killed off every fortnight. Globalisation and migration are the main culprits. Economic pressures force people to move from their village to the cities, local languages are coming under threat from the lingua franca of the workplace. Children also play a key role in the killing of a language, such as a child growing up speaking Mayan and Spanish soon figuring out that Spanish is better because it's spoken in school and on television.

A study by Dr Harrison and Greg Anderson, the director of the Living Tongues Institute, has identified five hotspots for endangered languages around the world – Northern Australia, Central South America, Oklahoma and the south-west USA, the Northwest Pacific Plateau and Eastern Siberia.

In the course of their research they came across Australian Charlie

Mungulda, an Aboriginal living in the Northern Territory who is believed to be the last speaker of Amurdag, a language previously thought to have been extinct. Dr Harrison plays a recording of the elderly Charlie, recalling words spoken by his late father. There's a long pause after the voice fades away. "Those are some of the very last words we will ever hear in Amurdag," the linguistics professor says with a sigh. That is unless someone shows a natural pronunciation gift when faced with the 100 or so words, such as "aburga" (rainbow serpent) that the linguists managed to scribble down.

Losing languages means losing cultural insights. The often-quoted examples of Eskimos having many words for snow, or Africans having many words for rice are perhaps overly-familiar. But did you know that the 200 or so people who speak Toratan on the Indonesian island of Sulawesi have a word for waking up and finding something's changed? Open your eyes and find you've fallen out of bed in the night? *Matuwuhou!*

Or find yourself herding reindeer with Todzhu people of Siberia and want to point out a particularly charming, five-year-old castrated reindeer that can be ridden? The word you're looking for is *chary*.

And the loss of languages also often means a loss of identity. Serge Sagna, a Senegalese PhD student at the School of Oriental and African Studies in London, who returned to his village recently to study its Bandial language, can personally testify to that. "My identity is completely bound up in my language. It reflects a unique view of the world, and a whole history without which we cannot move forward."

Bandial has been pushed aside in Senegal, not only by the former colonial language French, in which most professional business and education is conducted, but also by Wolof, the language of hip-hop, the streets and the national mbala dance craze. Even Mr Sagna reluctantly admits that, in two generations, his native tongue will be no more.

But perhaps more important than the individual words and cultural diversity are the vast chunks of human knowledge that accompany languages to the grave.

"We live in the information age, where information and knowledge are supposed to be of value, and we're running the risk of jettisoning millennia of knowledge," Dr Harrison said. "Most of what we know about endangered species is encoded in languages that have never been written down. So in saving languages we may be able to help save species and eco-systems."

As Exhibit A, take the two-barred flasher butterfly of Central America. It was long assumed to be a single species but the native Mexican tribe, the Tzeltal, knew better. They had a well-honed system of distinguishing between the different larvae, depending on what crops they attacked. Eventually, Western science caught up with them and biologists confirmed at least 10 species of the butterfly.

Similarly the 4,000 speakers of Brazil's Kayapo tongue differentiate between 56 folk species of bees, based on anything from flight patterns to the quality of honey.

The Kallawaya herbalist healers living in Bolivia, have gone one step further. For the past 500 years, they have encrypted their knowledge of thousands of medicinal plants in a secret language handed down in the practitioner families from father to son. It's patenting by language, as it were.

"Kallawaya is an excellent example of a language that could be patented for both its form and content, for the economic well-being of the community that invented it, and for protection against predatory pharmaceutical corporations that seek to exploit that knowledge without recompense," says Dr Harrison.

So what can be done to preserve these languages and the knowledge that they articulate?

In Australia, Doris Edgar is one of the last three remaining speakers of Yawuru. Ms Edgar, in her 80s, visits schools in the town of Broome, Western Australia, imparting to eager pupils the Yawuru names of local plants and their traditional uses.

Dr Anderson reckons it takes three to four years to adequately document a language at a cost of up to £200,000. "We have people and communities that desire our help to save their language, what we lack are the funds to do that," he said.

The Independent 19 September 2007

"Run! There's a thesaurus coming!"

Prospect, March 2008

Mastering French manners, the hard way

Caroline Wyatt BBC News, Paris

"A history of politeness in France", might strike the uncharitable as being a very short book indeed. But Frederic Rouvillois' definitive study of manners through the ages in France weighs in at a crushing 550 pages. It joins Nadine de Rothschild's best-selling bible of politeness in offering advice to those in need of guidance on how to behave in that oxymoron, "polite French society". For this season of festive meals can be a minefield for those uneducated in French ways. Oh, if only I had read their advice before venturing out to my first Parisian dinner party.

I had arrived punctually at the chic Parisian flat on the Left Bank, on the dot of eight o'clock in the evening, as per the invitation, bearing flowers for my hostess. I wondered why she seemed slightly put out. I realised, when the other guests – politicians, a philosopher, a banker or two and their wives – finally arrived an hour later.

The conversation was in rapid-fire French, no allowances made for the only foreigner in the room. So, to make myself feel more at ease, I reached over to a bottle of wine, to pour myself a second glass. The entire table suddenly fell silent as the wine emerged loudly, and in slow motion, into my glass. A deep froideur descended as 10 pairs of steely Parisian eyes turned to stare. I smiled weakly and remained quiet for the rest of the meal, fleeing as soon as I politely could. Clearly, I had committed an unforgivable faux pas, although what it had been I wasn't sure.

Cardinal sins

It was only this week that I discovered just how many terrible solecisms I'd committed under the strict laws of French etiquette. My lesson came courtesy of Constance Reitzler, director of La Belle Ecole – "the beautiful school" – which aims to give Parisians and foreigners alike that special polish. It teaches the "arts de vivre", that uniquely French concept which encompasses everything from how to appreciate your wine and food, to whether to eat your sorbet or ice-cream with a spoon or a fork. It's a fork, for those who want to know. And never spread your foie gras on your toast. Eat it with a fork, and the toast separately.

Constance patiently explained that a lady never, ever grabs the bottle of wine to pour her own drink. She must wait for her host or another man to pour it for her. And more than one aperitif before dinner is considered the sure sign of an alcoholic, or an Englishwoman. We are, after all, a nation renowned in France for 'le binge-drinking'.

And I had compounded the offence by wishing those at the table "bon appetit", before noisily expressing my appreciation of the food.

Both, apparently, cardinal sins in the Bible of French etiquette.

"Wishing someone bon appetit is seen as very vulgar in polite circles," Constance explained, as I realised to my horror that I must have wished almost every French person I have ever met at a meal "bon appetit".

Paris 'syndrome'

So why didn't the BBC send me on this course before I began my job in Paris?

And apparently in France it's good manners to keep your elbows ON the table, and your hands visible. The custom dates back centuries, to when noblewomen did so to display their dazzling rings, to show off their husband's social status. Keeping your hands above the table shows that you're concentrating on your meal. And, I thought, unworthily, that you are not using them to get to know the husband next to you rather better than his wife might like. I, of course, had politely kept my elbows off the table, and my hands beneath it while not eating – goodness only knows what all the wives had thought. But I wondered who was ruder: myself, for not understanding the local customs, or my hosts, for making me feel so ill at ease.

It's not that the French are necessarily rude – but Parisians certainly can be. A psychiatrist has coined a term for its effect on Japanese visitors to the city: "Paris Syndrome". Every year, several Japanese tourists have to be repatriated from Paris after falling prey to severe culture shock at the hands of the less than polite Parisians. Waiters who fail to understand their order, taxi drivers who take them to the wrong place and then charge double. All this is too much for some to take, as their dream of the city of light crumbles into a nightmare of darkness, creating a sense of rejection and paranoia.

'Bon appetit'

Yet I know exactly how they feel after my encounter at a dress shop last week. I picked up a skirt to try on, and as I took it to the changing room, the shop assistant shouted out across the crowded room: "I wouldn't bother if I were you – it'll never fit!" The phrase, "the customer is king", has clearly lost something in translation. Or perhaps the French think it a reference to the Revolution, a chance to cut the customer down to size. Madame La Guillotine may no longer be available, but a sharp tongue can do the job just as well.

Perhaps Constance can help both sides. As I rose to leave the Belle Ecole, she politely handed me a two-page guide to etiquette, with an expression of sympathy, though whether for my past and future hosts or for myself, I wasn't sure. I glanced at it. It could have been tailor-made for the oafish, drunken Englishwoman who came to dinner. "Never down your drink in one", and "ne jamais ecraser le buste vers l'assiette" or "don't put your bust in your plate" and "never make noises of satisfaction at the dinner table". And never, ever say bon appetit.

So now I know. And in spite of that, I'd like everyone across Britain to join me now in wishing all in France a very bon appetit indeed this Christmas.

From Our Own Correspondent
BBC Radio 4
23 December 2006

"Before we start, we'd like you to read through zis."

A Shameless generation that has never learned to work

Jayne Dowle

Just what can be done about the Shameless generation? Dame Carol Black is looking for the answer. She is the Government adviser overhauling the incapacity benefits system.

Her first priority is to tackle the culture of worklessness which infects our towns, villages and cities and undermines all attempts to build strong communities. Dame Carol calls it a "terrible legacy". No wonder she despairs.

Nearly three million Britons claim long-term incapacity benefit, and one in five children is growing up in a family where one or both parents rely on out-of-work benefits. Not working has become a three-generational lifestyle choice for many of these families – grandfather didn't work, neither did dad, neither does son – hence the tag "Shameless generation" after the television drama series that chronicles the lives of the welfare-dependent inhabitants of a Manchester council estate.

It's entertainment. But it's not funny. Pity the poor children born into the real-life version. What stultifying, dull and ultimately pointless lives they end up living. How can these Vicky Pollards even get their heads around the idea of getting up in the morning and taking responsibility for themselves if no-one they are related to has ever done it?

John Dunford, secretary of the Association of School and College Leaders, complains that the failure of such dysfunctional families to impart even basic skills means that teachers are becoming surrogate parents, and have to teach simple manners and necessities such as using a knife and fork.

You might think that Ministers would be better employed in cracking the causes of such fundamental social breakdown that attempting to paper over the cracks with ridiculous citizenship ceremonies. It is hard to imagine a teenager who can't even look an adult in the eye standing up with his hand on his heart to swear allegiance to the Queen. Chances are he won't know who she is. There are some genuine cases who can't work because of unfortunate events. But I see the idle evidence that they are in the minority every time I leave the house. At my son's school sports' day, an elderly family friend was amazed that so many dads had turned up. It took a while for it to sink in that most of them were there because they didn't have anything else to do. In her day, it would have been unthinkable.

Caroline Flint, the Housing Minister, took a lot of flak for her proposal that anyone who lives in a council house should actively seek work or face eviction. Yet, despite the flaws, she highlighted an issue which has at best become glamorised as entertainment and, at worst, underscores every social ill from child poverty to feral teenagers killing their neighbours.

The truth is that we have millions of people actively choosing not to work and to claim benefits instead. If Britain is to prosper and compete on equal terms with the world, something must be done. The Blair government's answer was "education, education, education". The ultimate aim was to get 50% of all young people into university by 2010 so they could be better-equipped to find decent jobs. It doesn't look likely.

Not working has become a three-generational lifestyle choice

Now it emerges that universities are to be paid bribes of up to £1,000 per admission to accept students with D and E grades on to degree courses. Lecturers are told to spend the money on remedial sessions to support less-able students and improve drop-out rates. You can see the thinking – it is aimed to reduce the number of Neets (young people between 16 and 24, not employed or in education or training), which currently stands at 1.24 million, and is reported to have risen by 15% since 1997. Where I live, in Barnsley, 8.1% fall into this category.

The problem is that being a Neet goes beyond hanging out on the street corner. It leads to higher rates of alcohol and drug-dependency and teen pregnancies, and effectively lays the foundation for the next Shameless generation. Forcing non-academic teenagers into formal education will only alienate them even further and cause drop-out rates to spiral.

Rather than bribing beleaguered universities to accept kids with no aptitude for academia, surely it makes better sense to spend the money on raising confidence and aspirations at primary and secondary level, and then creating career-orientated practical options for 14 to 17-year-olds, like the over-subscribed construction courses at Barnsley College.

Trades like plumbing, hairdressing and even mining, reported to be taking on new recruits for the first time in decades, are in demand. There are jobs out there. And there is no shame in hard work. We hear a lot about legacy-building. Much of it is political posturing, but turning around the terrible legacy of the Shameless generation could turn around the country.

Yorkshire Post 13 March 2008

Curriculum Vitae

What's your problem?

Jeremy Bullmore

Q **I was fired from my last job at a legal firm for sending an e-mail about my stag weekend to my e-mail address book, some of whom were clients. The story got some local press and I'm finding it quite difficult to explain away the situation in job interviews. I realise it was a stupid thing to do, but found it quite funny at the time and never thought it would get so serious. I've had four interviews so far and no-one finds it amusing. What's my best bet in explaining this in future ones? I'm getting worried about this.**

A You'll go on being worried – and with good reason – until you finally come to terms with what you did and how it strikes other people. It's clear from the way you pose your question that, although you now realise it was a pretty stupid thing to do, you're still surprised that nobody else seems to find it amusing, particularly potential employers. To you, it was just a bit of a jape, a harmless enough lark, maybe in retrospect a little unwise but surely not a hanging offence? C'mon, guys – where's your sense of humour?

At the risk of joining the ranks of the humourless, my sympathies lie more with them than with you – because you're still failing to distinguish between the jape itself and the questions it quite properly raises about your judgment.

Had you still been a carefree student, banging off a hilarious account of your stag weekend to your entire unedited e-mail address book would have been innocuous enough; and if it really was hilarious, would have given fleeting pleasure to quite a lot of people. Maybe a maiden aunt or two would have registered silent disapproval, but most would have read, laughed a bit – and then quickly forgotten all about it.

But you're not still a carefree student and your mistake – and it's a serious one – was your failure to imagine how this apparently innocent act would inevitably seem to others. It's clear from the fact that your e-mail went to clients that you weren't using your own e-mail account but your firm's. Immediately, as you should have realised, your message takes on a different significance.

So that's the mistake you made: not the firing off of an account of a racy weekend, but the total failure to foresee its effect on others

Had it been from your personal e-mail address, the local press wouldn't have been in the least bit interested. There was only a 'story' because a company was involved – and a legal firm at that. You really should have seen that coming.

So that's the mistake you made: not the firing off of an account of a racy weekend, but the total failure to foresee its effect on others. To any potential employer, and particularly a law firm, that's worrying stuff.

Next time you get an interview and the e-mail incident comes up, stop trying to laugh it off as a mildly regrettable bit of silliness. Make it absolutely clear that it's taught you a lesson that you'll never forget. And the lesson is not that you should forever suppress your sense of fun and mischief-making, but that you'll never again fail to think through the possible consequences of everything you do.

If all this sonorous advice strikes you as coming from yet another person with a sense-of-humour bypass, then I'm afraid you still haven't managed to get it.

Management Today November 2007

Low status kills

Why working for Tesco will shorten your life

Peter Wilby

According to a study just released by the financial firm Pension Capital Strategies, you should avoid working for British American Tobacco, Imperial Tobacco, Mitchells & Butlers or the retail divisions of Whitbread. They will all kill you off early. They occupy four of the bottom five positions in a league table of FTSE-100 companies, showing employees' life expectancies. A 65-year-old man can expect to live to less than 82 if he is retiring from Whitbread, but to nearly 90 if he is retiring from the property investment company British Land, which tops the table. The gap for women is similar.

The obvious explanation is that the four killer companies are all in the drink or tobacco industries and their loyal employees presumably overindulge in the products they make. But is that the whole story? The identity of the fifth company in the bottom five, Tesco – which, compared with Whitbread, gives a mere one extra year of life to male employees but nearly three to women – suggests it isn't.

Life expectancy is an immensely complex area with enormous implications for public policy. Most of us know three things. First, UK average life expectancy is improving sharply – at the rate of two years every decade, or five hours every day, according to the latest calculations. Second, the rich live longer. Poor blacks in downtown Washington, for example, live on average 20 years less than affluent whites in nearby Montgomery County, Maryland. Third, now that developed countries have conquered such diseases as typhoid and cholera, and eradicated extreme poverty (in the sense of people literally suffering starvation), bad habits, particularly drinking, smoking and poor diet, are the biggest causes of early death.

We tend to ignore an important rider to the first: that the rise in longevity is much greater for the affluent than for the poor.

We tend also to link the last two: booze and fags, we deduce, drive the poor into early graves. In fact, lifestyle is only a partial explanation.

A classic study of British civil servants found that, with each step down the hierarchy, average age of death fell. Smoking, blood pressure, cholesterol, obesity and lack of exercise accounted for at most a third of the differences between the civil service grades.

Professor Sir Michael Marmot, author of the study, found further significant differences between the grades in their experience of the workplace: how much control they had, how fairly they were treated, how interesting the work was, and so on. Such findings have been replicated across the world, and not just in humans. Whether in the wild or in captivity, dominant monkeys and baboons contract fewer diseases than their subordinates.

In other words, low social, economic and occupational status is a killer, not only through making people more likely to abuse their bodies through bad habits, but through some more direct mechanism. As Marmot told the Royal College of Physicians last year, that failure "to meet the fundamental needs of autonomy, empowerment and human freedom is a potent cause of ill-health". If he is right, the entire western world has got it wrong. It is true that economic growth generally leads to better health and higher life expectancy. But only up to a point.

According to Richard Wilkinson, professor of social epidemiology at Nottingham University (The Impact of Inequality, Routledge, 2005), average income levels aren't the main explanation for differences in death rates between US cities. The extent of inequality in each city fits the mortality data much better. The differences between the most unequal cities and the most equal ones is equivalent to the combined loss of life in a single year from lung cancer, diabetes, road deaths, AIDS, suicide and homicide.

It took policymakers 50 years to absorb fully the importance of tobacco in premature death and, though smoking has fallen dramatically among the affluent, the poor remain stubbornly addicted. It may take as long to absorb the research on the role of economic and social status, most of which is barely a decade old. Governments may then conclude that nagging people to change their lifestyles – for example, the recent proposal to weigh schoolchildren and send letters to their parents warning of obesity – isn't cost-effective. The link between low status and a self-destructive lifestyle may prove too powerful to overcome. And stress, lack of autonomy and other psychological factors may have physiological effects that are more important causes of premature death.

The implications for Tesco and Whitbread? I don't, as the social scientists say, have enough data to advise them. But perhaps they should look, not only at their overall pay rates, but also at the differentials, the work routines, and the quality of relationships between managers and workers. Not that they have any incentive to do so: they'd just have to pay out the pensions for longer.

New Statesman, 29 October 2007

The minimum wage will drive small shops under

Inflation-busting increases to the national minimum wage are disastrous for small shopkeepers struggling with soaring costs

In how many industries does the boss often earn a lot less than their most junior staff member? Welcome to the Alice-in-Wonderland world of small shops, as the national minimum wage goes up by more than inflation yet again. In how many government departments does the office junior get far more holiday entitlement than the top mandarin? Yet while statutory holiday entitlement goes up by four days for their staff, many shopkeepers hardly ever have a weekend off, let alone a proper holiday.

We have reached the point where a large number of people are worried about the widening pay gap between the bosses and the workers – and it is the shopkeepers who are coming off a decided second-best.

I have recently spent a lot of time in village shops. While trying to help sub-postmasters to keep their shops open after the post office income is taken away (clue: it takes a lot more than a bit of prudence, Mr Brown), I have seen many of their financial accounts. These often show wages making up half or more of their total overheads. With ever-rising electricity bills (all that refrigeration!), supermarkets selling at prices below the levels that small shops can buy at (thanks, Competition Commission, we're glad it is nothing to do with abuse of market power) and then an inflation-busting pay increase for staff, many independent shops will be running out of options.

Mark Hooley

"I have often seen shopkeeper accounts that show wages making up half or more of the total overheads"

Small shopkeepers are nice people. They want to be able to pay their staff well. Often their employees are also their neighbours: parents of young children getting back to work, young people back from college with a degree in media studies waiting for their big break, older people who have been made redundant from bigger jobs but who still want to work and contribute.

Of course these people would like to be paid as much as possible. But a job a few minutes' walk away, with no expensive commute, offering some flexibility, and actually quite interesting, is better than earning a few pence per hour more in the town centre – and certainly far better than no job at all.

As a result of the minimum wage rising faster than inflation for several years, there will be fewer employed hours in the small retail sector. Some proprietors will work even longer or take less holiday. There will be shops that will put their prices up and become less competitive. For some, investment in the business will be reduced – the old noisy chiller will have to last another year (fingers crossed).

More proprietors will envy their staff as they make up their wage packets or as they wish them well as they go on holiday.

In some cases, the rising wage bill will be the straw that breaks the camel's back and communities will lose out as their local shop closes.

In the grand scheme of things, this doesn't matter. After all, we are only talking about a few thousand micro businesses, most a long way from London. A few dozen extra closing is easily lost in the statistics. The lives of only a few hundred customers are diminished. An old lady who, without her local shop, cannot cope and finally has to move into a residential home. A single parent who has to catch two buses to get to town. A green campaigner who has to concede defeat and buy a car.

Clearly we are all in favour of paying staff a fair wage. But I am also in favour of leaving a fair return to small shop owners as well... perhaps even enough for just the occasional day off?

Kenneth Parsons, chief executive,
Rural Shops Alliance

Reprinted by kind permission of The Grocer
© William Reed Business Media 2008
15 March 2008
www.thegrocer.co.uk

Pipe dreams:
why we all want to be plumbers

The prospect of megabucks is luring office workers into joining the trades
Anushka Asthana

Tales of plumbers who earn £80,000 a year have led to a surge of interest in the job, according to new figures that show traditional trades are back in vogue.

Bored office workers are lining up to become electricians or plumbers, according to figures from the Learndirect careers helpline, which has fielded more than 900,000 calls from people looking for a change in the past 12 months.

The data shows that the most asked-after job last year was that of a domestic energy assessor – the official who checks a property's energy efficiency for home information packs (Hips), which are now compulsory when selling a house. The huge media interest in Hips has led people to think there is a lot of work for assessors, according to Oliver Burney, a careers coach at Learndirect.

Burney said the resurgence of interest in plumbing stems from the 'considerable myth' that tradesmen can earn up to £80,000. 'That is only true if you work very long hours, manage a company or are doing the Channel tunnel,' he said. 'The more realistic figures are below £20,000 for a newly qualified plumber, and then £30,000 with experience or £35,000 if you are supervising people. It may be a little higher in the south east.'

He said the typical call was from an IT consultant or office worker who had a degree but felt they were working below their potential. 'They think, "Why am I doing this?"' said Burney.

Tradesmen can earn up to £80,000. 'That is only true if you work very long hours, manage a company or are doing the Channel tunnel'

Andy Powell, chief executive of Edge, an organisation that promotes vocational learning, added: 'We know from research that people who are most successful and happiest are those who pursue a career they enjoy. I'm delighted and encouraged by this emerging trend towards people in the UK pursuing traditional trades careers. Far too often it's academic qualifications that are seen as the only route to securing a good job.'

The Learndirect figures come as other research reveals that leading company directors are planning to target the over-55s in an attempt to fill skills gaps. A global study of chief executives, board members and senior executives found that 43% thought it would be beneficial to recruit older workers, while one out of 10 felt that the ageing population would lead to serious talent shortages over the next three years.

The research was carried out by the Economist Intelligence Unit on behalf of Stepstone, a company that provides online talent management services to 20,000 companies, including the Royal Bank of Scotland and Cadbury Schweppes.

'This research shows that there is a huge potential sitting there and companies have to be much more pro-active about attracting it, nurturing it and developing it,' said Colin Tenwick of Stepstone, who argues that older workers needed to be offered more flexible working patterns and better pension provision.

B&Q became the first British company to target older workers, arguing that they were no less productive and had great rapport with the customers. Last year the company had one member of staff who was 91. Sainsbury's also launched a campaign to recruit 10,000 'mature' workers across Britain.

Richard Wainer, principal policy adviser at the Confederation of British Industry, said companies had to start targeting different groups if they hoped to fill skills gaps. 50% of CBI members were struggling to recruit suitably qualified staff, especially those with maths and science skills, he added: 'They have to spread their net as wide as possible.'

The Observer 27 January 2008
© Guardian News & Media Ltd. 2008

Putting our money where our mouths are

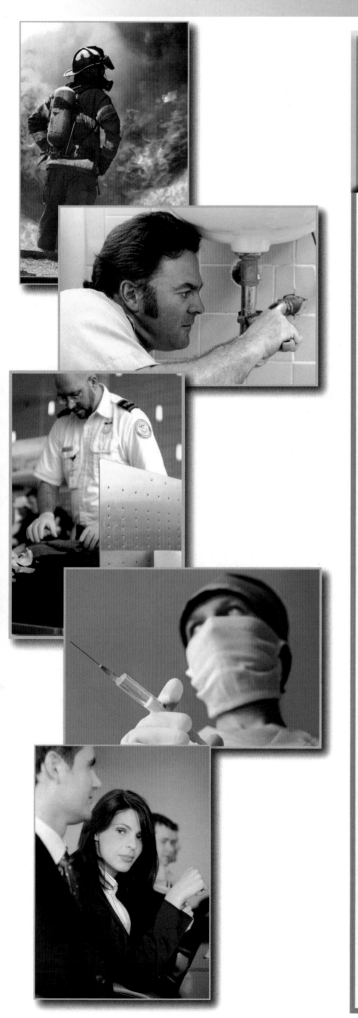

City bosses saw the biggest increases in pay but dentists came a close second

When it comes to pay it seems that to those that have, more shall be given. Directors and chief executives of major organisations saw their pay increase by more than 30% in 2007, according to the Annual Survey of Hours and Earnings. This bumper increase brings their average pay up to £212,910 per year and puts them at the top of the earnings list according to data collected by the Office for National Statistics.

Second are City brokers whose pay averaged £94,293 even though their increase was only 0.9% over the previous year. It seems that anyone dealing with money is certain to be earning a good salary, accountants average £37,000 – and a financial manager at nearly £78,000, earns more than three times as much as a firefighter (nearly £26,000). Aircraft traffic controllers (£51,911) and pilots (£63,664) are, perhaps unsurprisingly, amongst the highest earners.

Dentists had the highest percentage increase, at 24.7% but their average earnings of £31,747 don't put them in the highest earning league.

Library Assistants emerged as the worst paid of the 300 trades and professions surveyed, with an average salary of £10,479 and a pay increase of only 0.9%. Security professions do scarcely better at £10,779 (though security guards have a separate entry at £18,228). Since the minimum wage for adults is £5.52 per hour, anyone working a full 40 hour week ought to be earning at least £11,481 a year.

Plumbers earn almost exactly the average British wage of £25,485

But averages disguise a great deal of difference both between and within professions. Legal professionals average a salary of £50,469 – lawyers, judges and coroners earn more than £52,000, but for a legal secretary £17,000 is the most likely sum.

The average British salary is around £25,000 (but two-thirds of the population earn less than that). Nurses average £23,044 and midwives £25,586. At the other end of life, undertakers and mortuary assistants can expect only £16,219.

Within a secondary school, the average teaching salary is £31,000, however teachers in further education are the least well paid at £24,906. School secretaries are amongst the lowest paid workers at £12,850.

A little above the average earning level are estate agents (£27,872) while below are the careers advisers (£23,000) who might have suggested the job in the first place. Firefighters are actually at the mid point of the 300 jobs surveyed. They are joined by healthcare practice managers, printers and IT technicians. And earning almost the exact average of £25,485 are plumbers.

OUR CULTURE FIX:

The government is pledging to provide young people with five hours a week of cultural activity. But what will this consist of?

> In the five hours a week, I'd like to see dancing and the chance to learn about art from around the world. It gives you a different experience and you can learn about how other people live. It's good to have these activities in youth clubs as you don't always have them in school.
>
> I did a project on manga art at the Surma Centre [in Camden] and our drawings were shown around the estate. I enjoyed learning about Japanese art. We've also done breakdancing and are about to start a cookery course about world dishes."

Altaf, 15, Camden, London

> At the Knowle West Media Centre we come to a group called Mouth of the South every Tuesday after school. It's a team of young people who meet to put together a local newsletter and website. We also read, write and create articles and are learning about podcasts. What I really enjoy most is editing.
>
> I think it is a good idea for all young people to get five hours a week of activity but it should be in small bits. The government should offer the chance to learn computer skills and do the kinds of activities we do at Mouth of the South. It has really helped us with our school work."

Serena and Levi, 11, Knowle West, Bristol

> I enjoy playing the guitar but singing is more my thing. We do a lot of karaoke here as part of the arts events organised by Connexions. Dancing is another popular activity – street dancing mainly.
>
> The government should let everyone do these things and give young people the chance to be filmed so they can see themselves performing. We recently went to Manchester and danced in front of an audience on a stage with flashing lights and a sound system. There were loads of people there and it was a bit scary, but it's made me feel more confident."

Maggie, 18, Barrow-in-Furness, Cumbria

> I love acting because it gives you the chance to be in someone else's shoes and learn about people from different backgrounds. Personally, I would like to see anything that's got to do with learning about people from different cultures and can get everyone working together.
>
> I'd like to see more acting opportunities because there's nothing going on at the moment. And it would be good to be able to go to recording studios because I love rapping. Everyone is into rapping so that would definitely be a good idea."

David, 18, Woolwich, London

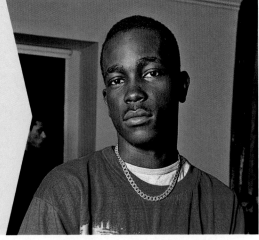

> I think I've got a creative mind. I like to make stuff up but we don't get much chance to do that at school. I'd like to see cooking classes offered to young people – I like all types of food. And filmmaking is a good thing. I did it as part of my media project. We used video cameras and editing equipment. It's quite technical, as you have to learn about the different types of shots, camera angles and lighting. So, when I'm watching a film I now see it all differently – you remember what you've been taught. Creativity matters because it means people get to express what they feel."

Rahib, 16, Tottenham, London

> I helped to design the new building at Knowle West Media Centre as part of the Archimedia project. It's helped me to see that I can do something with my life and find a career – it's got my confidence up and I am now hoping to study graphic design at university. We've also studied the abolition of slavery and learned a lot about Bristol's history.
>
> I think the government's plan is good, but there should be more than just five hours a week as there is nothing to do on weekends. It needs to be a mixture of fun and education and should include music, as it is a big part of young people's lives, as well as art and design."

Chad, 17, Knowle West, Bristol

WHAT WE WANT

Far from the opera or ballet, rap and street dance are closer to what it is they want, as **Tom de Castella** discovers

> Helping with the Archimedia project [a £3m scheme to replace dilapidated media facilities] has helped me a lot and made me change the degree I wish to study.
>
> The government plan is great but young people are constantly on the go so creativity shouldn't be limited to five hours a week. Youth projects might be able to offer young people something that schools can't, such as a place for them to be themselves and not worry about fitting in or getting an academic score.
>
> The cultural activity could include architecture and design, digital technology, creating newsletters and anything else that helps young people express themselves and find their hidden talents."

Sarah, 19, Knowle West, Bristol

> I'm into music. We can listen to music here at the youth club, but we haven't got a studio in the building to make our own. I also like sport so it would be good to do cultural activities involving that – I wouldn't mind making a video about sport. And I also like acting but I haven't really had the opportunity to do it that much.
>
> Culture is important because it gives you something else to talk about, other than what you've always done. If I wasn't coming here I'd probably be out on the streets. I wouldn't be up to any good."

Deniz, 17, Wood Green, London

> I'd tell Gordon Brown to set up cultural festivals where everyone brings their own food and shows off their cultures and traditions. Making films would be fun and I'd also like to do photography and go on trips to learn about culture.
>
> I also love martial arts like kung fu. You don't just learn the kicks and punches, but also about the history of it – where it's from in China and why they use it. I also went to a DJing workshop and learned to mix and scratch. Arts activities keep people occupied and stop them loitering in the streets."

Jimi, 17, Archway, London

> I enjoy photography. Without the media centre I would never have known what my passion was. Now I can just book out a camera and go for a walk, taking pictures of things that catch my eye.
>
> In the five hours of culture a week, all aspects of media should be looked at – photography, film, editing, animation, graphic design, music production. I strongly believe you've got to let young people decide what they want to do. For example, a lot of young people would love to learn how to use music software as their rep would be boosted massively by being able to make beats."

Marcus, 17, Knowle West, Bristol

> The five hours a week should allow you to make something you can show people at the end of it. It could be a CD or a DVD – something that you can show your friends and family afterwards. Singing would be my choice followed by dancing as they both help you to meet new people and keep out of trouble. I'm not shy but it has given me more confidence to know I can do stuff in front of a crowd of people.
>
> We're doing a residential exchange project called Lifeswap with a Manchester youth group, which is also to do with singing and dancing."

Briese, 14, Barrow-in-Furness, Cumbria

> There should be more cultural activities available, as schools won't do them. I'd like to see people doing a bit of everything – video, photography, music or whatever. Until you've tried something, you don't know if you're going to like it or not. You need to give young people a taste of it all in different workshops and it's good to have youth workers and experts to introduce the activities.
>
> I'm mostly into photography and I'm doing a silver Arts Award [a national project funded by the Arts Council and Trinity Guildhall]. It's very isolated in Cumbria but these activities bring young people together and help them come out of themselves."

Ryan, 20, Barrow-in-Furness, Cumbria

> Five hours a week is a good idea, but I don't think they'll be able to stick to it. It's a big promise for every young person to get that.
>
> People should be able to follow their interests. If they're into sport then they should be able to get special coaching, if they're into DJing then there should be a place available with microphones, decks and recording equipment for them to practice and perform. I'm into making music and music production. I love hip hop and I make my own recordings at home, but I'd like to try filmmaking too. Being creative broadens your mind and helps to raise your self-esteem."

Bret, 17, Barrow-in-Furness, Cumbria

27 February-4 March 2008

EMILIE SANDY

Photo posed by model

Natasha Farnham's warning to bingers:

I drank so much my liver failed at 14

By Emily Cook, Health Correspondent

Schoolgirl binge drinker Natasha Farnham is the youngest person in Britain to be diagnosed with liver failure – at the age of just 14.

Drinking from the age of 12, she was downing four bottles of wine a day by 13. Two years later, she was rushed to hospital after drinking 16 bottles of wine, cider and spirits during a three-day bender.

Here Natasha, of Bath, Somerset, describes how she was gripped by drinking and crime before entering rehab – all before her 19th birthday...

'I didn't think my drinking was a problem because all my friends were getting wasted every weekend as well. I suppose I thought I looked grown-up and would drink as much as possible – sometimes passing out.

I would save my dinner money all week and spend it on booze. My mum didn't know what I was doing because I would say I was staying at a friend's house. It was so much fun and it was never hard to get our hands on alcohol – that was easy. The hardest part was paying for it. Soon I was stealing to pay for alcohol. I would also sell DVDs and CDs I found in the house.

At 13 years old, I hit my lowest point. I was drinking up to three litres of wine a day (four bottles) and a litre of vodka.

I was missing school but it was fun. I was too young to understand what an alcoholic was, let alone understand that I was one. At 14, I upset my mum by dropping out of school.

After a very heavy New Year's Eve in 2004, I was feeling tired and my mum said that I looked yellow. I had been drinking a lot with my friends – it was the Christmas holidays and we were drinking even more than usual. I was taken to Royal United Hospital in Bath for 10 days before being transferred to Birmingham Children's hospital.

When the doctors there told me about the liver failure they looked shocked. They said they hadn't seen liver failure in someone so young. When I detailed how much I'd been drinking, the doctors and my mum just looked at me in disbelief. They warned me to clean up my act or die. But I didn't listen to them – I was too young.

In the four years after I was diagnosed, I was in and out of trouble with the police and now have a number of convictions. I have four convictions for being drunk and disorderly, two public order offences, one burglary and a caution for assaulting a police officer. When I drink, I turn into this horrible, angry person who just wants more and more alcohol. When I don't drink, I am happy and my family are happy.

I finally started to sort out my life when I was arrested for burglary. I've been in rehab now for a couple of months. I didn't really believe I had a problem until recently. I know it sounds stupid but it was just acceptable to get so drunk. But now I have no short-term memory and doctors warn me that if I drink any more, I'll die.

I am finally listening to the doctors – perhaps because I now realise how stupid I've been. But I'm not alone, everyone I know has drank as much as me and they will probably end up with problems in the future. But it's too late then. I would just tell kids - don't end up like me. I have been a binge drinker, had liver failure and been in rehab, and I'm still a teenager.'

Daily Mirror 15 April 2008

BOOZE BY NUMBERS

In a national poll 42% of youngsters said they started boozing before they were 13

40% annual rise in under-18s in alcoholic treatment programmes last year to 6,707

1,000 children under the age of 14 are being admitted to hospital every year as a result of binge drinking

95 under-eights needed emergency medical treatment for alcohol abuse in 2007, bringing the total since 2001 to 624

There are more young people on the planet now than ever. In fact 17% of the world's population is aged between ten and 19 – potentially that's 12 billion people with raging hormones and a stroppy attitude. But it's not their fault.

On-going studies have shown that just as teenagers are having to adapt to major physical changes, their brains, are far more susceptible to emotions – particularly, anger.

Many parents and teachers may have asked themselves why teenagers exist at all – why there can't be an instant transition from charming child to responsible adult, or at least a long period of hibernation so that young bodies and brains can develop without imposing their angst on the rest of the world.

The period of intense physical growth and mental adjustment known as adolescence is unique to humans. Other species make the transition from child to adult without a prolonged interim stage. But humans, perhaps because of our more complex physiology and social structure, require time for a more radical rewiring of the brain to take place. Studies have shown that the brain's internal structure is not completely fixed at the end of childhood, some areas mature later, a process that continues into the early twenties. Amongst the areas which develop latest are those which are responsible for the judgement of risks, the understanding of consequences and the need for self control.

Scientists in Australia set up an experiment in which they observed young people aged 11 to 14 discussing various issues with their parents. These interactions were designed to provoke disagreements – with the subject matter covering homework, lying, bedtime, use of the internet and mobile phones.

WHERE'S YOUR HEAD AT?

WHY THE TEENAGE YEARS ARE SO DIFFICULT

The study group then scanned the young people's brains, looking in particular at the amygdala area of the brain which controls impulsive reactions, and also at two pre-frontal areas which control more thoughtful responses. They found that the children who responded most aggressively to the problem-solving tasks were those with bigger amygdalas. Their brains were set up for impulsive, emotional behaviour rather than rational responses. "In the more aggressive children, the 'thinking' prefrontal cortex just isn't exerting enough control over the amygdala to regulate behaviour," says team member Sarah Whittle.

Professor Nicholas Allen who led the study, explained that children had been chosen because

THESE KIDS ARE STILL STRUGGLING TO ADJUST – THEY ARE A WORK IN PROGRESS

BUT HUMANS REQUIRE TIME FOR A MORE RADICAL REWIRING OF THE BRAIN TO TAKE PLACE

they wanted to monitor behaviour immediately after the onset of adolescence. "We were interested in the relationship between the brain structure and the kids' behaviour. The amygdala was one of the most important parts." It is the dominance of the amygdala that transforms the smiling child into the surly adolescent.

Professor Allen suggested that this went some way to explaining why teenagers who one day approached tasks with a maturity beyond their years could act with immaturity the next. "If you talk to parents of early adolescents, a lot of them will tell you they have quite a job adjusting to the changes in their child. These children can be moody, they can be argumentative, they can be angry. The brain is undergoing a lot of change.

"These kids are still struggling to adjust – they are a work in progress."

Sources: Various

Teenagers need to be taught the facts of death

By Tom Brown

act by adolescents, with their lives before them, to choose death? Each one is a future ended and promise unfulfilled and we all feel cheated. What contributions, what achievements, what families, what happiness might they have brought to others? We'll never know now. In such perplexity, it is easy to play the blame game. The media, the internet and the pressures of modern life have all come in for criticism – and some of it is justified.

Emotion

Yet the explanation could be more simple and sad. Could it be that the youngsters have fallen victim to a lethal combination of immature emotion, sentimentality and the empty cult of celebrity? When "catching the bus" trips off the tongue as code for self-slaughter, it shows a shallow and juvenile attitude to death. Let us be clear that we are not witnessing a suicide cult or 'club', as more sensational reports have claimed. Bridgend is just the latest locality for a teen suicide cluster.

In one village in Northern Ireland last year, three 15-year-old boys

Ask any disgruntled teenager (aren't they all?) what is wrong with them and the odds are you will get the cliché answers: "I'm bored." "I'm fed up." "Nobody understands..." But there are times when the stock answer hides a darker truth – and the vague unhappiness of the cartoon teenager becomes the desperate horror of self-destruction.

The teenage suicides in Bridgend may be a local abnormality, a tragedy for one community and an appalling burden for individual families. But they should affect us all and act as a terrible warning to anyone, anywhere, with adolescents in the family.

Why

Hundreds of thousands of words have been expended in answer to the baffled question that is always asked when young life is needlessly snuffed out: Why? What could possibly explain the deliberate

Death is fatal, final and forever. Not a happy-ever-after, but an unending sense of grief, loss and waste

killed themselves within a month and the health minister met internet companies in a bid to stop websites being used to promote suicide among young people.

Across the United States and on the other side of the globe in New Zealand there have been similar epidemics and suicide prevention programmes have been set up. Nor are these clusters new; in at least one town in Scotland in the 1930s, there was a young male suicide every week. It was ignored and no investigation made but it was assumed these men in their late teens and early twenties were in despair at unemployment and poverty.

What is different about the Bridgend cluster is the size and that it alerts us to the speed with which a suicide epidemic can spread among the young. It should make us all more aware of the need to watch our young more closely for the symptoms of alienation. In most cases, these are just a stage in the messy and chaotic business of growing up but Bridgend has shown how they can become fatal.

Isolation
The widespread adolescent feeling of isolation was confirmed by a recent Unicef report which ranked Britain last among developed countries for the happiness of children. Teenagers are telling us there is something missing in their lives and they, too, are being ignored. They probably do not know what that something is but it is up to us, their elders, to find out. Is it affection, attention, an aim?

When youngsters disappear into their bedrooms and spend hours in front of a computer screen, are they

playing horror games? Are they networking and comparing moans with other adolescents? Or are they checking out suicide sites? Do parents know, do they care – until it is too late?

Pain
Police and parents, perhaps to ease their own pain, said media coverage might have influenced later victims and the mother of Nathaniel Pritchard, 15, said: "We feel that the media coverage of the recent suicides put the idea into Nathaniel's head. It may have given Nathaniel the impression that attempting suicide was a way of getting attention without realising the tragic consequences."

I could face the same accusation with this column, but events have to be reported as they happen, particularly when there is cause for public concern. Where parts of the popular media can be faulted is in the manner of the reporting. Some over-sentimental treatment helped romanticise the young victims and played to the very cult of posthumous stardom which caused their deaths.

The role of the internet also needs more attention.

I know all the arguments about censorship but servers should be able to shut down suicide websites. It is clear that some of the suicides were beguiled by the idea of celebrity (what use is 15 minutes of fame when you are dead?) and the peer prestige evidenced by memorial websites.

Within hours, thousands log on and leave their tributes in message-speak: "Love you loads, your a star & always will be 4eva xx". "R.I.P. Clarky boy!! gonna miss ya! always remember the gd times!" "Sleep Tight Princess". Others – "Hope ur having a laff up there" and "Look after the others" – betray a childish attitude to death, in which the departed frolick together in some Elysian playground. It is like computer games in which characters are annihilated but are revived at the touch of a button.

By all means understand, counsel and cajole young people who despair of life – but also tell them the facts of death. Death is fatal, final and forever. Its legacy is not a happy-ever-after but an unending sense of grief, loss and, in the case of young suicides, senseless waste.

*Scotland on Sunday
24 February 2008*

> They are telling us there is something missing in their lives

> A childish attitude to death, in which the departed frolick in some Elysian playground

Missing children:

'Andrew, just tell us you're alive'

Seven months ago Glenys Gosden's 14-year-old son disappeared, joining the 200,000 people who go missing each year. She talks to Cassandra Jardine

The answerphone message at the Gosdens' home begins predictably. "There's no one here to take your call. Please leave..." Then there's a sharp intake of breath and Glenys Gosden's voice falters as she continues: "Andrew, if it's you, please know that we love you, we miss you."

Every day Glenys and her husband, Kevin, hope to hear from their 14-year-old son, Andrew, who disappeared seven months ago in circumstances as mysterious as those surrounding the vanished toddler Madeleine McCann. So far there have been a few leads, but no word from Andrew.

The evening before he vanished was unremarkable. After supper with his parents and sister, Charlotte, 18, Andrew spent an hour making a computer jigsaw with his father.

He then watched some comedy programmes – Mock the Week and That Mitchell and Webb Look – with his mother. "He didn't seem strange, but he was always a quiet, thoughtful boy," says Glenys, 43.

"On Friday September 14, he left for school at 8.05am; we went off to work shortly after. At teatime, he wasn't in his room, but I assumed he was in the basement playing on his Xbox.

When I found his school uniform on the back of a chair in his bedroom, I knew he'd come home and changed. We rang his friends, who said he wasn't with them. They said he hadn't been at school."

That weekend the police searched the bushes near the Gosdens' home in Doncaster, but found nothing. By Monday,

they knew he had taken £250 out of his bank account and had bought a single ticket to King's Cross. Another passenger had seen him on the train, but no one had any idea where the small, bespectacled teenager had gone, or why.

The story of Andrew's disappearance so intrigued Rachel Ford, a television producer, that she is using it to launch Missing Live, a month-long BBC series that highlights individual cases and explores general issues related to the estimated 210,000 people who go missing each year in Britain.

Running away is not a crime, so the hunt for missing people has until now been a low priority for the police and Home Office.

But that is changing. A new police-run national database, which has been operating for a few months, will provide hard facts about the ages, genders and movements of the missing. There are two groups who are most prone to vanishing – young men and older women.

> **That weekend the police searched the bushes near the Gosdens' home. By Monday, they knew he had taken £250 out of his account and had bought a single ticket to King's Cross**

Two thirds of runaways are under 18 and the vast majority return within 48 hours. However, the charity Missing People has 6,000 cases on its books.

Depression, illness, marital problems, debt and mental illness – particularly dementia – are the main reasons why adults leave. Some plot an escape – like John Darwin, who faked death in his canoe to start a new life in Panama; others leave believing their families would be better off without them.

Photo: Guzelian

They are usually wrong. Even suicide seems easier for relatives to handle than the limbo of not knowing whether someone is dead or alive, living it up on the other side of the world or lying dazed in the gutter. The burden of anger, uncertainty and guilt is hugely destructive.

Children who go missing have often fought with their families, or are plagued by anxieties. But Glenys Gosden cannot fathom why Andrew decided to leave for London.

"Our only thought is the Reggie Perrin theory – that, like one of his favourite comic characters, he just wanted to step out of conventional life. He'd just seen his sister get A-stars in her GCSEs and, even though he's just as bright – he's very gifted mathematically – maybe he wanted to step off the treadmill."

It's tempting to assume that runaways come from dysfunctional families, but the Gosdens don't fit that picture. Kevin and Glenys are both speech therapists – a profession that makes them "shrewd observers", according to Glenys.

There are Christian texts on the sitting-room shelves, but they haven't baptised their children because "you can't impose your views". Andrew had been reading Nietzsche's Beyond Good and Evil, so she wonders if he liked the idea of being 'the superman', 'in charge of his own destiny, without guilt or remorse'.

Upstairs, his room is full of the books more usually enjoyed by a boy his age – Harry Potter, Alex Rider, the Roman Mysteries; there's also a snooker table and Marilyn Manson posters. Charlotte's room next door is plastered with Goth material.

"She's dyed her hair black," her mother says, comfortable with teenage experimentation. Her tone changes as she says, almost to herself: "If there was something Andrew didn't feel he could say to us, he didn't give us the chance."

Drugs, drink? "He didn't even smoke"

Could he have gone to meet an internet contact? "We've only had a laptop in the house since June and he didn't even want an email address. We've checked the school computers too." Drugs, drink? "He didn't even smoke."

A belief in remaining strong has kept Glenys going through seven months of fear – where is Andrew living; what is he doing for money? – but Kevin collapsed under the strain. "Missing Andrew, going up and down to London searching – I had a nervous breakdown," he says. Charlotte, too, has had a 'very tough' time without her brother.

Part of Glenys's self-control is exercised in not blaming anyone for the failure of the investigation. Certainly, there have been blunders and delays that point to how the system could be improved.

Upstairs, his room is full of the books more usually enjoyed by a boy his age - Harry Potter, Alex Rider, the Roman Mysteries; there's also a snooker table and Marilyn Manson posters

For starters, when Andrew didn't turn up at school, the wrong family was contacted. That makes Bob Geldof's proposal, to be broadcast on Missing Live, of a text alert for parents seem a good idea.

But Glenys says it would have made no difference in Andrew's case. "The police wouldn't have done anything that day; they would have assumed he was just playing truant."

The first hours of a search are crucial. One of the police officers in the Gosden case made the kindly, but unwarranted,

> **"But now I just want to hug him. Our door is always open, the answerphone is always on. Just tell us you are alive"**

assumption that Andrew would 'just turn up'. It was unfortunate, too, that the police didn't trust Glenys and Kevin's conviction that Andrew would head for London because he'd always enjoyed family visits to relatives and museums.

Most serious of all, once he was known to have gone to King's Cross, 24 further days elapsed before his image was found on CCTV footage. Since it was the 27th day since his disappearance, and tapes are routinely wiped after 28 days, it was too late to follow his trail in a city of seven million people.

Further complications arose from the multiplicity of police forces involved – not just South Yorkshire and the Met, but also the parks and the river police.

"We need more co-ordination," says Paul Tuohy, chief executive of Missing People. "A child-rescue alert system exists to send news flashes to radio and television stations, but the police have only used it three or four times in as many years; in the US, they use their 'Amber Alert' system much more often." Madeleine McCann's parents went to the European Parliament in Brussels earlier this month to ask

MEPs to set up a further amber alert to track child-abduction cases across borders.

Technological developments could speed up future searches. Number-plate recognition and mobile-phone tracking are proving useful; automatic image tracking – sifting CCTV footage for a distinctive logo or bag – could save countless hours.

Equipment also exists to scan film for unusual incidents, such as a child being separated from a group. Biometric pictures can identify people who are confused or disguised, while age-progression techniques generate images of someone five, 10 or even 20 years on. Already the Gosdens worry that Andrew might look different.

All these developments could release families from the limbo of not knowing. For the moment, though, the Gosdens wait. The police say that because there is no body, they are assuming Andrew is alive, but his parents live on a knife-edge of hope and despair.

Was it their son who was spotted in Brighton recently? Could he have been the boy seen at the Natural History Museum?

Having caused so much pain, he might be frightened of making contact. "I was angry for a time," says Kevin. "I wanted to ask him, 'What is so wrong with a middle-class, middle-income, emotionally supportive family that made you disappear out of the door?'

"But now I just want to hug him. Our door is always open, the answerphone is always on. Just tell us you are alive."

The Daily Telegraph 18 April 2008
© *Telegraph Group Limited 2008*

Missing People helplines: sightings 0500 700700, runaways 0808 800 7070.

For up-to-date statistics on:

Alcohol

Animals

Body image

Britain & its citizens

Consumers

Disability

Drugs

Environmental issues

Financial issues

Food

Health

Internet & media

Law & order

Religion

Sport & leisure

War & conflict

Young people

as well as many other topics in Essential Articles see:

Fact File